ETERNAL

ALL ASSOCIATION INTERNATIONAL MATCH

WALES
v.
ENGLAND

NINIAN PARK, CARDIFF

RDAY, 19th OCTOBER, 1957

THE "YOUNG ENGLAND" WHO VISITED ITALY

'Big Dunc'—finest of all The Bab

MANCHESTER UNITED
FOOTBALL CLUB

er Man — DUNCAN EDWARDS

'Greatest Youngster
I've Ever Seen'

Says Matt Busby

(Manchester United Manager)

SOCCER STAR, March 1, 1958

Duncan Edwards—the lad who had

HERO OF A

by
GRA

This book is dedicated to
Keith Edwards
Tom Clare
Pat Foley
and Barry Shmeizer

Published in Great Britain and Ireland in 2023 by
Reach Sport, a Reach PLC business,
5 St Paul's Square, Liverpool, L3 9SJ.

www.reachsport.com
@Reach_Sport

Reach Sport is a part of Reach PLC.
One Canada Square, Canary Wharf, London, E15 5AP.

Hardback ISBN: 9781914197697
eBook ISBN: 9781914197703

Photographic acknowledgements:
Duncan Edwards family collection, Tony Park, Ray Adler, Mirrorpix, Alamy
Every effort has been made to trace the copyright.
Any oversight will be rectified in future editions.

Design and production by Reach Sport.
Editing: Simon Monk, Roy Gilfoyle
Cover design: Rick Cooke
Typesetting: Danny Lyle

Printed and bound by CPI Group (UK) Ltd,
Croydon, CR0 4YY.

DUNCAN EDWARDS

An intimate portrait of Manchester United's lost genius

WAYNE BARTON

Reach Sport

K.G., K.T., E.P., G.C.B., G.C.M.G., G

Chairman: Major-General O.P.J.R
Vice-Chairman: Colonel H. S. Calves
Hon. Treasurer: Colonel H. J. Mc
Secretary: Lieut.-Colonel G. J. Mitc

THE KENTISH CU
TRIANGULAR TOURNA
ween the FRENCH, BELGIAN and BRI

BRITISH AR
v
FRENCH AR

PLAYED ON THE GROUN

OF THE

DULWICH HAMLET FOOTBALL
CHAMPION HILL, DULWICH

ON

SATURDAY

Floodlit Football Match at The Cliff, Broughto

FINAL — GILGRYST CUP

MANCHESTER UNITED v. ASHTON UNITED
WEDNESDAY, 1st APRIL, 1953   Kick Off 7-3

MANCHESTER UNITED
RED SHIRTS AND WHITE SHORTS

OLIVE

FULTON   KENNEDY
                GREAVES   BARR
WHITEHURST   EDWARDS   SCA
McFARLANE   VIOLLET   WEBSTER   Mr. E. C. ALLEN
                                   Mr. G. MERRIMAN
        Mr. G. READLE (Stretford)
WRIGHT   MOSES   ROSS   RADCLIFFE   SID
HOLDEN   McNAB   KNIGHT
        BRICKELL
                McBRIDE
            ASHTON UNITED
        YELLOW SHIRTS AND WHITE SHORTS

TO READ—HOLD PROGRAMME TO LIGHT   ★

MANCHESTER UNITED

JEFFREY WHITEFOOT   JACK ROWLEY

MATT BUSBY (Manager)

TOMMY
TAYLOR

DUNCAN
EDWARDS

BILL FOULKES

BERRY   DON GIBSON   HENRY COCKBURN

DUNCAN EDWARDS of **DUDLEY** won his Junior
International "cap" last season and has represented England in
two full internationals this season. He will be playing for
England against Scotland next Saturday. He has also played
for the B'ham & District County side and the Worcester County
side this season, and still has another year at school.

LEN COOPER has played for his area side for three
seasons and represented the South of England against the North
at Dudley   He has also been a regular member of
the   sides.

McGuinness (7)
Charlton (10)   Chapman (8)
Edwards (6)   Harrop (5)   Colm
Rhodes (3)   Beswick (2)
Clayton (1)

MANCHESTER UNITED
A. Savle

TARJETA POSTAL

FOOTBALL
ASSOCIATION

ENGLAND
–v–
SCOTLAND
(FOR THE 'VICTORY' SHIELD)

THE FOOTBALL LEAGUE TEAM

Contents

Acknowledgements

Even for an author who loves Manchester United, the prospect of writing a biography of Duncan Edwards is not one accepted blindly. Duncan is one of the most precious names in the history of football and he remains such a presence that it almost feels like he belongs to a number of different families; that of Manchester United, of the England football team, the town of Dudley, and, of course, his own. It was therefore an immeasurable honour to be asked by Duncan's family to write this book, with one theme kept in mind – that I stayed true to how down to earth he was. I didn't ask why; I presumed it was because they saw him as Duncan, and not the mythical superhuman he became after he left his hometown. He was an ordinary boy with an ordinary upbringing, and therefore his journey and the heights he hit should be seen as aspirational rather than unobtainable.

To tell Duncan's story in such a way was a challenge, primarily because any perceived embellishment of his legend wasn't merely a consequence of his tragic death. Most of the praise was said contemporaneously, and so, to humanise him almost felt, at times, blasphemous. However, ultimately, it was quite the opposite. Duncan had flaws in his game. He wasn't perfect. But he was already the greatest of his time and, most crucially of all, he was improving. It is impossible to know how great he could have been – this is one of the tragedies – but I have tried, where possible, to offer a reasonable projection of where those improvements might have come and how they would have benefitted his club and country.

To achieve this version of Duncan's story I required an incredible amount of assistance. First and foremost, I have to thank Laurence Brownhill and Keith Edwards for their support and blessing of this book.

Laurence and Keith have, in recent years, been the biggest public champions of Duncan from his family, and I dearly hope I have achieved their wish of portraying their cousin how they would have liked. Tragically, Keith passed away during the writing of this book; I will never forget his generosity and faith. Thanks also to Michelle Brownhill and Leanne.

It was important to have as much of Duncan in this book and in his own voice as possible. I am grateful to everyone who assisted with this and in particular I wish to thank Nick Sharples, of New Kelmscott Press, who gave permission for Duncan's words from his only book, *Tackle Soccer This Way*, to be used. I naturally recommend anybody reading this to acquire a copy of that book too.

To achieve a completely full picture of Duncan it was important that the words of his mother were used. The words of Sarah-Anne Edwards, Bobby Robson, Tom Finney, Walter Winterbottom and Bill Foulkes were spoken to Rose Cook-Monk for her documentary 'And Then Came Munich', and used with permission.

David Gaskell, Johnny Giles, Frank Blunstone, Wilf McGuinness, Harry Redknapp, Alan Wardle and the late Harry Gregg are all people I owe a debt of gratitude towards for being so forthcoming with their time speaking about Duncan. I also have to thank Duncan Armfield for sharing his father's memories.

No story of Duncan would be complete without the story of the team in which he played and no story of that team would be truly authentic without the scene of the time being accurately set; and so I must put on record how truly grateful I am for the conversations and support of Tom Clare, a gentleman of the highest order.

For complete balance I wanted to get as complete a world view as possible and so I wish to thank Richard Wilson (@TimoMouse on Twitter) for his assistance in finding interviews with players from Red Star Belgrade. Thanks also to various staff at Athletic Bilbao and Real Madrid for their assistance in acquiring archive local newspaper reports. Thank you to Graham Brookland from the Army FA for his help.

I have to thank Nick Walters for his belief in this book. As usual, I have to articulate my deep and sincere gratitude to everyone at Reach Sport for their work and support. Paul Dove, as always, your support has meant everything, and Claire Brown, you are just the best, there's no other way to say it. Every book is a collaboration and I have to thank Simon Monk for his tireless work as editor, and Roy Gilfoyle, whose careful attention to detail has enhanced this book.

Thanks to Barry Shmeizer – the first person to read the first draft, Barry, you gave me tremendous reassurance that I had taken the right path with the way I told this story. Thanks to Roy Cavanagh, a man who has written wonderfully about Duncan in the past – I am so grateful that you gave me your support when we spoke all those years ago.

A huge thank you to Tony Park, for everything.

Thanks to Barney Chilton, Eifion Evans, Alan Monger, Rory Tompkins, Andy Gillespie, Lindsay Roe, Paul Holmes, Brian Greenhoff, Angie Best, Phil Marsh, Lee Lawrence, Mark Foster, Jimmy Williams, Richard Fenton, Matthew Smallwood, Chris Culkin, Ben Allen, Ben Greenwood, Luke Smalley, Nipun Chopra, Keane Franey, Jamie Andrews, Marc Biggs, Steve Hobin, Stan Chow, Andrea Morrissey, Alan Keegan, Judith Jennings, Gary Thompson, Ben McManus, Dan Kersh, Des McKibbin, Ed

Barker, Rich Walters, Bjarte Valen, Paul Anthony, Tony Bil, Ray Adler, Jesus Rodriguez, Andy Birkett, Steve Crabtree, Helene Britt and Dave Coleman, Roy Taylor, Justin Eagleton, Keith Norris, Peter Wood, Kyle Diller, Mike Bartlett, Michael Garvey, Mike Carney, Dips and PJ, Sarah Truscott, Stuart Hardman, Therese Visnes, Oyvind Enger, Ronald Stephenson, Chris Lepkowski, Tom Malone, Jane Gregg, Danny Woodvine, Matt Galea, Tyler Dunne, Mark Foster, Tom Boswell, Bob Bolton, Darren Hall, Steve Whittle, Matt Battle, Stel, and Conor Minchin. To the memory of Andy Bode. A sincere thank you to Kerry Rutkin and Craig Park, you fantastic, generous men.

I'm so thankful for the help, support and kind words of Paddy Barclay, Danny Taylor, Rob Smyth, Leo Moynihan, Adam Crafton, David McDonnell, James Robson and Simon Mullock.

A big thanks to Norman and Dee Whiteside, Martin Edwards, Paul Parker, Sammy McIlroy, and to Nick, Paul, Stephen and the entire Murphy family.

The other Murphy family, practically my own; Dave, sincerely, thank you mate. You are always looking out for the best for me.

To Dan, Kim and Alex Burdett – Dan, you're truly the best mate. To Steve and Gem, the love is real. Hayley, Els and Gruff. Thank you to Mozza. Mike Pieri, you're a legend, thank you for everything. To the Gatts, Mikiel, Phil and Charlotte, you are all too wonderful for words.

Steven Marrable, your continuous support means more than I ever say to you, and the same is true for all of my in-laws. Mum, your belief in me has always helped me believe in myself. To my wife, thank you for always pushing me to improve even and especially in the frequent moments where I doubt myself.

Finally to my nephews, Freddy, Noah and Logan. You are all so extraordinarily precious to me.

Prologue

Wednesday February 12th, 1958

It was never an enviable task.

The staff discussed which of them should face the reporters today; and, as ever, the responsibility would fall upon the shoulders of the individual who wasn't required for the latest emergency.

There are few more noble vocations than becoming a doctor or a nurse. Anyone who dedicates themselves to this life does so fully aware of the highs and lows they will face. It doesn't make the hard moments easier, but there is at least some acceptance that they will come.

Medical professionals are in the industry of saving lives. They do so with dignity and often with neither the requisite credit nor financial recompense for their heroic contribution to society. They are not celebrities, even if their work is worthy of renown.

Professor Georg Maurer was more inspirational than most. In addition to his day job, his life's purpose was to push for the creation of a medical school in Germany to provide a better educational system for the doctors of tomorrow. It was an ambition realised in 1967. It was an accomplishment to be proud of and yet, given the nature of these things, it was an achievement only really acknowledged by his peers and wife Erica. If that had been his life's work, he could have been satisfied with his contribution to mankind in a way that not many others can claim.

Fate had chosen a different path for Georg Maurer.

He could scarcely have imagined that less than 13 years after helping to save British lives in the Second World War, he would be required to do so again following a tragic incident just six miles away from where he worked, at the Rechts der Isar hospital in Munich, Germany.

A plane carrying an English football team had crashed upon take-off, killing several passengers. Some survivors were mortally wounded. Others were fighting for their lives. It wasn't always clear who fell into which category.

The football team were Manchester United, known as 'the Busby Babes', an alliterative term to reference both the manager – Matt Busby – and the youthful age of his team. That youthfulness had captured the imagination of the country thanks to their exciting style of football. They were hero-worshipped by the local boys and girls of Manchester. The strength of that bond was reflected in the grief which had consumed Manchester and England as the names of those who had died in the crash were told.

It was the responsibility of the doctors to inform the press of the status of casualties and survivors. Dr Maurer and his colleague Dr Lang would take turns with Dr Graham Taylor, the medical officer from British European Airways, to update journalists outside the hospital. There would be regular conversations and official bulletins throughout each day.

Almost a week after the crash, most cases of life or death were established. A small handful remained in the balance. One was one of the co-pilots, Kenneth Rayment. One was Matt Busby. Another was the 21-year-old star player, Duncan Edwards. "He was full of life, full of football," Matt once said of Duncan. "He would play every day in the week if he could."

On Wednesday February 12th, it was this young man's life that was the primary subject of an update, following a race against time where an artificial kidney had to be rushed from Freiburg, over 200 miles away.

Duncan had been in and out of consciousness since the crash. After showing signs of lucidity, he had regressed into a coma. With his life in the balance, the emergency-upon-emergency procedure had been temporarily successful.

It was the turn of Professor Maurer to tell the journalists. Maurer had a kindly yet serious face. He carried a warmth which was perfect for diplomatic international relations. His expertise made him the right man for the job he was employed to do; his natural demeanour made him a good choice for the unenviable duty he was now obliged to. He provided the news in the matter-of-fact way. The young man's life had been saved just as his heart was about to stop beating.

Before he returned to the ward, Maurer paused. Perhaps in normal circumstances, he wouldn't do this. But he had been struck so powerfully by the emotional force of the incident that he was compelled to share what he'd experienced. He had noticed Duncan in a state of semi-consciousness and what he witnessed could not be shaken from his mind.

He took a breath, sighed, and said: "You know, he seemed to imagine he was still playing football... and once shouted, 'Goal, goal!'"

Chapter 1
Making An Impression

Almost all of the major milestones in the life of Duncan Edwards seemed to feature an element of fate. As if created by a storyteller, a timeline featuring what, at times, would have been seemingly inconsequential coincidences; then, when looking back with hindsight, they perfectly weave into a theme best summarised by a Portuguese term, *saudade*. The closest English translation is bittersweet, but *saudade* is much more loaded. It is melancholy, it is longing for something that will never be, while at the same time accepting that nostalgic dwelling of this nature has a propensity to pull you out of your present state of mind.

It is arguable that no other sportsman in history evokes this feeling quite like Duncan Edwards. On February 6th each year – a date on which he wasn't born, nor did he die, and yet remains eternally linked to – there is a commemoration which propels Duncan back into the British national consciousness; thousands of conversations occur which emphasise the message that his name must not be forgotten, as time eventually removes us from the generation fortunate enough to have witnessed him play football. It is incumbent upon us all to remember Duncan, and those who passed with him, and it is just as important for his memory to be honoured by representing who he was in an accurate manner. This is no easy feat, considering the circumstances.

Duncan Edwards, more than any other player in Manchester United history, is drenched in hyperbolic tributes. This will forever be the case, because most of those tributes are and were paid by those who knew him and those who watched him play. For those who were not quite so fortunate, the questions are asked. How could a man who never quite reached six foot be spoken about as though he were two feet taller? How could it be possible that he was described as the perfect footballer? The complete player? How realistic is it that he could have no weakness in his game? Is it even possible to tell the story of his life without being carried away with the plaudits? The nicknames? Tank... Atomic... Superman. Great names, except for one thing. Duncan Edwards wasn't a tank. He wasn't Superman. He was an ordinary human, capable of extra-ordinary things. Recounting the life of a sportsperson provides a certain licence to indulge in the romantic embellishments.

Is it disrespectful to start on this note, or is it doing what Duncan actually achieved a disservice by elevating it to a metaphorical state which is unrealistically attainable? Considering the life he led, this writer feels the greatest tribute is to recount what he did, as he did it; allowing those tributes to come from the mouths of those who knew him, and letting the reader make their own mind up.

The very life of Duncan Edwards, when simplified, almost contradicts itself.

It is defined, ultimately, by bad fortune, but it is equally true to say he was a very lucky young man.

He died young. Tragically young. And still, events which occurred during his life could well have taken it even earlier still.

The first of those events was his very birth. Duncan arrived weighing 9lbs 8oz, notable for his size even when entering into the world. It was fortunate that his mother, Sarah-Anne, did not suffer badly with complications due to the size of her baby; at that time, it was not inconceivable that the birth could have been much more problematic.

Duncan was born on October 1st, 1936, at the Edwards family home of 23 Malvern Crescent, in the Woodside area of Dudley. His father, Gladstone, was a metal polisher for Bilston-based ironworks manufacturer Joseph Sankey and Sons. Bilston is a market town in Wolverhampton, five miles north of where the family lived. Gladstone and Sarah-Anne were childhood sweethearts born and bred in the area. They grew up living next door to each other. As kids, Gladstone told his neighbour, "I'm going to marry you someday." And he did.

The national mood was one of cautious optimism. The Midlands was not immune to the impact of the Great Depression of the early 1930s but seemed to have the potential to thrive once more. The coal-mining industry was in a slow decline, but the area still had a strong industrial presence, producing weaponry and machinery for the Army.

Investment was made locally to help young families. Dudley Council was in the process of building the Priory Estate, with a commitment to create more than 2,000 houses to rehouse families from what were bluntly described as slums. The new homes had gardens, electricity, running water and indoor toilets. The Priory Estate was only two miles away from Holly Hill but it might as well have been Hollywood, such was the luxury – and Sarah-Anne (known as Annie or Sarah to friends, or even Nance to family) and Gladstone were thrilled when their application to be rehoused was accepted.

Throughout the late 1930s, however, there was the ominous international threat of war. Adolf Hitler's Germany invaded Poland on September 1st, 1939, prompting England and France to declare war two days later. Every family in England had suffered in the First World War, and the Edwards' were no different – Duncan's uncle Sidney had been killed in battle in January 1917, when Gladstone himself was just a child. Gladstone was spared the trauma of enlisting as his job was considered an essential service – however, the region's vital role in assisting the military made it a prime target for German air raids, most prominently during November 1940. More than 40,000 British civilians lost their lives during the Blitz and almost four times as many were injured.

The Edwards family were fortunate to escape the physical consequences of war but, like everyone, they lived with the mental trauma of it. As a four-year-old boy, Duncan was given a gas mask to carry at all times, and many nights were spent reacting to the factory sirens warning of German planes approaching; the family would race out to their air raid shelter and pray that they would be spared.

Even without the dread of war, the move to the Priory Estate had not quite heralded the idyllic lifestyle Sarah and Gladstone had hoped for. Other rehoused families did not seem to have the same community pride as the Edwards' and before long, the council estate was not much better kept than the slums from which the families had moved. This did not prevent Sarah and Gladstone from being sociable characters; they were proud Midlanders, as friendly to neighbours as they were resourceful. When rationing began in January 1940, the family made the most of their new garden, turning it into an allotment-cum-zoo; Gladstone grew vegetables and had a chicken coop. Like many parents, when times were particularly hard, they always made sure Duncan was well-fed even if it meant going without themselves.

These tough early years had a definitive influence on Duncan. Sarah would be desperate to protect her son from the horrors of war; on their bomb shelter evacuations, she would make up stories of fantasy to distract Duncan. This was coupled with the one great hobby on the male side of the family – football. Gladstone was a big fan of Wolverhampton Wanderers, who had been one of the best sides in the land prior to the war. When the First Division resumed almost seven years later on the last day of August, 1946, Duncan was almost 10 years old and was a burgeoning footballer in his own right.

"He was kicking a ball before he could walk," Sarah recalled. "I'd have to buy reins for him and hold the straps at the back. We'd put a ball on the floor and Duncan would be stretching the reins and kicking it." Pushing against the resistance of the straps, the infant Duncan was developing his strength; and, particularly in times of austerity where football was such an accessible game across the working classes, the fascination with the ball was encouraged.

Sarah made Duncan a football kit and bought him his first boots. "We were constantly having to replace them because of either wear and tear or his feet were getting bigger," she remembered.

Football was the main activity of the boys of the estate. Duncan and his friends would dribble a ball to and from Priory Road Junior School and spend their break times playing at the waste ground at the back of the school. After school they would play on Priory Park or even on the grounds of Dudley Castle.

"Every evening and Sunday morning I would be in the park playing with lads of 19 and 20, getting used to the hurly-burly of the game, and giving, I hoped, as good as I took," Duncan said. "For most of these games I would play in my ordinary walking shoes, which caused friction at home. On one occasion my mother bought me a new pair of shoes and within two hours of putting them on I arrived home with them invisible beneath great cakes of mud. My popularity was at a low ebb that night."

Duncan participated in all sports at Priory Road, including as a wicket-keeper during cricket games against local school Wrens Nest, but football remained his primary love, and he played at right-half or centre-half for the school team on Saturdays. "My early recollections of Duncan were when we met at the Priory School on Saturday mornings and walked up to Kates Hill School with our kit on and our boots slung around our necks," schoolfriend Mike Jones told the *Dudley News*. "I was then a right-winger and Duncan played behind me."

Another primary school friend, Colin Perry, recalled being in the same team. "Whoever was on the same side as Duncan was never on a losing side," he said.

There was no question that Duncan was learning to handle himself against boys twice his age; even though he was still small by their standards, he managed to make an impression. "The time limit was when it became too dark to play any more, but the games, with anything up to 20 lads, were very intense," DM Elcock of Russell's Hall told the *Black Country Bugle*. "Then one evening a fresh-faced lad stood watching and shouted out, 'Can I have a game?' He was younger than the rest but the answer was, 'Sure, kick up hill, they need some help', which raised a laugh. That was the first appearance on Priory Park of Duncan Edwards... there wasn't a lot of room, so players soon had to learn to use both feet quickly and be prepared for some hard tackles. Duncan took to the game quickly, and soon became equally good at shooting and passing with both feet. He also learned to take and give hard knocks – some of us were five years older than he was. At the end of the game we would make our way homewards, singing at the top of our voices and young Duncan loved it."

Another of the boys who joined in was Tom Whorton. "I first came to know Duncan Edwards when he was about 10 or 11 years old," he said. "I was about 16. We had to scrape a few coppers together to buy a football, which we took turns to keep overnight. We very often burst the bladder which delayed us playing. This is where Duncan was a blessing, due to his father buying him a completely new football, enabling him to dictate whether to play or not. The age difference was quite big but Duncan more than held his own."

In one such game, the youngster suffered a moment of embarrassment. "I can remember the moment I decided that if ever I was going to be any good at football I would have to learn something about the arts of the game," Duncan said. "All the other boys were both bigger and older than I, yet somehow it fell to me to take a penalty... fully aware of the responsibility, I carefully placed the ball and decided to impress everyone by toe-punting it into the goal harder than it had ever been toe-punted before. But the ground was wet, and as I swung my foot my legs shot from under me, my boot scraped the ball so that it rolled very gently about five yards wide of the pile of coats forming one of the goalposts, and I was left on my back gazing at the sky listening to the hoots of laughter. It was at that moment I solemnly decided that I would learn from my mistakes."

In his school team, Duncan's natural ability and his insatiable desire for the game were evident immediately. Priory Road Juniors faced off against St John's Primary School, who were coached by teacher Gordon Meddings. "It was obvious he was something special, even though he was only 10 years old," Meddings recalled. "He covered every inch of the field, taking goal-kicks, throw-ins, corners and free-kicks and also managing to halt every attack… his play inspired the Priory Road boys to a 3-0 victory."

Duncan's dedication to football sometimes distracted him from his schoolwork. "He went out with a ball, and came back with the ball and would spend hours heading and kicking a ball against the wall," Sarah said. "Even if he was dressed up on Sunday, he couldn't help kicking stones, and when we went on holiday we always had to buy him a ball. He liked his school work well enough. He was a good drawer and he liked history. He liked the open air life, fishing and cricket. But football was his first love."

Duncan and his friends James Dunn and Donald Bradley often went down to the streams near the Crooked House pub in Gornalwood; their exploration led them to discover bird eggs, which they would take and swap with their friends - back in the days before wildlife conservation was commonplace. He was also a keen cyclist, and would ride 10 miles to Kinver or even more than 15 miles to Bewdley just to keep active.

Bert Bissell was a local probation officer and founder of the Young Men's Bible Class at Vicar Street Methodist Church. In 1936, he climbed Ben Nevis for the first time, and did so again in August 1945 with a group of young men from the class. This became an annual pilgrimage, and in August 1947, Duncan joined the walk and made it all the way to the top. He loved the school holidays when he would visit family and spend time with his cousin Keith, swimming and fishing in local lakes. Even when Sarah and Gladstone did not take a ball, this did not deter Duncan, who would kick anything that remotely resembled a spherical object, including a pig's bladder.

Another of Duncan's cousins, John, recalled how close the family were. "My dad was born and bred in Dudley so we would go over and play with our cousins once or twice a year," he told the *Coventry Telegraph* in 2011. "If there was a brick in the street, Duncan would go and kick it. You never saw him without a football at his feet. Duncan was always full of life. He was 5ft 8in when he was 14 and we used to call him The Tank. The last proper memory I have is of going to the swimming baths with him. He could swim like a fish and was a natural sportsman. He used to love to go on the diving platform and do a bomb into the water, he was great fun."

Just as life in Britain was beginning to return to some sort of post-war normality, the Edwards family suffered a devastating personal loss. Sarah had fallen pregnant and given birth to a daughter, Carol. Duncan adored his sister, but Carol died in 1947 at just 14 weeks old after contracting meningitis – crushing Duncan and his parents.

Not quite 11, Duncan had experienced plenty of trauma in his young life, and found football a constant source of comfort. The professional game had resumed, but Gladstone could not afford to take Duncan to watch his beloved Wolverhampton Wanderers. They went once – and before half-time, Duncan was pestering his dad to leave. "He hated watching football, he only wanted to play," Duncan's cousin, Laurence Brownhill, recalls. "His dad couldn't even get his interest for a full game at the Wolves. He was Manchester United mad and none of us could understand why. It was Manchester United this and Manchester United that."

Wolves were now managed by Gladstone's hero, Stan Cullis,

and even though they were a good side, they did not capture the public's imagination with their style of play, so sportswriters or radio broadcasters rarely spoke about their thrilling matches. The Edwards' did not own a television and in any event, football was rarely broadcast.

The 1948 FA Cup final – the last before Duncan left Priory Road to join Wolverhampton Street Secondary School in Dudley town centre – was contested between Manchester United and Blackpool. Blackpool boasted the midfield talents of Stanley Matthews, renowned as the greatest player in the country. On this day, however, even Matthews could not inspire his team to victory – Matt Busby, the recently-appointed United manager, had earned plaudits for his attacking style, and after 70 minutes of a final which his team threatened to lose 2-1, United scored three times in a blistering 13-minute spell to win the cup. Edwards listened to the match on the radio and, like thousands of youngsters inspired by the cavalcade of late goals, rushed out to play football with his friends at full-time.

"I am always striving for perfection, and it was not until the 1947/48 season that I really saw such perfection from the players at Manchester United for the first time," Busby later said. "United beat Blackpool in a match regarded by many onlookers as the best final ever played on the famous Wembley turf."

United's entertaining style was the buzz of the sport. The young Edwards was drawn to the story. Even when Wolves won the cup the following year, their win over Leicester did little to thrill Duncan in the same way as the 1948 final.

Duncan, meanwhile, was becoming the talk of his own neighbourhood. In every group of boys, one has to be the tallest. In the Priory Junior School football team 'league champions' photograph of 1948, Duncan's size was noticeably different to that of his peers, with him and a boy by the name of Malcolm John towering over the rest.

Malcolm's older brother Roy had also gone through the same school and shared a pitch with Duncan many a time. Roy said Duncan showed considerable promise: "He could do anything even with a tennis ball outside his kitchen in Elm Road. His mum said he was so good with a ball his brains must be in his feet. You can talk about Pele, Eusebio and Maradona, this boy would have been better than the lot of 'em – the best and greatest world player ever. I have seen Duncan place a football – the old leather kind – on the penalty spot and boot it into the goal – at the other end of the field with one bounce only – and that was when he was only 11 years old."

Priory Juniors had an almost-perfect record. Their one blemish came against Wren's Nest, who achieved a 4-2 win. In the return match, Duncan was geared for revenge, and inspired his team to a 5-1 victory – their goalkeeper was Thomas Millinson, who was so good he was already playing for the Dudley Boys team, but he could do nothing to stop a 'blockbuster' of a strike from the young Duncan.

It wasn't just father and son in the Edwards family who carried the football bug. Sarah's father had played locally, while Gladstone himself and his brother George had played in the local league. There was professional blood, too. Ray Westwood, Duncan's uncle, had played six times for England, over 300 times for Bolton, and, at the time of his nephew's move to secondary school, was still playing professional football for Chester City. Bolton were keen on another member of the family – Dennis Stevens, an inside-forward, a first cousin once removed who was almost three years older than Duncan. Dennis was hotly tipped to make it into the professional world – and, although he would become a legend for at least one club, his younger relative was taking early steps to a status that would make even that word seem insufficient.

Chapter 2
Education

Although it is fair to say that Duncan Edwards was not intended for greatness academically, it was clear he had an internal desire to better himself, while he showed capability in areas other than football which may have one day helped him develop a career. Professional football back then was a career dictated as equally by a club as by a player's talent. This was an era of small playing squads, of no substitutes, of older entry into the professional game, of fewer competitions, and of dual trades for those who were lucky enough to get a chance. Secondary school would be spent learning a trade. Duncan showed promise in woodwork and was encouraged to consider a career in carpentry.

Duncan had actually chosen to go to Wolverhampton Street – many of his friends went to Park Secondary School, but the boy had been captivated by the talk of the many different activities Wolverhampton Street had. They had a football team, but also a successful Morris and sword dancing team, which seemed to seal the deal. The teams were run by Stella Cook, and Duncan progressed to the senior dance team in his first year. Mr Reg Baxter, Duncan's music teacher, recalled: "It was like watching ballet seeing him perform with bells on his ankles. Duncan was a pretty hefty boy but so light on his feet. He loved to dance."

Aside from dancing, there was always football. Duncan was picked for the first game his new school team played. School friend Don James played with Duncan at this age and said he was able to play with boys of 16, already their equal in size and "already getting way beyond them in soccer ability".

The first game of the school season was against Northfield Road school in Netherton. Northfield Road were coached by Mr Geoff Groves, who could scarcely believe what he watched unfold. "He played centre-half amongst all these boys of 14 years of age and told them all what to do – including the referee," Groves said. "I wrote to a great friend that very night and told them I had witnessed the greatest thing ever seen in football. I added – not only would he play for the English Schools' Football Association but also he would play for the England senior side. He completely dominated the game. We were all talking about him afterwards. Nobody really had to teach him anything about soccer. The game was born in him. He was a genius."

In addition to his role as a teacher, Groves was a trainer with the Dudley Schools Boys team, and immediately asked young Duncan to play. The following Saturday, Duncan turned out at outside-left alongside his relative, Dennis. On October 23rd, at the age of 12 years and three weeks, Duncan Edwards' name appeared in the newspaper for the very first time as he played his second game for Dudley Boys. The *Dudley Herald* reported on his side's 5-2 win over Nuneaton in the English Schools Shield with a passing mention of "Edwards, the right winger, at 12 was the youngest player on view… "

It was reported that Dudley's opponents in the next round would be Kings Norton, away – and that's where Duncan had his first taste of cup disappointment, when his side were eliminated.

Also in the Dudley Schools team was old foe Tommy Millinson, who now attended Wolverhampton Street and quickly struck up a friendship with Duncan. "You hear a lot of people saying they discovered him, but that's rubbish," Tommy told the *Express and Star* in 2008. "That lad didn't need discovering. It was obvious how good he was. I remember the two of us practising for hours against the wall at the back of the school. I would cross the ball and he would knock it in. It didn't matter how bad my cross was, he'd always manage to get on the end of it. We got on very well together. He was a smashing lad, modest, but confident about his football."

Against ordinary schoolboys for Wolverhampton Street, Duncan was unstoppable. In the return game against Geoff Groves' Northfield Road boys, he left his mark once more. Youngster Fred Barnett told the *Dudley News* how he remembered "sitting on a grassy bank on Netherton Park and watching my school play a school from Dudley and seeing one of their players hit the ball from near the halfway line and watching the ball stay one foot from the ground all the way into the goal… I later learned it was Duncan Edwards."

Duncan developed such a strong local reputation that teachers would arrange for boys like Tommy Millinson to lay off passes for Duncan to strike shots against the wall of the school. The wall became known as 'Duncan's Wall' and retains that name even today, more than 70 years later. He was a special case.

Already a class above among his peers, it was when the net was cast further afield, when Duncan was playing against older, more talented boys, that the true measure of his ability could be noted. Eric Booth had been the secretary of the Dudley Schools FA since 1935 and had been notified of Edwards when he was at Priory Road. "We knew right away that we had something special," Booth said. "In his first year at Wolverhampton Street School, he was chosen to play for the Dudley Schoolboys side, where he came up against boys of 15. For once in his life he looked a comparative midget, but he was still a wonderful player for his age."

Booth took a particular interest in Duncan's development. The opening in the Dudley Schools team had so happened to come at outside-left. On Groves' advice, this freakishly talented centre-half had to be put into the side, and Booth decided that in the absence of natural left-footers, they should give a chance to this precociously gifted child out on the left wing. The game ended in defeat, but Duncan was a natural, while Booth tried to help the boy by telling him to work on his left foot.

Later, Duncan would comment on how Booth helped various aspects of his game. "He taught me how to trap a ball, how to head it," he said. "Probably the most important thing Mr Booth taught me was the necessity of being two-footed. The natural testing ground for my left foot was the park in the evening games among the local lads. I started by using my left only when I was in the clear. As it strengthened, so I began to use it when I was in difficulties, and eventually I would try to go through the whole of these games using only my left foot."

Booth was equally complimentary about his student. As he entered his second year at secondary school, Duncan was moved from a position where he could settle into one where he could influence play. "He was exactly what one wanted," Booth said. "I told him not to let the defenders tackle him – to get the ball into the middle. And he did it as if he were 29 years old. We were astounded at his accuracy. He passed to a team-mate on an exact course and height. He played for his junior school, his secondary school and his town. In the following year he played at right-half in the town team."

People were noticing. One interested observer was Jack O'Brien, a scout who covered the Midlands area for Manchester United. He sent a hand-written letter to manager Matt Busby: "Have today seen a 12-year-old schoolboy who merits special watching. His name is Duncan Edwards, of Dudley. Instructions please." O'Brien was told to keep going with that special observation.

The Worcester School's Football Association reports of the following years read almost as a tribute book to the prodigious Edwards. On December 2nd, 1949, Duncan was named in the 'B' team in a trial to represent the county team against

Northamptonshire on the 29th. The trial was successful. Eric Booth took the opportunity to nominate Duncan as a potential player for England Schoolboys, and so English School FA representatives Bert Tunnicliffe and Bill Ward attended the game at Worcester City's Claines Lane.

Edwards did not score but inspired his team to salvage a 2-2 draw; the national assessors later selected him to play for the England Schoolboys against Ireland at Boundary Park in Oldham on May 6th, 1950.

As the date approached, Duncan grew in confidence, signing his name on scraps of paper and giving them to schoolmates with the promise those pieces of paper would be worth something one day. This, however, was simply an immature reaction to an increased level of attention – Duncan quickly became embarrassed by the attention. "He was quiet in class," his teacher Stella Cook said. "He never bragged about football. He became shyer as he became well-known."

Duncan was excited about playing for England but was sad at the same time; his call-up meant he was ineligible to play for his school in the School's Cup final, while he also had to withdraw from the dancing team who were due to take part in the National Festival in Derby. "The only time in years we managed to get to the Dudley School's final, Duncan couldn't play because of an international match due in a few weeks, but he turned up to watch," Cook recalled. "We had an offside given against us which looked doubtful so I asked Duncan how the referee made that out. I was impressed with his quiet and easy answer – the decision was quite right although it was against us, and the spectators thought otherwise." Clearly, Duncan had a sporting fairness that outweighed his competitive desire to win.

The international call-up alerted all of the local professional clubs who weren't already paying attention. Under FA Schoolboys' rules, a teacher had to accompany Edwards on the trip to Oldham, and Eric Booth decided to be the chaperone. He visited Duncan's parents, reassuring them that he would take good care but also giving them a warning. "You'll be swamped with scouts from many clubs," he said. "For heaven's sake don't let Duncan sign anything, no matter what rewards are being offered. He'll be better still in the future – and he'll render himself ineligible to play for English Schools FA if he is attached to a professional club."

Duncan had impressed so much in his trial that he had been selected in an unfamiliar role as centre-forward – a position that coaches at lower age levels would usually place the best player in the team if necessary. Lining up on the left-hand side of Duncan were Ray Parry of Derby Schools, and 14-year-old David Pegg of Doncaster. Duncan's place in this team was a matter of local pride for the likes of Groves, and Meddings, who was also on the local schools committee – it was the first time in 40 years a boy from Dudley had played for the junior England side. Thirteen-year-old Duncan – described as strong and two-footed, and a "splendid distributor, especially with long cross passes to wings" in the match programme, starred in a 5-2 win.

In August 1950, Duncan traded holidays in the Black Country for the relatively glorious setting of Blackpool. Meddings was attending a preliminary FA coaching award for schoolboy internationals, so he took Duncan along with him. In Blackpool, they stayed at the Romford Private Hotel on South Shore – a small hotel owned by Stanley Matthews and his wife Betty. Duncan renewed acquaintances with Parry and Pegg, the boys who had played with him three months earlier.

The boys indulged in the local fun – tormenting a local youngster in a 'Beat the goalkeeper' stall at the Pleasure Beach amusement park so much that the stall holder eventually let them play for free to attract an audience, so unerring was the accuracy of Pegg and Edwards.

Meddings, however, was there for serious business; as were the other course attendees, one of whom was Joe Mercer, the 36-year-old Arsenal captain. Meddings was keen to get the professional's view on who he felt were the outstanding prospects from the 20 pupils. "He immediately named Duncan, Ray Parry and David Pegg," Meddings recalled.

The following year, Duncan continued to grow, both physically and emotionally. He had the weight to match his height and it often meant difficulties for anyone brave enough to try and tackle him. In one Birmingham and District trial one such young boy went in for a challenge and broke his leg.

"On the following Saturday we were playing South Birmingham away," Meddings recalled. "The injured boy was standing on the touchline, his leg encased in plaster. Duncan had a terrible game. He was afraid to make physical contact because of the sight of the boy and was most upset about an incident which was not his fault."

He quickly got over the unsettling reality of physical consequences. "The young Edwards was never afraid to go in and tackle," Geoff Groves said. "He had legs and thighs already like oak trees, and yet was so light on his feet. He could almost have played blindfolded. Duncan was completely two-footed, he was very brave."

In another game at Birmingham at Henry Road in Yardley, Duncan went on a run and, after beating three players, hit a shot with such ferocity that it broke the wooden crossbar in half and caused the game to be stopped.

In Duncan's third year at secondary school, Eric Booth invited him to spend time with him at Park School – where Booth taught – in order to further his football education. This would most commonly occur just after games, where Booth would run through elaborately-sketched tactical drills on the blackboard, and began to suggest that Duncan had as much to bring to his game from an intellectual perspective as a physical one.

"It's your job to distribute the ball to the rest of the team," teacher told student. "If you think all you need to do is to hold the ball and take it through, what will you do to your team-mates? When you play in bigger games you'll have a bad habit."

Duncan, aware of Booth's influence in his progress, accepted the lesson, and also became more vocal in his tactical encourage-ment to team-mates. "He taught me the rudiments of the game very well," he later said of Booth.

He had become the most prominent local schoolboy by a distance. An inter-county trial at Stourbridge on November 16th, 1950, was navigated and Duncan was called into the Worcester team to face Gloucestershire on December 10th, where he lined up wearing the captain's armband and the number 10 shirt at inside-left. He retained the shirt and captaincy to face Northamptonshire at Rushden on February 10th, 1951. He continued to impress, too, for the Dudley Boys team. Having defeated Mid-Warwickshire 8-0 in the second round of the District Schools Shield Competition, Duncan's side scored another eight against Tamworth at Dudley Sports Centre to win 8-1. "A feature of the early play were the long crossfield passes of Dudley's international Edwards, who kept up a steady stream of passes to his forwards, and himself scored with probably the hardest shot of the match," read the report in the February 24th edition of the *Dudley Herald*.

On the field, players were almost afraid to go near Edwards. On the side of the pitch, Eric Booth had the opposite problem, and couldn't fend off one scout without another assuming the vacant position. Booth had talked the matter over with Duncan, Gladstone and Annie, and gave every scout the same response. "I'm not interested in which team he joins but in seeing that the lad gets a square deal. If he doesn't make the grade, what will your club do for him? What help will you give him to become a qualified carpenter between the time he signs amateur and professional forms?"

Scouts from Aston Villa and Wolves suggested that he could repair their goalposts. It did not seem a well-considered solution. Manchester United, however, as represented by Jack O'Brien – this was a different matter.

Chapter 3
Enter United

Manchester United Football Club is such a strong commercial entity in the 21st century that the words 'Football Club' have been removed from the crest. Many supporters feel the commercial growth of the game has caused an irreversible conflict between supporters and the sport, and at Manchester United, that feeling could be traced to the summer of 1998 – the first time the club released a strip where the crest was missing the words 'Football Club'. Fans of a cynical disposition started to believe that anything that could be, was commercialised. Stick a crest on it, preface it with three magical words – 'Official partner of' – and you can attach anything between the first two words. Such as a diesel engine partner. The idea of associating that with Manchester United in the 1940s would have been alien.

In fact, the idea of associating Manchester United with commercial power at all would have been laughable. It would be closer to the truth to say they were destitute, a situation exacerbated by damage to Old Trafford suffered during the war, and it was partly this issue which created the circumstances in which their greatest quality would be born.

That greatest quality, for clarity, was the development of their famous youth system.

Louis Rocca was one of the key figures in the early history of the club, originally known as Newton Heath L&Y – being an offshoot of Newton Heath L&Y railway works. Rocca was there through the highs and lows, and many financial challenges, while he also claims to have suggested the new club name of Manchester United at a meeting in 1902. He was also there when local businessman James Gibson invested £2,000 to save the club from financial oblivion in December 1931.

By then, Rocca had been joined at the club by someone equally passionate in the shape of Walter Crickmer, who among many other achievements, was responsible for setting up the MUJACs (Manchester United Junior Athletics Club) – a groundbreaking youth system devoted to unearthing the finest talents from across Manchester and beyond. Crickmer drew up a list of rules, a gymnasium was equipped for the boys and a trainer and coach engaged for them. A committee was formed, representing different areas of Manchester and district, each committee-man covering his own area and bringing in the boys who had represented their county or country. All this spade work was supervised by Walter. Boys were delighted to play for the MUJACs, and they ran away with the Chorlton Amateur League in their debut 1938/39 season. The idea of pride in where you were from and a sense of together-ness and unity developed in a young band of brothers helped the overall quality and also helped to forge a strong relationship with the supporters, who were more inclined to be vocal and attached to their team if they knew the boys were local lads.

Another seminal moment came in 1942, when the name of Matt Busby, a former Liverpool midfielder, was suggested to then-chairman James Gibson as a potential manager, to lighten the load on Rocca and Crickmer.

Aged 36, Busby was coming to the end of a fine career as a player. Liverpool offered him a role as assistant manager and Busby verbally accepted the proposal. There was a growing sense that the war would soon end and football clubs were beginning their preparations for the return to action. Word reached Manchester of

Busby's informal agreement; by now, Gibson, Rocca and Crickmer had concluded that Busby would be a wise choice as manager. Rocca sent a letter to Busby's Army unit, saying he did not know what his "old friend" planned to do at the end of the war, but that he had a "great job for him" if he wanted it.

In February 1945 Busby travelled to meet Gibson in Manchester. He had a couple of bold demands. He wanted complete control over the senior squad, including player recruitment. He also wanted the three-year contract offered to him to be revised to five. Gibson agreed on both counts.

While in Italy with the Army, Busby had rekindled relations with the former West Brom midfielder Jimmy Murphy, who was coaching his own Army team. Busby was compelled by both Murphy's intense instruction of effectively meaningless games, and his players' response. He offered him a job as his assistant when he was demobbed. Murphy accepted.

Busby gave Murphy complete control of all playing matters beyond the first team. This enabled Rocca and Crickmer to concentrate more on recruitment and administration. The pair were suitably impressed by the new hierarchy, in particular the heightened sense of ambition amid humble surroundings. Busby was here to win.

"I did not set out to build a team," Busby said in his book *My Story*. "The task ahead was much bigger than that. What I really embarked upon was the building of a system which would produce not one team, but four or five teams, each occupying a rung on a ladder, the summit of which was my first XI." The club decided on a policy of youth development. Players would have to be found in local youth clubs or as soon as they left school. "I wanted to build teams of world-class footballers, and to do the job efficiently, had to get hold of them young," Busby said. The new United manager felt a team comprised of big signings might not cultivate the team spirit he desired. "I am not normally a fussy individual," he said, "but when it comes to the business of signing footballers, nothing but the best will satisfy me. By that I mean the lad must have something more than soccer ability: he must be a worthy representative of United, on and off the field, amenable to discipline, and good living."

Busby himself was proactive when it came to finding the best young players. He remembered Joe Armstrong, a 5ft 4in Post Office messenger boy who didn't grow tall enough to become a postman, so became a telephone engineer.

When Busby arrived in Manchester, he made Armstrong his second signing, following Murphy. Armstrong's connections were crucial in helping to discover new talent. Timing was crucial. Armstrong would watch teenagers play in youth games all over the country. He relied on his honesty, diplomacy and persistent nature to charm the parents of boys who he felt would be good enough to play in Jimmy Murphy's youth team. Murphy was assisted by Bert Whalley, a former United player who had to retire early due to an eye injury.

The first team success helped, as did the style in which United played. The summer that United won the FA Cup, Mark Jones, a centre-half from Barnsley, accepted Joe's invitation to go to Manchester. The year after, Jeff Whitefoot and Dennis Viollet – a midfielder and striker respectively, both of immense talent – were brought in. They were followed by David Pegg, Duncan's team-mate at international level.

"The first thing you look for is ball ability," Armstrong said. "I worked with Jimmy and he taught me the job along with the boss, coupled with Bert Whalley. The four of us were the people who really formed the Busby Babes. In my day, scouting was very hard because you didn't approach a boy. I'm afraid I did many things where I broke the rules. I waited around corners, I travelled on trains where teachers would be with the boy. I remember there was one boy who became an international… in the hotel just outside Carlisle station, I'll always remember dodging in a toilet there and locking the door while the player concerned followed me in. I was able to talk to him and then unlock and let him out!"

Armstrong and Rocca's network included scouts across the land. One of these was Jack O'Brien. They knew exactly what to say to make United look like an appealing proposition. When Eric Booth asked O'Brien how Manchester United would help Duncan, the response was impressive: a promise that United would arrange for him to attend a local technical college to learn carpentry until he was 17.

Both O'Brien and another of United's local scouts, Reg Priest, had been instructed to take a closer look at Edwards following a missed opportunity which was bothering Matt Busby. He had seen a young inside-forward by the name of Alec Farrell. Busby approached old friend Joe Mercer for help, partly due to the coaching courses he had been attending. "I asked Joe if he could do anything to help," Busby said. "Joe had been coaching the schoolboys, so he knew their capabilities better than anyone, but he was not very hopeful when I told him of my interest in Farrell."

Farrell was an Everton supporter and so when his boyhood club made an offer it was a formality that he would move there. Busby was still disgruntled about it the next time he met Mercer. "I don't know why you were so concerned about young Farrell," Mercer told him. "The best player of the whole bunch was a 14-year-old giant called Edwards. He's the one who'll make a world-beater, or I'm a Dutchman."

Mercer's judgement was correct. Duncan's performances at local level were commanding attention. Further schoolboy caps followed. Duncan played against 'The Rest' for England on March 17th, and then again against Wales at Somerton Park in Newport on March 26th. That date was Easter Monday – 24 hours later, Duncan was rushing about to play in a county match against Bedfordshire. The game was scheduled to be played at St George's

Lane, but heavy rain had made the waterlogged pitch unplayable, so the game was switched at the last minute to Perdiswell. There was no case of fatigue for Duncan, who inspired his side to a victory which could comfortably be filed under 'comprehensive'. Per the school minutes: "The County boys again showed brilliant form and overwhelmed their visitors by eleven goals to one."

The win moved the Worcester boys into the cup final, where they faced Derbyshire at Worcester City. Duncan skippered his side to glory, going 2-0 up before half-time. It was the first county cup medal Duncan won, although he had been collecting plenty of trophies along the way. "He'd have his school bag, and when he'd bring it home after playing football it would always be full, either a medal or a plaque, I lost count," Sarah said. "He was never a show-off if he won anything. He just played because he loved it."

In April 1951, Duncan realised his first major ambition when his schoolboy representation for England finally led him to play on the biggest stage in football, as Wales visited Wembley on the 7th. It was a moment recounted famously in a school essay Duncan wrote that December entitled 'A true wish', where he talked of his boyhood ambitions to play at the famous stadium.

At Wembley, in front of 100,000 people, Duncan wore the number six shirt. The match programme described him as standing 5ft 8ins, and weighing 10st 12lbs. To put this into a contemporary perspective, the average height of every grown man in the country in the decade was 5ft 7ins.

The end of year school report made special mention of the star: "The outstanding boy in the county was undoubtedly Duncan Edwards, our captain... Achieved great distinction by gaining three 'caps' with the national team, and also by captaining the junior team versus Ireland. An excellent team player, he was the inspiration of the county side."

Duncan spent some of his summer hop-picking with friends in Ledbury, as well as fishing, though these activities were merely distractions until he could get his feet on a ball again. Still a school-boy, he could not yet sign forms with any club. He and his parents had heeded Eric Booth's advice to not agree anything formally. However, Manchester United were making serious overtures, and felt confident that Duncan would eventually sign for them. Busby: "I watched Edwards. Jimmy Murphy watched him. Bert Whalley also had a few looks. We all compared notes, and were unanimous in endorsing the opinion expressed by Joe Mercer, but the next problem was to try and persuade the youngster that the North was a better place in which to live than the Midlands… and that he would be wiser to join Manchester United than Wolves, or Aston Villa, or Birmingham City, or West Bromwich Albion… As soon as Duncan Edwards left school at 15, I was ready to match word for word with any of my rivals!

"There was no necessity to 'sell' Manchester United: my battle was won before I started to fight it. As soon as I introduced myself he told me, 'I think Manchester United is the greatest club in the world. I'd give anything to play for your team, Mr Busby.'"

So United relaxed. Edwards entered his final year of school, finally allowing himself to dream that he could become a foot-baller, and at the same time taking in the prospect of a move north. "Not until I had become a youth international did I seriously think of earning my living at the game," he insisted. "Of course I wanted to join United. I could think of nothing more marvellous. But before I answered I faced up inwardly to all those doubts that came crowding in at moments like this. It was a chancy game and perhaps I wouldn't be good enough. It meant leaving home and living in Manchester… oh, and so many other small niggling doubts flashed through my mind."

In the summer of 1951, Duncan again represented England at left-half, with David Pegg in front of him at outside-left, against Scotland at Chesterfield. As he returned to school for that last year, Booth was keen to impart some final words of wisdom. The teacher was greeted at the first school's meeting of the year with a letter of congratulations upon the successes of Duncan Edwards, so he could feel as though he had played his own part, but he was still not quite done yet. He had witnessed Duncan's growth and was particularly impressed with the assured performance at left-half, which would be a deep-lying midfielder today. Formations were more rudimentary; the right-half and left-half would be tasked with winning the ball, carrying the ball, servicing the ball to the forward five players, and bringing up the rear at all times. They were, then, responsible for dictating the entire tempo of a team's play, and therefore, the most important players in a team.

"It is as well to listen to advice as long as it comes from a person with real experience in the game," Edwards remembered. "As a boy I always had a yen to be an inside-forward. One day the schoolmaster, Mr Eric Booth, came to me and said, 'You know, Duncan, your position is left-half.' And that was as good a piece of judgement as I have ever heard."

Booth had taken his lead from observing Duncan's performances in the international side and when the county trials teams were announced on October 22nd, 1951, Duncan was in at left-half having spent most of his school 'career' at inside-forward. After coming through the game at Halesowen on November 3rd, he was selected as captain against Gloucester on December 22nd.

On New Year's Day 1952, Duncan made the national press for a game played on December 29th, billed as a 'North vs South' trial match. The *Daily Mirror*'s Willie Evans had seen Edwards in action before but was clearly taken aback by the growth in the meantime, writing: "Duncan Edwards was the star player of the game. He was a dominating figure, both in attack and defence. He has grown and put on weight since last year, and his display is the best I have seen this year from a schoolboy. He also has developed a most deadly shot."

Later that month, Duncan received his first negative press in the *Sports Argus* on the 26th, when he was described as being "played right out of the game" for Dudley against South Birmingham. There was consolation a month later when the *Birmingham Gazette* ran a glowing feature:

For Duncan Edwards, the 15-year-old schoolboy international from Dudley's Wolverhampton Street School, the next two months can well be among the most memorable of his young life. Duncan is rated as one of the finest schoolboy footballers in the country and when the England boys meet Scotland at Wembley Stadium on April 5 it is expected that he will lead England as their skipper. If he plays against Wales at St Andrew's, Birmingham, the following month he will equal the all-time record of Derby's Raymond Parry, who won nine school International caps, inside 12 months. Play-anywhere-Duncan is primarily a wing-half but he has appeared as centre-forward, on the wing and in both inside positions. He was only 13 when he gained his first junior school international cap. Last year he won three senior caps and another junior cap against Northern Ireland at Belfast when he captained the side. Quietly modest, Duncan is a team player first and foremost. Listen to what Mr Eric Booth, secretary of Dudley Schools' FA, who coaches Duncan, has to say of this boy star who thinks nothing of putting in three hours' individual ball practice a day in his own backyard.

"Duncan is a great team man. His wonderful stamina and ability to turn defence into attack by uncanny ball distribution make him the most mature wing-half for his age I have yet seen," said Mr Booth, who thinks the boy has the hardest shot in schoolboy football. "He lives only for playing and will work himself to a standstill to perfect any fancied weakness in his play."

Mr Booth has been coaching Duncan since he was 11 and although it was at first thought advisable to shield him from senior football because of his age the lad's outstanding talent forced him into the Dudley representative side long before his 14th birthday. Naturally they are proud of this hefty, 'football crazy' lad at Wolverhampton Street. Says sportsmaster Mr. E. Martin, "Duncan is definitely an outstanding schoolboy player." At 11st 13lb and topping the 5ft 9in mark he has all the physical attributes needed… and he is still growing. The lad is fully aware of the interest in him by League clubs but until he leaves school this interest must be of the watching kind only." Duncan is intent on making professional football his career. "When I leave school I would like to go to a club where I can get on," he says.

On April 2nd, Willie Evans reported in his *Mirror* column: "I know that one of London's best clubs would like to sign him." Another team, however, convinced themselves that they were the favourites to snap up the hottest prospect in football. Bolton Wanderers believed they had two trump cards, and that was quite aside from the presence of Nat Lofthouse, one of the game's most celebrated forwards, in their team. No – the Wanderers had something closer to home they felt might help them get their boy.

Bolton scouts Frank Pickford and George Taylor went to the Midlands to watch Duncan play, with Pickford taking Gladstone out for a few pints to convince him to talk to his son. Duncan was then taken to Bolton to be shown around, where he was told how well he could settle in the area because his relative Dennis Stevens was now a professional at the club. The charm offensive continued even when Duncan returned home. Frank took Ray Parry, the Derby boy they had signed, down to try and talk Edwards into signing. Parry had made his professional debut for Bolton a few months earlier at the age of 15, and the suggestion was that Duncan could be next.

On April 4th, Duncan lined up against Scotland at Wembley. He apparently confessed to the *Daily Herald* the day before the game, "I know I shall get butterflies in my stomach at Wembley." However, returning to school, Duncan appeared frustrated, according to Stella Cook: "He came into school and said, 'You don't want to believe what you read in the papers'. He said he had said nothing of the sort [about butterflies]. He was cross about printing 'lies'. If he had 'butterflies' he kept them to himself and he wouldn't have known the expression."

His first press misquote – although, considering he would use a similar phrase in the future, perhaps he was protesting too much out of embarrassment.

Edwards continued to attract attention as he made England appearances. In recognition of his first game as captain, he was presented with a travelling case by the mayor of Dudley, George Marlow. One local newspaper referenced Duncan asking the mayor for advice about which club he should join. The mayor's response was quoted: "We reminded him of his local ties but he was determined to join Manchester United, the team he had favoured from a small boy." Marlow also passed him a pen, "in case you need it one day for autographs."

The night before the game, Duncan and his team-mates trained at Highbury. He was the only one from this schoolboy group to have played at Wembley, so as captain he gave his new colleagues some "useful advice" according to Leslie Nichol of the *Express*. There was a definite maturity in his performance in a 1-0 win, said the *Birmingham Gazette*: "Edwards played a real captain's part for England at left-half and his through passes to his forwards were a delight."

Having made the Dudley Schools and Worcester county teams the talk of the country for two years, Duncan was forced to end his schoolboy days on an anti-climatic note. In the President's Trophy competition against Halesowen & Stourbridge, at the Grove in Halesowen, Dudley tasted defeat after playing with 10 men for the entirety of the second half.

At least he was on the pitch. Due to his participation in England's schoolboy match against Scotland at Aberdeen's Pittodrie stadium, Duncan could not play against Staffordshire in the final county match, with the report describing the game thus: "Our team, although lacking the inspiration of the captain, Duncan Edwards, of international fame, put up an excellent show."

On May 3rd, Duncan was again representing England, this time against Wales in Birmingham, with the Victory Shield on offer for the victors. Peter Morris of the *Birmingham Gazette* may have been applying local bias when giving his pre-match assessment, but he was probably speaking the truth: "England must start favourites. Their great strength lies in the half-back line, where the two Midlanders, Frank Bolton (Rowley Regis) and Duncan Edwards (Dudley), have played brilliantly so far."

Morris did not need to express bias after England won 5-1. "Thirteen thousand people left St. Andrew's on Saturday convinced, in spite of drizzling rain and mud, they had seen some of the best schoolboy footballers in the world," he wrote. "England Boys, led by Duncan Edwards, of Dudley, beat Wales 5-1, but more important than the result was the form shown by all these talented youngsters. A number of League club scouts were there watching… Dominating the game was England's captain and left-half, Duncan Edwards. This heftily-built, tremendously strong youngster got through the work of two and never wasted a ball."

Duncan had been outstanding but he still had energy to burn. The team coach dropped him off in Dudley town centre. He walked home, a 20-minute journey, and found his friends on the park waiting for him to play another game. He dropped his bag back with his mum, and still in his national team dress, ran on to the park. In actual fact, the boys needed a goal post, so Duncan put his England blazer down to create a goal.

Jimmy Murphy was utterly convinced with what he'd watched earlier in the day. "From the first time I saw him as a boy of 14, Duncan looked like and played with the assurance of a man, with legs like tree trunks, a deep and powerful chest and an unforgettable zest for the game," the United assistant said. "One look was enough, but there was scarcely a club in the First Division who did not have scouts watching Duncan. You could not miss such a talented player. Joe Armstrong, Bert Whalley and myself kept close watch on his progress. We were helped by the fact that Duncan himself, impressed by the stories he had read of Manchester United's first great team just after the war, was attracted by the idea of coming to a club that placed football skill and entertainment at the top of its priorities. In a sense this was a real cloak and dagger operation, for with such a potential star nearby, there were great pressures on Duncan to stay in his own area in the Midlands."

As it transpired, United were anticipating an urgency that for one reason or another did not exist as far as the other local clubs were concerned. The one exception to this had been Wolves and Stan Cullis. Cullis *had* been desperate. So desperate in fact that one week he drove to Elm Road every single night and parked outside the Edwards house, hoping to convince the boy and his family that staying local made sense. Every time Cullis received the same response: Duncan was set on going to Manchester United.

Busby and Murphy had an eye on the calendar. England had one more schoolboy international during the 1951/52 season – against Ireland at Dalymount Park in Dublin on May 31st, where Duncan would be captain once more and play for a record ninth time over three years for a schoolboy. After that game, he could theoretically sign for a professional club and it would not affect his ability to play for England, as his schoolboy days would be over.

The boy himself had no idea about the planning that was going on. He simply wanted to play football. England lost 1-0, so it was in a disappointed mood Duncan travelled home the following day. A miscommunication undoubtedly helped Manchester United finally seal the deal. In the afternoon, Reg Priest heard that Bolton were planning to make a move, so contacted United and told them to act in haste. Jimmy Murphy ordered Bert Whalley to travel to Dudley with a contract. The United assistant had to make a judgement call as Busby was on United's post-season tour of America. "Bert had set off for the Midlands to clinch the deal and his car broke down," Murphy remembered. "He had to hitch a lift and got back to Manchester in the early hours of the morning. I had already had an urgent call from Reg Priest informing United that there were a lot of moves to get Duncan to change his mind, especially from a famous Lancashire club. There was nothing for it, we had to get back on the trail, so we hired a car and, tired out as he was, Bert Whalley went back to the Midlands. In fact, Bert had to knock up the Edwards household in the early hours and Dunc came down in his pyjamas rubbing the sleep from his eyes."

In actual fact, Priest had either heard incorrectly or was trying to push United into action – the Bolton scout Frank Pickford was in Belfast, looking at another player. Duncan himself seemed utterly bemused when Whalley was sitting in the living room at 2am. "What's all the fuss about?" the boy told the United coach. "I already said that United are the only club I want to sign for."

Amid the inconsistencies of stories, Duncan's comment after being awakened remains one factor which is present in almost every retelling of his signing for the club. What is clear is that Matt Busby was not there – despite later memories told by Duncan himself that the manager was. United's late-dash urgency adds to the drama, and perhaps they were prompted by an unnecessary panic, but prior to that they had seemed relatively assured of having got their boy. Allegations of inducements in the form of payments or gifts to parents often followed United's acquisition of these talented kids but were never proven. However, most were happy to put on record the fact that everyone from United had laid eyes on him, and all of the significant senior figures had, at one time or another, spent time with the boy and his family prior to June 1st, 1952. Another element which is certain is the drama: that United did send Bert Whalley to rubber-stamp the move upon hearing of Bolton's interest. With confirmation in the form of a signature on an amateur contract, Bert Whalley returned to Manchester.

However, on this occasion, there *was* an inducement that someone went on record admitting. Although the Old Trafford contingent had laid on the charm offensive – and Sarah and Gladstone were quite happy to leave the decision up to Duncan – they had not quite factored in Sarah's down-to-earth personality. She was satisfied by Joe Armstrong and Jimmy Murphy reassuring her that Duncan would be looked after, but she was not particularly bowled over by the presence of Matt Busby in the way that young players would be. She had no airs or graces, whoever was in her living room. Busby appreciated that. He asked her if there was anything she needed. Sarah pushed her luck. "A twin tub washing machine," she said. A few days later, she answered her front door to discover a twin tub washing machine was being delivered. It became the talk of the Priory Estate. The Edwards' had a twin tub. The neighbours would knock with the pretence of being social and conversation would quickly turn to the machine. *Could we bring our washing around, Sarah?* And every time, Sarah would say no. The twin tub remained unused for weeks. Sarah could not work out how to use it, and couldn't face admitting that in front of her friends.

By the time she had worked it out, her son was already in Manchester. The price of commitment, the price of reassurance that the best young footballer in the country would sign for Manchester United? A washing machine.

Chapter 4
Apples

Duncan Edwards might have had cause to think again if he had realised Matt Busby and Jimmy Murphy intended to look to the future instead of the present. The youngster had been captivated by the 1948 FA Cup team. He had been intoxicated by the attention paid to him during the multi-year courtship to lure him to Old Trafford. And he had been dreaming of integrating himself into the Manchester United team which had just won the First Division championship in 1952.

Busby, however, saw the judgement of the press – a hearty congratulations for the achievement, but a verdict that this was the crowning glory of a team whose best years were now behind them. He couldn't disagree. Reg Allen, Allenby Chilton, Henry Cockburn, Stan Pearson, Jack Rowley and the great captain Johnny Carey were all the wrong side of 30. Not for the last time, it appeared to critics as though the manager had been too loyal to his long-standing servants.

All things considered, it was an announcement worthy of the description 'bombshell' when, at that year's shareholders meeting, Busby answered questions about the ageing squad with the statement: "We have at least £200,000 worth of talent beyond the first team." How much of that fee the newly-acquired Duncan Edwards accounted for is unclear, but for context, the record transfer fee in England at the time was £34,500.

You could call it fortune, or you could describe Busby as a master of opportunism and timing – either way, a competition had been created that could prove the United manager right, and still provide him with enough time for patience to be exercised. He certainly championed the creation of the FA Youth Cup, a competition devised to pit the best young boys against each other. It almost seemed it had been designed especially for Busby.

A competition for young amateurs assigned to professional clubs, it was deemed there would be a greater interest than at county level, while also showing clubs how those players were progressing. Players had to be between 15 and 18 years old, while clubs were encouraged to use their own first-team stadiums to add a big-match feel.

Meanwhile, Busby's demand for complete control, and subsequent success, had more than justified the choice of Crickmer, Gibson and Rocca – the latter of whom sadly passed away in June 1950. If the manager's proclamation of youth team value had been greeted with scepticism outside of Old Trafford, that couldn't be further from the truth internally. The powers that be were delighted that their long-term plan was finally looking as though it was to bear fruit – indeed, Jimmy Murphy described the young players at the club as "golden apples".

On June 7th, Duncan officially became recognised as the latest of those apples when the Midlands press reported of United's summer signings. "Manchester United certainly believe in capturing them young, for their latest signings include three 15-year-olds," read a column in the *Leicester Evening Mail*. "They are Dudley-born Duncan Edwards, a left half-back who has played nine times for England as a schoolboy; Gordon Clayton, a goalkeeper from Cannock; and Allan Rhodes, a full back from Chesterfield. There should be some good results from such a trio."

Indeed, the *Sports Argus* referred to Edwards and Clayton as two of the "brightest schoolboy football stars" from the region. The pair travelled on the train to Manchester London Road that weekend, where they were met by Bert Whalley. Duncan had promised

Gordon he would save him a seat on the train, as he was getting on at Dudley and Gordon was getting on at Stafford. Sure enough, as the train pulled in, Duncan was waving out of the window. He'd been good to his word – even though the train was empty!

United's venture into signing out-of-area boys had necessitated all kinds of non-football arrangements. As they could not yet sign as professional players, the more pressing matter was their employment. So, as good as it was for United to make a promise to look after Edwards' carpentry ambitions, they also had an obligation to do so anyway. They arranged an apprenticeship for Duncan at a local cabinet makers. Then they had to take care of his lodgings. United had a roster of landladies who looked after a few boys each on a permanent basis, but in the summer months, they also had landladies near their Cliff training ground in Lower Broughton serving as, effectively, halfway houses. These were temporary lodgings necessary to take in the new young boys while those who had not been offered professional terms by May 31st were sorting out their own future.

Duncan found the first few weeks strange. The majority of the first-team squad were still away and he would report for training on Tuesday and Thursday evenings at the Cliff with the rest of the new young faces; these were introductory sessions in front of Jimmy Murphy, Bert Whalley, Jack Pauline, Arthur Powell, Bert Fishburne, Harry Ablett and Joe Travis, coaches who looked after the various teams. Duncan and Gordon were told they would be moving into Mr and Mrs Watson's house at 5 Birch Avenue, just off the Warwick Road stretch between the two Old Traffords; the cricket ground which housed Lancashire County Cricket Club, and the football stadium of Manchester United.

Pre-season training was due to commence on July 13th, so before then, both United and Duncan's new employers were lenient with time off. He was permitted to return home at weekends and also for a midweek event at Dudley Technical College on July 2nd, where the precocious 15-year-old was named as guest of honour alongside the local man who had recently established himself as England's first-choice goalkeeper, Birmingham City's Gil Merrick, at a Dudley School FA presentation. Edwards was surprised by the news that one of the local competitions had been renamed in his honour, and it was with considerable pride that he presented the 'Duncan Edwards Trophy' to Dudley Grammar School.

Though Duncan took a little longer to settle in Manchester than his garrulous new friend Gordon Clayton, he was enjoying his new surroundings. Clayton had no problem talking to his new landlady, and in comparison, Duncan seemed almost introverted. As the first-team players returned, Mrs Watson's filled up with its regular residents – Johnny Berry, 26, the former Birmingham City outside-right who had starred in the First Division team with six goals in 36 games; Jackie Blanchflower, the 19-year-old Northern Irish boy with one first-team appearance to his name; Mark Jones, also 19, with seven senior appearances; and David Pegg, who was yet to make his first-team bow but was of course known to Edwards from their time together in the England set-up.

Blanchflower recalled his initial meetings with Edwards and Clayton, admitting that he, Jones and Pegg felt "disturbed" by the new arrivals and that he was jealous of Mrs Watson's attention to Duncan, as she had mistaken his shyness for homesickness. There was an additional wariness for Blanchflower, who was a left-half – the position Duncan was known to play. But United had placed their youngsters carefully. Even within the walls of digs, there was a hierarchy of progression which highlighted the virtue of patience and the rewards for hard work. First there was Berry, who had spent his entire post-war career in Birmingham, so could discuss Duncan's home area with him. Jones was the most senior of the homegrown boys – he was also physically taller and broader than Duncan, another perceptive move from United to place their new boy in lodgings with someone literally bigger than him.

Blanchflower was a little different. He had been battling for a regular place in the reserve side, usually wearing six, but occasionally the number four at right-half before an injury had ruled him out for months. Jeff Whitefoot was an emerging left-half but in the final weeks of the previous season, senior player Billy McGlen saw out the Central League campaign in the number six shirt. Now close to fitness, Blanchflower was bracing himself for a new rival, and the reality that he would have to find a new place in the team.

David Pegg, meanwhile, had just dipped his toes into the reserve side. The 1951/52 Central League season had started with Roger Byrne scoring a hat-trick in the number 11 shirt but by the end of the campaign, owing to Byrne's own progression, Pegg had become first choice outside-left for the second string. Pegg was smaller than most of the other players but size was compensated for with hype, with Matt Busby himself speaking of the Doncaster boy's potential. His position in the reserve side was evidence that opportunities would be given with talent the decisive factor.

Duncan quickly became popular with his housemates. He had a keen sense of respect for those around him so he made sure to repay Mrs Watson's kind attention with an almost over-the-top approach to cleanliness in his first few weeks; Clayton nicknamed him 'Brush' due to how many times he would sweep his bedroom clean. That quickly became the name Berry, Blanchflower, Jones and Pegg called him.

"So off I went to Manchester, a raw 16-year-old living with eight other young United players," Edwards remembered. "By day I worked as a joiner and on every Tuesday and Thursday I had two hours' coaching in heading, throwing, kicking, and trapping. Each week the lesson was different, but after four or five weeks we would suddenly come back to it again so that the coach could see whether we had improved. We would be watched to see that we were incorporating our lessons into actual match play. I found myself picking up club spirit in the most humble role when I first joined… I was often little more than a general labourer, helping to clean out dressing-rooms and baths. It was hardly an edifying job yet it helped me to get to know professional footballers. People like Jack Rowley, Stan Pearson, and Johnny Carey, the top men of the day. I watched them to see how they conducted themselves. I began to realise what was going to be expected of me if I made the grade… my football education reached its climax playing alongside people like them in five-a-side games. I learned things in those games it would have taken 12 months of coaching to have taught me."

Duncan loved the idea of being around football all the time and was envious of the young players who had been given jobs on the ground staff at Old Trafford instead of an apprenticeship. He decided early on that he did not want to pursue a career in carpentry, but it would be a while until he was brave enough to tell his parents.

It was this conscientious approach which defined Duncan's first few weeks at United. He admitted that the first time he met the other players at training, he wondered if he was at a football club at all. "There were so many other youngsters that it seemed almost like being at school," he said. "I found it very easy to make friends."

On the first day of 'official' pre-season training, all of the players were gathered together. Matt Busby later said: "At the start of a season, Jimmy Murphy, Bert Whalley and I get the boys together for an informal chat… Following one such talk, I pulled Jimmy Murphy to one side and said, 'Jimmy, you see the big boy in the corner of the room. All the time I have been talking his eyes have been on me, taking everything in.' That is the way he has been ever since. Always ready to listen to something that may be to his benefit. The boy's name – Duncan Edwards."

There were other new boys. Brian Lowry, a local forward player, Alan Morton, an outside-right from the north east, Alan Rhodes, a wing-half from Chesterfield, Colin Webster, another goalscoring forward from Wales, and Walter Whitehurst, a left-half like Duncan who was also a youth international. But Duncan had his own reputation and one of the existing players, Bill Foulkes, remembered being "in disbelief" when he was told of Edwards' age.

"The first time I met Duncan, I was a part-time player training twice a week," Foulkes said. "One Thursday afternoon Duncan showed up. I couldn't believe the ability that he had. The strength and maturity, as a schoolboy. He was a terrific person to know, always friendly, always polite."

But 15 he was, and as a new boy on day one, Duncan was placed in the care of Bert Fishburn, Jack Pauline, Arthur Powell, Harry Ablett and Joe Travis, the men charged with looking after the Junior and Colts teams. A week before the opening league game of the season, the club held what was publicised as a 'public trial match' at Old Trafford; these events were actually mini-curtain raisers with the new youngsters playing at 1.45pm before another match between the first team and reserve team at 3pm. These games were billed as 'Reds' v 'Blues'; Duncan was in the Reds team which won 5-0. The Blues were no mugs. They included Albert Scanlon and Eddie Lewis, two boys of tremendous promise, as well as Eddie Colman. The potential was just as great on Duncan's team, with Pegg, full-back Geoff Bent, and defender Ronnie Cope. One local report of the afternoon's proceedings carried the line of the Reds half-back line proving "too strong" for their opponent.

In his programme notes for the following week's *United Review* as the first team welcomed Chelsea to Old Trafford, Matt Busby insisted: "I think all who saw the United juniors in action last Saturday will appreciate that we have some of the greatest young-sters in the country."

There would surely have been one or two nodding heads in the terraces from supporters who would have spent their morning at the Cliff watching Edwards play for the Colts side in the opening match of Division One in the Manchester Amateur League against Heywood St James. The Colts – with Gordon Robbins at right-half and Duncan at left-half – won 6-1. There was similar comfort in 3-1 away victories against Roebuck Lane and Dukinfield Town both before the end of August.

Robbins and Edwards had sufficiently impressed to be called up to the A team to face Ball Haye Green in Leek. A 4-3 win for United encouraged Jack Pauline to recommend that Clayton, Edwards, Robbins, Scanlon, Doherty and Noel McFarlane, an outside-forward, should all be called into Jimmy Murphy's first ever FA Youth Cup team.

Murphy certainly treated the competition seriously. United fielded six schoolboy internationals in their team to face Leeds United on October 22nd, and held the match at Old Trafford. Clayton, Cope, Edwards and Pegg had played for England, with Paddy Kennedy and McFarlane having represented Ireland schoolboys.

In spite of all of the preparation, the *Manchester Evening Chronicle* complained of "only about a couple of hundred spectators present when the game began", although that was partly due to the fact it had kicked off at 3pm on a Wednesday afternoon.

Leeds had some promising talent such as defender Jack Charlton; but without even a game being played at this level, the reputation of Duncan Edwards – now only just 16 – preceded him, and the Yorkshire side had made a specific plan, asking one of their forward players to mark a midfielder. "I was switched from my normal inside-left role to inside-right in order to combat left-half Duncan Edwards as I was 6ft 2in tall," remembered Mick Evans. "However, I didn't get a kick all game."

United scored early on through Albert Scanlon; the hosts then plundered three late goals in quick succession, evoking memories of the 1948 final in what one report described as a "monopolised" display. *Daily Mirror* sportswriter Willie Evans drew the comparison. "Matt Busby, the Manchester United manager, says he has a team of young players worth over £100,000," Evans wrote. "Believe me, he's right! Tempted by the Busby bouquet to the boys I took a trip to watch his young stars play. How they played! I came away with the conviction that here was the best junior side I have seen for some time… these Manchester United lads have that same rhythmic, cultured and planned look as the cup winning side United turned out in 1948. Floodlight training is working wonders for United. Every Thursday evening, they are watched and coached by Jimmy Murphy and Bert Whalley. On Tuesdays, Murphy and Whalley join in the practice matches. Each member of the United side is a former schoolboy star of international, county or town class… it is hard to be outstanding in such brilliant company. But the lad who was able to do just that was Duncan Edwards, left-half, last season's England International skipper. He was great."

The reward for conquering Leeds was a match against another local rival, albeit of lesser stature – Nantwich, who were so thrilled to be drawn against United that they forfeited home advantage to play under the floodlights at the Cliff on Tuesday November 4th. Some 2,600 spectators crammed around the pitch, providing a tidy gate receipt of £216 which Nantwich were allowed to keep. United's generosity didn't end there. Although the Cliff had flood-lights, they were not very powerful, and so the hosts provided their visitors with bright amber shirts which officials had picked up on the post-season tour to America.

And then kick-off came, proving the pleasantries were well and truly over. United were three goals up in six minutes and, by half-time, had struck 10 times – with Eddie Lewis, who had been the '12th man' for the first team at the weekend (the reserve in case of a drop-out, in the days before substitutes) netting a hat-trick in the first 45 minutes. Edwards had notched one of the 10 – his first United goal at any level – and was probably expecting Jimmy Murphy to congratulate him and his team-mates for a strong performance. Instead, the Welshman urged them to try even harder in the second half, barking: "You haven't won the game yet!"

Driven by the fear of their interval chastising, United relentlessly tormented their amateur opponents, scoring 13 more goals, hitting the woodwork four times and forcing the goalkeeper Brian Thorley into probably as many saves as conceded goals (the watching Matt Busby actually signed Thorley shortly after, and the young goalkeeper played a handful of games at junior level for United).

In the final tally of 23 goals to nil, Duncan helped himself to five, as did Pegg and Doherty. It was a record victory for United at any level – it still is – and rightly attracted the attention of the national press. A sportswriter for the *Daily Mail* decreed Edwards as: "The greatest junior prospect I have ever seen. That is no exaggeration." Another reporter described the Dudley boy's passing range as "being the equal of anything I have seen from full international players".

Later that month, Bury were the opponents in the third round of the cup at Old Trafford. United made short work of controlling the tie.

Duncan was revelling in his football. He had struck up a close friendship with Eddie Colman, the boy so Salford that he grew up on Archie Street, the cobbled terraced street in Ordsall which served as the inspiration for the television soap *Coronation Street*. Colman was an extrovert, and emboldened with a cocksure attitude which was only intensified by the opportunity to play for his local club. Colman would joke that he was only picked to play football to make up the numbers but had so impressed Busby and Murphy in a performance for Salford Boys at the Cliff that they immediately signed him up. He was partly right – no proper professional club had taken much interest. Murphy couldn't believe his luck. In the early weeks of this campaign, Colman would normally turn out for the Colts as Jack Pauline *et al* expressed concerns about his size, but whenever he and Edwards played in the half-back line together, it was clear they had a style which was complementary in the extreme.

This was no doubt aided by their off-pitch friendship. Edwards' football style was already speaking for itself so he needn't compensate by compromising his laidback demeanour. Colman and Clayton could be the loud ones. Together with David Pegg, the boys would often go to the Plaza, the Locarno or the Continental in Manchester to dance. Pegg loved his music such as Frank Sinatra, and loved a dance as much as Colman, but even though he had a history for it, Duncan – as Wilf McGuinness later recalled – would prefer to sit at the table rather than get up on the floor.

The grace he showed for his size was still noted on the field of play, however, with one local report picturing Duncan in the tie against Bury as part of a "ballet-like" ensemble as he rose to head the ball. Nothing graceful associated with his involvement in the opening goal; seven minutes in, he strode forward with purpose, unleashing a shot of venom which Eddie Lewis diverted past the goalkeeper. A resolute Bury were relieved to come away with just a 2-0 defeat, after Lewis added his second later on.

Edwards was once again the most impressive player on the pitch, commanding the pace from left-half. Sportswriter Edgar Turner declared afterwards: "I am sure Matt Busby could give him a game in the first team now."

Such talk gathered momentum after a sterling performance and a goal in a 4-3 win against amateur side Northern Nomads in a friendly game at the Cliff on December 3rd. The report in the *Manchester Guardian* read: "Edwards is remarkably strong for his years, is fast, and tackled well, but best of all shot with real power in either foot."

Three days later, Edwards was called into the reserve team for the first time to play in the Central League game at Burnley. With Blanchflower once more established in the number six shirt, Duncan's promotion found him at inside-right in the number eight shirt. It seemed a step too early – Burnley won a physical game 1-0. Nonetheless, Edwards retained his place for the following week's visit of Preston, as Jimmy Murphy and Bert Whalley kept an eye on him with the next round of the Youth Cup not until February. The second reserve game went much better, finishing 2-1 to United.

By Christmas, Edwards was back in the A team and scored twice against Everton to strike genuine fear into a team who were due to face these same United players in the Youth Cup. Sure enough, ahead of that tie at Old Trafford on February 4th, 1953, the young Toffees players were given a stern warning. "Before the game, our coach Gordon Watson told us all to keep an eye on the left-half as he'd played against Everton Reserves and scored two goals," remembered goalkeeper Cyril Hatton. "It was proved correct how good he was by scoring the winner against us. The goal I can remember as if it was last week. A corner was hit to the far side of the area where Duncan Edwards stopped it, trapping and hitting all in one movement. I never saw the ball and just heard it hit the back of the net. It was an absolutely brilliant goal."

The shot was struck with deadly precision, low through a "forest of legs" according to the *Daily Dispatch*. In United's narrowest cup game yet, once more Edwards had proven to be the difference. The contribution came with a reward – another call-up to the reserve team, and a homecoming to boot as Edwards was named as inside-forward in the number 10 shirt at Wolves. It was one of those occasions where everyone went home happy – everyone local, that is, anyway. With friends and family in attendance, Duncan was delighted to get his first goal at this level, sliding the ball in from a narrow angle. The home side, however, had registered goals either side of that 54th-minute shot to send the Edwards family home in a good mood.

It had been an eventful first season at United for Duncan Edwards and it was now approaching the business end. United faced Barnsley at Old Trafford in the FA Youth Cup for a place in the semi-final. Some 12,400 were at the game, almost 5,000 more than the attendance for Barnsley's first-team game against Birmingham at Oakwell on the same day. Also in attendance was the new signing Tommy Taylor, ironically enough from the Yorkshire side, and acquired in the same cloak-and-dagger style as

Edwards' own arrival; a story which featured Busby and Murphy in a Barnsley theatre to watch a movie, and asking the ticket-seller to alert them if a 'tall, thin man' – Cyril Spiers, the Cardiff manager who was rumoured to be interested in Taylor – arrived to watch the movie. Spiers did, and having directed him to his seat, the seller walked past Murphy and Busby to give them the nod – the United party relaxed, knowing that for the next couple of hours at least they would not have to worry about missing out. Taylor was duly signed for a fee of £29,999, with Busby giving the Barnsley tea lady a pound coin so as not to burden the forward with a £30,000 transfer fee.

The Youth Cup tie was played at a frenetic pace, with Barnsley deciding the only way to match this United side was to go hell for leather themselves. Something had to give. Just before half-time, United were awarded a free-kick 30 yards out. Due to the weight of the balls it was rare to see players take on a shot from a set-piece, but that is precisely what Edwards did. The powerful shot appeared to be on target, but to make sure, John Doherty showed either remarkable bravery or stupidity to get in the way of it, diverting it past the goalkeeper. Barnsley grabbed a shock equaliser – but their first goal concession of the tournament merely stung the pride of United's kids, who enjoyed two quick-fire strikes to put the tie to bed.

Edwards starred again for the reserve team in a 3-1 win over Newcastle; a performance strong enough to prompt George Follows, in his *News Chronicle* column of April 1st, to proclaim: "Like the father of the first atom bomb, Manchester United are waiting for something tremendous to happen. This tremendous football force they have discovered is Duncan Edwards, who is exactly 16-and-a-half this morning. Though nobody can tell exactly what will happen when Edwards explodes into First Division football, one thing is certain, it will be spectacular. What can you expect to see in Edwards? Well, the first important thing is that this boy is a man of 12st and 5ft 10in in height. That gives him his first great asset of power. When he heads the ball, it is not a flabby flirtation with fortune, it is bold and decisive. When he tackles, it is with a mantrap bite, and when he shoots with either foot, not even Jack Rowley is shooting harder. Add to this, body swerve and bravery and the sixth sense in a tight corner that distinguishes the truly great player and you have 'the boy who has the lot'. If you think this is a lot to write about a lad of 16, I can only say you obviously haven't seen this boy Edwards."

That evening, Edwards proved the point by scoring in a 4-0 win over Ashton United to help his team win the Gilgryst Cup at the Cliff; this 'A' team line-up included the likes of Scanlon, Lewis and Dennis Viollet, who scored the other goals. Edwards had also scored in the semi-final of this secondary competition.

By now, Duncan had given up his apprenticeship and convinced the club to put him on the ground staff, though he was still yet to tell Sarah and Gladstone. He was sweeping the terraces of Old Trafford on the morning of Friday April 3rd when he was told Matt Busby wanted to see him in his office. Duncan had watched his young housemates all get further opportunities in the first team that season. In addition, John Doherty had taken his chance with two goals in five games, and Eddie Lewis had done even better, getting seven in 10 league games. Duncan could expect he'd get his fair chance – but those boys were at least a year older than him. Duncan expected he would have to wait until next year at least.

Busby, however, had other plans. He'd seen enough. The sportswriters were already making a case for the young boy and even they, as early as they seemed, were late to this particular game, with the rave reviews from Pauline, Whalley and Murphy all serving as the surest cast-iron endorsements Busby needed.

"Go and get your boots," he told the youngster, "as you are playing in the first team tomorrow against Cardiff City."

In the years which followed, the legend of Matt Busby would transform him into a man to be feared and revered in almost equal measure. The reputation was set in stone once United's success was established, but in the years when that was not the case, there wasn't necessarily a great terror associated with the manager. Or, at least, not as far as Edwards was concerned, as he was brave enough to ask if he could use Busby's telephone to call his parents to let them know the good news.

Busby smiled and granted the request; Duncan then raced back to Birch Avenue to tell everyone he could. It had been a late decision taken by Busby due to an injury suffered by regular left-half Henry Cockburn. So late, in fact, that Cockburn's name appeared on the team-sheet of the match programme, though not so late that the newspapers were not able to acquire a quote from Gladstone for their Saturday editions.

"We are as excited as a couple of kids," he said of he and Sarah, who were planning to make the last-minute trip to Manchester. "Duncan is the calmest member of the family just now. He is used to playing before big crowds."

Edwards later agreed, saying the thought of making his debut for United was "not terrifying, after having played at Wembley three times before I was 15."

United's travails that season might have helped the result seem less of a nightmare, but it still did not make a 4-1 home defeat to Cardiff any more palatable in isolation. Busby's side were two goals down inside 15 minutes and couldn't muster any momentum to break down a disciplined Cardiff defence. Just about the only player who didn't let themselves down on a horrible day was Duncan Edwards, whose performance was more of a consolation than the penalty Roger Byrne scored just before the end of the game.

Edwards' partner in the half-back line was Don Gibson, a steady squad player who deputised at right-half when Johnny Carey was not available. Club captain Carey was intending to retire in the summer with Gibson never likely to be a permanent replacement; these were the moving pieces Busby was working with as he sought to implement his long-term plan. It was this sort of phasing which had resulted in the inconsistency of the season. Stan Pearson, in front of Edwards at inside-left, was also a veteran close to the end of his career; a complete contrast to the inexperience of Duncan and Pegg at outside-left.

Big things were expected of Edwards but this was an era of more realistic assessments. Hyperbole was the language of tomorrow. The general lethargy in United's play as they plodded towards the end of the season was mirrored by the dropping attendances – 52,590 had turned up for a game against Preston in early March, but only 37,163 were in the stands for the Cardiff game. It was difficult for Edwards to impress, though he did as well as anyone could expect.

"The only ray of sunshine that filtered through the United gloom," wrote Alf Clarke in the *Manchester Evening Chronicle*, "was the display of boy debutant Duncan Edwards, who did all that was asked of him, including taking a shot from 30 yards that was only just wide."

Clarke's generosity was barely matched by other reporters. In the *News Chronicle*, Frank Taylor remarked that Edwards "looks a wonderful prospect, tackles well, hits a lovely long ball – but he looks a bit thick round the hips," while the *Manchester Guardian*'s assessment was that Duncan "showed promise of fine ability in passing and shooting, but will have to move faster as a wing-half. However, he cannot be judged on this match". There was a more munificent assessment in the *Liverpool Echo*: "Setting an example for coolness to his more experienced colleagues in the early stages was League debutant 16-years-old Duncan Edwards. It was a striking commentary on the superiority of Cardiff's defence that, apart from a dangerous overhead kick from Pearson, the best shots came from the young half-back."

There was no fairytale entrance into the first team for Duncan Edwards, then – just a hard reminder of the work to be done if the club were to return to the summit of English football.

Chapter 5
Bouncing Babes

When you think about it – really think about it – it is remarkable to consider just how different almost every aspect of life appeared to be in the UK in 1953. You can wind back a decade earlier and be wowed by this contemplation when you break it down into the smaller, everyday things. Go back another 10 years and it seems crazier still. Life for a young person living in England in the early 1950s seems almost primitive compared to how it feels in the 21st century.

It would be another 10 years still until the freedom of the Sixties but there is no doubting the liberation that was being felt in the post-war youth. Britain was emerging from the damage of the war. There was prosperity in the air, albeit with a pragmatic sensibility.

How did this affect football? Well, at Manchester United, their redevelopment of Old Trafford after the bombing featured the restoration of a roof on the Main Stand in 1951. That work was continuing throughout the ground with the intention to have all terraces covered by the end of the decade.

In the summer of 1952, the year Duncan Edwards signed for Manchester United, the average national weekly wage was £8.13s. The maximum football wage was increased from £9 to £14, and £10 in the summer (the cut in wages often meant that some footballers found jobs in the off-season). As Britain was cautiously navigating peacetime after two world wars, conscription was still compulsory, and was increased from 18 months to two years in October 1950 due to British involvement in the Korean War. That meant healthy males aged 17 to 21 years would be required to serve in the forces for 24 months, unless they worked in one of the 'essential services' industries – coal mining, farming, or the merchant navy. Footballers were not exempt.

The reputation of footballers was also very different to how it is today; different to how it was in the early 1940s, when, as Jack White's memory tells us, most people wouldn't know who was playing on the opposition team. Different to how it was in the early 1960s, when George Best stepped into the spotlight created for a sportsman by the pop culture wave the Beatles were riding on. It would be wrong to say footballers were derided by the average working man, but considering the average labour of being a footballer compared to being a miner, for example, there was a certain pride carried by the common man of how hard he had to work for his wage.

But football was becoming more accessible. It was enter-tainment. Families went on Saturdays. Towards the end of matches the gates would open, and instead of people leaving, hundreds of children would swell the crowd.

There was a greater accessibility to players, who were much more likely to live in the house next door than they are today. And if you were a United fan and you were lucky, you might live close to one of the digs, where a handful of your heroes were. For the younger boys of the 1950s, footballers were the real-life heroes. They were the most accessible creators of entertainment, and because Manchester United's were a mix of local boys and mostly young, there was something aspirational for the kids of Salford and Stretford.

"I can remember going to games on a Saturday and seeing workers who had come from the pits, with dark smudges all over their faces," remembers United supporter Tom Clare, a young boy of the time. "There was no television. This was the entertainment, this is what you did on a weekend. It made everything so much more special that these were just everyday lads you could see down the street. It gave you this extra connection to the club. I can remember idolising Eddie Colman and following him as he walked home from the game to his house on Archie Street. He'd walk, and noticed I was following him, this timid kid lurking 100 yards behind. Whenever he'd stop, I'd stop. 'Are you my bloody shadow?' he'd laugh... but it was all good natured."

Duncan Edwards' mode of transportation was a bicycle. He had made an instant impression on the young United fans who had most likely sneaked in to watch the youth games. "The first time I saw Duncan was in a youth team game," says Clare. "I was mesmerised. Nobody could take liberties with him. One or two players tried and they were quickly put in their place. He was so quiet. He signed autographs after the game – every bit of paper. Every cigarette card. Then he'd get on his rusty old Raleigh bike and cycle back up the Warwick Road."

The connection was made stronger by a number of factors. The accessibility, the youth. The fact that over the first year of the FA Youth Cup, United's youngsters had been the pride of the club, emphasising the idea that the transition was nigh.

It would make that feeling stronger still if United could go all the way in the competition. Their semi-final opponents were Brentford. Duncan – who had made his first-team debut a week earlier – was back in the youth team for the first leg at Griffin Park on April 11th. This was no demotion for him or David Pegg, who lined up in his usual number 11 shirt after also playing against Cardiff. For Manchester United this wasn't just about the Youth Cup; it wasn't just about winning something. It was about vindicating Busby's bold claims of less than a year earlier.

Brentford scored after just three minutes, and held that lead until half-time. But United were fired up by a Jimmy Murphy blast, and scored in even quicker time after the restart through McFarlane. In an eventful second half with both teams pushing for a second goal, Brentford missed a penalty, and Scanlon grabbed the crucial strike with 10 minutes left. As the United boys walked off the pitch, Murphy could be seen singling out Edwards and the captain Ronnie Cope to praise them for their efforts.

Brentford had looked daunted after Scanlon's goal; they feared the worst at Old Trafford, and those concerns were well-founded, although it still took Murphy's 'marvels' a while to get going. The visitors had the audacity to fashion an effort in the 29th minute, provoking United to hit back immediately through a goal from Lewis. A second, third and fourth goal followed. United were playing exhibition football and it seemed the Brentford players could only get close enough to foul their opponents. From one such illegal challenge, Edwards hit a ferocious free-kick which flew into the goal. A sixth goal, from Scanlon, followed.

Brentford manager Tommy Lawton described their conquerors as "the best youth team I have ever seen" and exclaimed that Busby "must be the happiest manager in the world". The main praise in the press was reserved for Eddie Colman, Edwards' half-back mate, who had delivered balls all evening to the forward stars.

Busby might well have considered his kids to be practically perfect in every way, but their opponents in the final were Wolverhampton Wanderers, and the Midlanders had an arguably even more impressive record in the competition (if we are to disregard the Nantwich game as an uncompetitive aberration). Their victories had come by scores of 5-0, 2-0, 5-0, 6-0, 5-0, and 6-0. The Wolves manager, Stan Cullis, shared similar ideals to Busby in the way to construct a football club, and this much had been proven by the club's emphatic Central League successes in recent years – three consecutive championships.

United's last Division One game, against Liverpool no less, would bring in 20,869 supporters two weeks after the first leg of the Youth Cup final against Wolves, which attracted 20,934 fans. The prospect of witnessing the best two young teams in the country demanded an audience that befitted the occasion. And United put on a show for the crowd, registering a blistering 7-1 victory, a relentless goal spree which made an emphatic statement. Tom Jackson, of the *Manchester Evening News*, put it into words: "Gallantly as the Molineux boys fought, they were gradually torn to shreds by a United team that, say in three or four years' time, could be among the elite of First Division football."

There was a new boy in the team – Billy Whelan, an Irish inside-forward who had recently arrived from Home Farm for a fee of £10,000. He made an instant impression, grabbing one of the seven. Edwards had not been among the scorers, but he was nonetheless pictured and described as "the star" of United's team by the *Wolverhampton Express & Star*, who led their report of the game with the headline 'Dudley boy the inspiration in Manchester United's Youth Cup lead'. "Edwards, whom I interviewed as a Dudley schoolboy just 12 months ago, was, to all intents and purposes, the complete wing half-back," wrote their correspondent. "Strong man in a strong side, he failed only once in the whole game to make good use of the ball and if for nothing else, I would remember him for the uncanny accuracy of a series of long raking passes across the field on the inside of the full-back, not to mention the urgency with which he played throughout."

Success in the competition was now practically a formality. United arranged a special service with British Rail to leave London Road for Wolverhampton at 12:25pm on Saturday May 9th, so fans could "roll up and cheer the boys". The maturity of the performance that greeted those supporters was worthy of seasoned professionals. Wolves scored early on, but United were able to manage the game with assurance. That much was thanks to the influence of Duncan and Eddie, the two half-backs, who constantly took the sting out of the play. This coolness was rewarded with two quick goals just before half-time, as Lewis and Whelan put any question of a comeback to rest. Wolves salvaged a

2-2 draw but the impressive firefighting skills of the half-back line had completely doused any tempo the hosts tried to generate.

Two days after the final victory, Edwards was included in a post-season youth team trip to Ireland, where he took his first flight on a tour led by Murphy and Bert Whalley. All three games were won convincingly with a local report praising United's "magnificent display of football, well above their grade, splendid team work, and a sound knowledge of the best type of positional play that was a credit to their club". And for Duncan there was the personal accolade of *Daily Mirror* journalist Willie Evans' "outstanding junior player of the season", as he wrote on May 13th.

The creche of Busby and Murphy had delivered its first reward, and it could scarcely have come in more comprehensive fashion. There were beneficial consequences. This was not a recruitment system that would rest on its laurels after one impressive result. United scouts were constantly on the hunt for new talent and used the success of their youth team to convince the very best boys to sign for them. Wilf McGuinness, captain for England schoolboys, recalls: "I first saw Duncan when he captained England Schoolboys and he was marvellous. He joined United and I was unsure whether to sign as they were interested in me. I went to the final of the Youth Cup against Wolves. I saw this giant playing at left-half and recognised him as Duncan... I was a right-half at the time. I thought how wonderful it would be to be in the same team as him. It was my main reason for joining."

McGuinness had gone on the trip to Ireland, but was not included in the playing squad, and he remembered the time as almost like a "carefree family holiday"; he spent much time with the boy he had succeeded as national skipper, wondering if the reason Edwards didn't speak so much was because he was conscious of his thick Dudley accent. McGuinness might have had a point. A feature of Jimmy Murphy's often-politically incorrect team-talks would be to denigrate the locality of the opposition. Though just for effect – Murphy was embracing as anyone could be of different cultures and ideas – Edwards had grown accustomed to saying less while everyone around him was happy to state their piece.

Another quiet lad was set to join the ranks. Earlier that year, Joe Armstrong had been on one of his scouting missions to the north east. "It was a thin February morning with frost upon the ground," said Armstrong. "We had to peer through the mist but what I saw was enough for me. This boy is going to be a world beater." Jimmy Murphy described Armstrong on his return to Manchester as a man "with the excitement of a gold prospector who had struck it rich". The boy was Bobby Charlton. Joe Armstrong was able to charm Bob Snr and Cissie, the parents of the youngster. The former telephone engineer enlisted the help of Murphy, who spoke of being a similar age when he'd left home to play football, and how his own career had helped take his father out of the coal-mining industry. He assured the parents that the club would look after their boy.

Charlton arrived at Old Trafford in July 1953. He was met at London Road station by Jimmy Murphy, who was taking him to his new digs. Charlton recalled how Jimmy had been obsessed with one boy already at the club: "When he first met me at the station his entire football universe seemed to be filled by big Duncan. On that journey, Jimmy had said with shining eyes, 'Bobby, I've got a player you will find hard to believe, he is so good. He has everything. He is tall and powerful, but he also has a wonderful touch. Right foot, left foot, it doesn't matter. I'm going to make him such a player. Just look at him – and then remember I haven't knocked the rough edges off him yet.'"

Charlton thought to himself *surely nobody could be that good*. As he made himself comfortable in his new home at 5 Birch Avenue, he awaited the return of his housemate with the legend growing in his mind.

Duncan had spent the summer back in Dudley with his parents. His laidback demeanour made him bashful in the face of all the attention he received back home. He was at his happiest talking to old friends, telling them stories that were hardly even to do with football, such as the food he ate when he travelled. Tommy Millinson, his old goalkeeper friend from the Dudley boys team, would joke that he should still think about joining Wolves.

Edwards was excited to return to Manchester for the new season. He wasn't even yet a professional, but it was almost certain he would this time not be beginning in the Colts or even the A team. And it was as certain as anything could be that he would be a professional on October 1st, his 17th birthday. At Birch Avenue, he met his new housemate, and struck an instantly close friendship. Charlton was similarly reserved, and equally passionate about football. Duncan appreciated the quiet shyness, and spent much time with the new boy to help him settle. Bobby was appreciative of the time taken by the player everyone was raving about.

Though Edwards' performances had earned progression, the influx of new players like McGuinness and Charlton meant that spaces in teams were at a premium. The number of half-backs at the club meant that some players who demonstrated their versatility – Edwards being one – would probably be tried in different positions. This was part of the normal process. It was a results business, but United's coaches generally relied on the players being good enough to win because they had the talent. They could afford to try new things because trying a player in a new position could possibly yield something much more beneficial over a longer period of time than the short-term setback of a defeat.

Against Liverpool on the opening day of the Central League season, United's strength down the middle was almost embarrassing, with Mark Jones as the central defender, and Jeff Whitefoot and Jackie Blanchflower as the half-backs in front of him. Edwards played as inside-forward in the number 10 shirt, and put in an impressive shift as his team won 3-2.

The question for the reserve team coach Jimmy Murphy was not whether Edwards could play there, but whether it was getting the best out of him for both himself and the team. At any other club, they could well have played Edwards at inside-forward and built the team around him as the best player. United could do that and still have a very good team. But the challenge Murphy faced when developing any young player was not necessarily being the best when compared against the opposition, but moulding them into the best player they could possibly be.

Even looking at it at the age of 16, the discussion around what position Duncan Edwards should play is one of fascination. Over time people have looked on Edwards as an all-round player, able to play anywhere, and when discussions are held about greatest ever teams, Edwards often gets shoehorned into a free position for two reasons – one, people say he was good enough to play anywhere, and two, some find it hard to define the role a half-back played.

Edwards' style may well have redefined how an inside-forward was meant to play. One thing that was becoming clear from the different sort of characters and players United had in their team was that individuality was embraced. Duncan was *so* unique that Murphy and Busby had a conundrum within a conundrum. While he was light on his feet for his size, he was not as slight as the likes of a Dennis Viollet or Bill Whelan, both of whom seemed almost genetically engineered for the silky stylings of a Busby inside-forward: gliders who could move the ball on with a deft touch, goalscorers who might disappear from a game and then reappear with a devastating finishing touch. There was no hiding place for a player like Duncan Edwards. The education process was how to ensure that remained a blessing without even so much as a hint of it becoming a curse.

Of course, the same principle applied to other players who showed promise in different positions. After a promising run of form, Edwards was moved to half-back in the number six shirt, with Blanchflower shifted to the centre-forward role, for a Central League game at Stoke on September 19th. United lost 3-2, but

Duncan had done well enough to get another chance in the senior fold. A strong performance alongside Colman in a 7-0 win over a Sheffield and Hallamshire representative team in the Tomlinson Trophy, earned praise from Busby, who called the performance a win of "high skill". "The wing half-backs – the men who mean so much to any side – were at their best," he said. "I refer, of course, to Duncan Edwards and Eddie Colman."

Alf Clarke of the *Evening Chronicle* agreed with the manager's assessment. "Edwards was outstanding again… they played brilliant football. By far the best I've seen all season."

On Thursday September 24th, the *Mirror* reported that Duncan had been named as captain for Lancashire Boys in a game against Liverpool on Saturday 26th at the Prescot Ground. When he reported for training on Friday morning, however, Duncan learned he would not be going to Liverpool, nor would he be playing in the Central League against Preston at Old Trafford – he would be travelling as 12th man with the first team who were playing at Tottenham Hotspur. From a pick of three games, the youngster sat out the last weekend before he became a professional, kicking his heels in frustration.

It did not dampen the occasion of October 1st; Duncan duly signed professional terms, a mere formality but still a relief to his parents. Edwards cheekily contacted his old schoolteacher and mentor Mr Booth, saying: "Mr Busby says that now I have signed professional forms could I have your approval to drop my carpentry training?"

The reality was that the club had permitted him to do that in the summer. In fact, Duncan had become so used to his morning lie-ins that he had started to grumble at the noise his new roommate, Bobby Charlton, was making when he got up to go to his own apprenticeship.

Bert Whalley personally called Booth to thank him for all he had done; Booth asked if he could have a ticket the first time Duncan played in a cup final at Wembley. United obliged, and continued to provide Booth with complimentary tickets for over a decade. Perhaps Booth had passed on some advice for Whalley, the same advice he'd given his pupil a few years earlier – that Duncan was best suited to left-half. That was the position he played in reserve games at Burnley and Bury, a 2-1 defeat and 3-1 win respectively.

It was then time for a new season of the FA Youth Cup. United were drawn at Everton in the first round, one of their sterner tests in the previous campaign. Edwards found himself in the unfamiliar role of centre-forward in the number nine shirt, with Colman and McGuinness at half-back. Bobby Charlton, Alan Rhodes, Ivan Beswick, Brian Lowry and Sammy Chapman all made their Youth Cup debuts. It was the boys who had been there before who made the difference. Colman's outstanding volley was the only goal, while the Everton match programme for their next game opined: "United were full value for the win and it appeared that the experience of their young stars, Pegg and Edwards, did much to sway the game in their favour."

As United's junior side continued to operate smoothly, results looked as though they were beginning to pick up for the senior side, after a start to the season that made the previous season's look positively thrilling. No wins from the opening eight games were followed by a run of four wins and a draw from the following seven, but few were convinced by a 1-0 win over Aston Villa on October 24th. In only three games that season had United mustered more than a single goal.

"How can football sink so low as in this game at Old Trafford?" blasted one writer. "You expect £15-a-week players to serve up something better than this... drastic United changes might be expected."

The following days have gone down in legend. They are often presented with the general theme that Busby had seen enough and wielded the axe. It can most certainly be traced as a turning point in the club's history, but the manager was hardly as ruthless as the story goes. If you were to go by the myth, you might believe Busby used the midweek friendly in the following days against Kilmarnock as a chance to make wholesale changes to his team. But he made only one change of his own accord, dropping Rowley and calling up Dennis Viollet. Stan Pearson was also dropped from the team, but he was unwell and left back in Manchester, with Blanchflower taking his place.

In the first few minutes, Henry Cockburn scored a fine lobbed goal, but then succumbed to injury. Perhaps sensing the manager's decreasing patience with his veteran players, Cockburn insisted he could continue. Eventually, it was clear that he could not, and, with it being a friendly, Busby was able to bring on his 12th man as a substitute. Enter Duncan Edwards. United – who had seemed vulnerable – suddenly looked in complete cruise control, and scored two more to win 3-0.

"After 20 minutes our international wing-half, Henry Cockburn, left the field injured," Edwards recalled. "I went on in his place and have never been dropped from the first team since. Moments like that make all the months of gruelling work worthwhile."

The next First Division game was at Huddersfield Town. Cockburn's injury would rule him out for a week or so. The number six shirt was given to Edwards. It had been a gradual rather than sudden change but Busby's team now had an average age of just 24, with Wood, Foulkes, Whitefoot, Taylor and Viollet all in the side alongside Edwards. Without Allenby Chilton and Jack Rowley, that average age dropped to 21.

Huddersfield were enjoying a good season, and were third in the table. United's kids held no fear and chased for the win. Although the game ended goalless, there was a much greater sense of adventure than had been on show the previous week, and the endeavour was greeted with a warm reception by the press. It was

Alf Clarke of the *Evening Chronicle* who could be credited with the earliest coining of a famous nickname when he wrote "Busby's Bouncing 'Babes' Keep All Town Awake".

The home fans at Old Trafford still needed some convincing. Only 28,000 turned out for the home game against Arsenal the following week, as Busby kept faith with the same side. But the kids started in magnificent fashion, scoring after just three minutes and making it 2-0 just before half-time. Edwards went close with a long-range effort. The Gunners recovered to get a draw, but the entertainment value had most definitely gone up a notch. Edwards' all-action display and full-blooded tackles against veteran professionals were announcements to the world that he was not going to stand on ceremony. Being called into first-team action and expressing yourself – as Edwards did to his credit against Cardiff and Huddersfield – was one thing, but getting involved in the heat of the battle to influence a physical match was something that shocked many observers. He had only just turned 17. "Edwards at left-half showed uncanny judgement and maturity," Don Davies wrote under his pseudonym 'An Old International' in the *Manchester Guardian*. "His tackling was strong, his ball play faultless and he alone was rarely at fault in following Rowley's promptings."

In an age where few people would be bold enough to make definite predictions, the *Daily Worker* were willing to stick their neck out: "Our tip is Manchester United to be the team of the year in 1955. Against Arsenal on Saturday they had six players aged under 21 – and they outplayed the Arsenal veterans. Duncan Edwards, star of United's youthful team, gave an outstanding performance."

United then played against Wrexham in the Youth Cup, but Busby instructed Murphy to leave Edwards out to give him a breather. In his stead, Charlton scored twice, making his first mark on the competition to help United progress 5-0.

Charlton had become a convert after just a couple of months observing Duncan's performances. "Every move the big lad made ridiculed the scepticism I had felt on that taxi ride from the station," he said. "He showed awesome power as he ran through the churning mud. His tackling was a series of tank traps, as ferocious as it was perfectly timed; his passing was penetrative and accurate; and, whatever the conditions and however heavy the ball had become, his heading was always immaculate in its strength and direction."

The freshness told in United's next senior game down in Cardiff. The energy and power coming from the half-back line of Whitefoot and Edwards had the hosts all at sea as they pushed up the pitch, harassing them into the concession of two early goals. Two similar patterns followed – goals in the 48th and 52nd, and then two goals in the last nine minutes, to secure a stunning 6-1 win.

Was this a fluke or a genuine turning moment? Judging by the Old Trafford attendance for the visit of Blackpool – 20,000 higher than the Arsenal gate – there was a certain curiosity to know.

"There was a good percentage of the crowd who, I'm sure, turned up just to see if the way people spoke about Duncan was true," says Tom Clare. "He was a spectacle… He was a big lad. It was probably more a case of seeing him for the first time and not really appreciating a boy of that age could be that size. Even if he was carrying a few extra pounds at 16, it wouldn't have been more than puppy fat, and he soon burnt it off. When he was a regular in the first team he was as fit as a butcher's dog."

Duncan's direct opponent on the day was inside-forward Ernie Taylor. The FA Cup final earlier that year had instantly been immortalised as the 'Stanley Matthews Final' because of the 38-year-old's exceptional wing performance in a 4-3 win for the Seasiders against Bolton. However, it was not Matthews, and not even the hat-trick hero Stan Mortensen, who Jimmy Murphy had judged the man-of-the-match. That accolade went to Taylor, whose industry had created the platform for others to shine. It was surely the case that he would provide Duncan with his sternest test yet – and, when Blackpool took an early lead, it seemed as though that would be the case. However, Edwards responded, seizing the initiative and driving United forward. Soon it was Taylor looking in vain for Edwards. United thumped three goals in reply before the half-time whistle, and another soon after the break.

"To get into the picture at all, Ernie Taylor had to wander far away from his youthful opponent Duncan Edwards," Don Davies wrote, continuing that Edwards "gives the lie to the adage that old heads do not grow on young shoulders. There seems little that time and experience can add to his present store of shrewdness and judgement, unless it be the reminder that there is such a thing as beginner's luck."

Poor Ernie Taylor, who was about to suffer even greater embarrassment. If the Kilmarnock friendly is erroneously seen as a tectonic shift in United's history, there can be no doubting the role of the match played between England and Hungary at Wembley four days after United's 4-1 win over Blackpool. Egos are always more brutally exposed when they are faced with uncomfortable truths in an unavoidable manner, and that was the case for English football on November 25, 1953.

There should have been no doubting the size of the task, as Hungary were the number one ranked side in the world and had not been beaten for 24 games. They were a goal up within 60 seconds, as Nándor Hidegkuti netted, and went on to bewilder their hosts, leading 4-1 after 27 minutes in a sensational spell of football inspired by Ferenc Puskás.

The most common formation in England was the WM shape, effectively a 3-2-2-3, but the Hungarians inverted this to control the middle of the park, dominating the play and running riot. To the embarrassment of almost all of the 105,000 fans in Wembley, a fifth goal came in the 52nd minute, and a sixth – the hat-trick goal by Hidegkuti – was volleyed in after some showboating. Hungary then took pity on the English, casually holding on to the 6-3 lead they'd established in under an hour. The visitors ended up registering 35 shots on goal, and the game was defined by flustered English defenders getting confused by the movement of Hidegkuti, who wore eight, and Puskás, who wore 10. Those numbers were commonly associated with the inside-forwards, and England's defenders simply did not know how to track their movement.

Criticism was levelled at the players. At the *age* of the players. At the manager, Walter Winterbottom, a former Manchester United player who had only experienced a short playing career and had no managerial experience before being appointed national team coach.

While it would take some time for greater formation shifts in the British domestic game, Busby and Murphy already had their finger on the pulse when it came to the soccer revolution.

After the match, Sándor Barcs, president of the Hungarian Football Federation, told reporters: "Jimmy Hogan taught us everything we know about football." The team coach, Gusztáv Sebes, echoed those words. "We played football as Jimmy Hogan taught us," he said. "When our football history is told, his name should be written in gold letters."

Hogan, a Lancashire-born former inside-forward, had become compelled by football abroad when playing for Bolton and seeing how uncompetitive games against Dutch teams were. He promised to return to Holland to "teach those fellows how to play properly". He did, spending time there, then in Switzerland, Hungary and Austria.

In a twist of fate, Jimmy Murphy bumped into Hogan while the latter was coaching some Austrian players in France. Murphy was enthralled. "Mastery of the ball and of the simple way of doing things were the basis of football," Murphy said. "I used a lot of Jimmy Hogan's ideas when I joined Matt Busby at Manchester United. He was a very influential coach."

Busby, however, had his own strong principles on how he wanted the game to be played, and he strongly endorsed the idea of individuality, allowing a player to express themselves within the team shape. "What is this pattern of playing I keep going on about?" Busby asked in his book *Soccer At The Top*. "Only the naive would imagine that it is a drill to be followed by every Manchester United player. It is a pattern formed by the players and the staff, formed by individuals who are all different, and therefore the pattern over the years will gradually change."

The United bosses had clearly already been employing the Hungarian approach to those rave reviews domestically. Though hardly a hidden philosophy, Busby and Murphy were scarcely given the credit they deserved for their foresight on this front – perhaps it was because United's own revolution still came with the caveat of British sensibility. And, at the time of the Hungary victory, there was nothing besides an FA Youth Cup victory which seriously suggested United were preparing to do something similar on domestic shores.

It was another young Busby side that went to Portsmouth on November 28th. Seven players aged 21 or under were in the team which earned a 1-1 draw; and earned was the right word, given the way they had to battle for a late equaliser through Tommy Taylor. It was another battle of a game against Sheffield United at Old Trafford; this one ended 2-2. A 3-1 defeat at Chelsea threatened to derail the confidence that had been building but United's response was impressive, first of all hitting Liverpool for five and then winning the next three games in the league, twice against Sheffield Wednesday on Christmas Day and Boxing Day, and then against Newcastle on January 2nd.

The key feature of the win at St James' Park was the autonomous and faultless effect of their half-back line, Whitefoot and Edwards. "I am almost tempted to say that Geoff (sic) Whitefoot, 20, is the best right-half in England bar none," Bob Ferrier wrote in the *Mirror*.

"Duncan Edwards, 17, is built like a Marciano. He almost ran Ivor Broadis right out of St James' Park, this giant of a boy."

With just 12 senior appearances behind him, Duncan was given his biggest honour yet on January 5th, 1954, when he was called up to the England under-23 side to face Italy in Bologna later that month with Whitefoot and Ray Wood, the goalkeeper. The *Daily Worker* reported the news with this glowing tribute: "Edwards, only 17 years old, has quickly built up a reputation as one of the best wing-halves in the country."

His reputation had not been done any harm by Tom Finney suggesting he was "one of our finest-ever Soccer prospects" in the *Halifax Courier* on December 19th.

Manager Matt Busby promised that his boys would deliver. "There's no fear of Wood, Whitefoot or Edwards qualifying for the 'Big Head' label," he said. "They will not let young England down."

Edwards' rapid ascent prompted the *Mirror*'s Arnold Howe to write a feature titled 'Boy Who Was Born To Be A Footballer' on January 6th. "The youngster never stood a chance of learning a 'useful trade', for he was not like the other boys at school," wrote Howe. "His feet were too educated. Manchester United watched this boy, Duncan Edwards, a score of times and then realised that this man-sized schoolboy was indeed a football prodigy.

"I was able to spend only seconds chatting to Duncan yesterday as he left a lesson in manager Matt Busby's Old Trafford 'academy'. Mr Busby, himself breathing hard from a spell of training, wisely advised this valuable footballer to keep on the move. 'He might catch cold,' explained Matt. Duncan added that he has never supported one particular team. 'I just went round watching Wolves, Villa and West Brom,' he said. He said, of course, that he was 'looking forward' to the Italy match. Matt Busby summed up the boy's feelings. 'He is a normal, healthy lad, so he is naturally thrilled.' Duncan was working hard on quick passing and sprinting. He often nips down to Old Trafford for an extra ball-kicking session. And just as surely as he strokes the practice ball to a colleague, so will he stride through more matches and more honours."

Not only did Duncan go down to the ground for extra training, he would also continue to go to the Cliff on Tuesdays and Thursdays, just as he did when he was an amateur, because he loved football and United so much, although initially that was under the guise of helping Bobby Charlton settle in.

The first significant disappointment of Duncan's career came in the FA Cup, as Burnley won a thrilling game at Turf Moor. The hosts had gone 2-0 up in five minutes, United were level by the seventh, but Burnley hit back again to win 5-3. It was a game that would not be forgotten, and still, according to George Follows in the *Daily Herald*: "For me, the final memory will be of the boy Edwards striding through the mud in hopeless battle, the bravest boy on the field."

Edwards had fought through the pain after being kicked on his leg and ankle, and at one point he was reported as doubtful for the following weekend's Manchester derby, but there was no way he was going to miss his first taste of this occasion. United grabbed a first-half lead through Berry, and Edwards' passing range was on point. With nine minutes to go, however, Edwards' eagerness to add a second was said to be at fault for City snatching an equaliser; a lesson in keeping a cool head when the pressure is on. United had to settle for a 1-1 draw, and though Edwards was once more the best player in a big game, he came away feeling frustrated.

The run of big games never seemed to stop for Duncan, and the next stop was Bologna for the under-23s. He travelled down to London to meet up with the England squad, where they played a 55-minute practice match against Chelsea's first team and managed a creditable 1-1 draw. In the England squad was Chelsea's own outside-left, Frank Blunstone. "I'd heard all about the name Duncan Edwards and the great Busby Babes," he said.

"My first encounter with him was when we played for the under-23s. He was so strong and powerful, such a big and strong boy. He was a nice lad, a typical Midlander. He was a very sensible boy."

After their practice game, the England players went down the road to watch Fulham play Grimsby in the FA Cup. Later still, the squad flew to Italy to play in their inaugural under-23 fixture. It was a bumpy journey, with many of his team-mates suffering from air-sickness. It was this reason that most players gave when trying to explain their embarrassing 3-0 defeat to the Italians, a result which did nothing to inspire faith in things looking better in the years to come.

Chapter 6
The Great Duncan Edwards

In spite of the England call-up, January 1954 was shaping up to be a pretty miserable month for Duncan Edwards. Even the positives had come with caveats – the call-up was followed by the loss to Italy and started a fear of flying he would carry with him, and even the man-of-the-match display against Manchester City had come with the asterisk that he was culpable for the conceded goal. It didn't get much better back home, as Bolton Wanderers came to Old Trafford and won 5-1, with his old friend Ray Parry scoring twice.

It would have been a welcome week off for Duncan after that if not for the youth team's first hiccup in the Youth Cup; they had drawn in their fourth round tie at Rotherham on the same day as United's first team were losing to Burnley. The replay against the Yorkshire side was set for January 27th, under the floodlights at the Cliff. Due to Rotherham's home colours being red, they were offered the amber shirts – but, hearing the legend of what had happened to Nantwich, declined. The replay meant that Murphy could call Edwards into his team, and almost instantly the difference was embarrassing. Duncan notched a hat-trick, single-handedly deciding the 3-1 win for his team.

The *Rotherham Advertiser* poured praise and scorn in equal measure: "It was a pity that Manchester United found it neces-sary to bring into the side Duncan Edwards, who played in the England side against Italy last week, and has made 14 (actually 13) First Division appearances. I know Edwards is only 17, but

I think it is against the principle of the Youth Cup to introduce professional players. It was my first glimpse of Edwards, and indeed he is an amazing player, almost of the John Charles stamp already. He was almost the entire reason for Manchester's superiority, for not only did he score all their goals, but he also dominated the play throughout... Edwards scored the opening goal, 15 minutes after the start, when he headed in from a corner. For 20 minutes of the second half Rotherham more than held their own... then Edwards threaded his way through to score with a brilliant shot."

Rotherham manager Andy Smailes quipped after the match: "When I see a player like that, it makes you think footballers should be handicapped like racehorses."

Perhaps that had been the instruction Smailes had given his players; Edwards suffered an ankle knock, and was a doubt for the next first-team game against Preston. One man who might have been secretly happy about that was Henry Cockburn – the veteran wing-half who had been displaced by Edwards and would request a move away in January.

However, Edwards was as durable as he was brave, and when the team-sheet went up for the Preston game, Duncan was in it. United won again. "I can remember the first time I saw him," then-Preston right-half Tommy Docherty recalled. "It was really the start of the Busby Babes. Duncan was awesome. He was everywhere. I could not get over that he was built like a man and was only 17 years of age."

Edwards was still in the side when Spurs came to Old Trafford, and put in another star display – creating the first goal for Jack Rowley and having an effort cleared off the line.

United's form was generally good, and though at times they were inconsistent, they usually responded well to setbacks, as proven by a league defeat to Burnley which was followed by victories over Sunderland and Wolves.

The routine wins against the smaller teams in earlier rounds of the Youth Cup meant that Duncan would probably have been expecting to travel to his homeland to play in a senior game against Aston Villa on Saturday March 13th, instead of travelling to the south east to play Bexleyheath & Welling. However, United had just announced their participation in that summer's Blue Star Youth Tournament in Zurich, Switzerland, a showcase event for top young players to face clubs of different nationalities. Busby had wanted to enter his team in the competition in 1953, but they had already arranged their post-season trip to Ireland.

On March 10th, it was clear that Edwards would be travelling with his youth team-mates. "Matt Busby has made this move because, with his Youth XI, holders of the FA trophy, booked for a big summer international tournament in Switzerland, he wants his strongest possible line-up of under-18s in Saturday's fifth-round tie at Bexley Heath," Tom Jackson wrote in the *Manchester Evening News*. Busby wanted to take no chance that his club would go to the tournament without being holders of the national cup.

What happened on the train journey to London was extraordinary. The trip was well underway when Jimmy Murphy took Duncan aside to speak to him about a private matter. Ronnie Cope, the defender, had been the captain of the inaugural Youth Cup team. Cope was too old to play this season, and David Pegg – by virtue of his international status and longevity at the club – had assumed the role. Pegg had 27 first-team appearances, but it was clear that Edwards was now effectively making a role in the first team his own too, and with his recent call-up to the England under-23 side, Murphy felt it may be time for a change.

"I'm making you captain," Murphy told him. "You're the most experienced player in the team."

Edwards nodded, thoughtfully, and returned to sit with his friends.

A while later he returned to where his coach was sitting and asked if he could have a word.

"Jimmy, I don't want the job," Duncan said. "It's not fair. Dave Pegg has been captain all season and I think he ought to keep the job."

Murphy nodded, accepting the maturity of his *de facto* leader, and acknowledging the class he had demonstrated.

Bexley Heath & Welling were, in effect, the nursery club of Charlton Athletic. They were coached by Bert Johnson, a former Addicks player who had a tremendous reputation of his own. A sign of their quality could be seen in their 4-2 victory over Chelsea in the prior round. The game had attracted plenty of interest – Johnson wrote in his programme notes he had been informed that the BBC would have screened the game if it had been held the previous Saturday.

The southerners started with purpose, with the *Kentish Times* giving praise for their defender Keith Cox whose hard challenging "completely upset the tall, well-built Edwards". There were 4,300 supporters packed around the pitch, and plenty of them were taking the moment to heckle Murphy and Whalley about their supposed stars who had yet to show their style.

"Murphy... where is this great Edwards of yours? We ain't seen him yet, mate."

At that precise moment in the 22nd minute, the ball bounced favourably in the direction of United's number eight (Edwards was playing further forward at inside-right). Duncan shifted the ball a few yards in front of him so that he could generate the power – goalkeeper Mick Topps got the faintest of touches to it, but could not stop the long-range drive (from either 25 yards, according to the *Kentish Times*, or 40, according to Murphy) from nestling into the corner.

"There's the great fucking Duncan Edwards," Murphy snarled to the naysayers behind him.

Bexley Heath managed to level the scores, but with the game reaching its conclusion, there was panic in the home defence, leaving an empty net for Bobby Charlton to send his team into the next round.

Edwards would, once again, be the one to make this youth team game go down in history, but in the dressing room after the game he urged his team-mates to give "three cheers for the captain, lads".

It could well have been that the 17-year-old was growing so self-conscious of what he felt was disproportionate praise, that he was almost over-compensating, in trying to make sure others received their own fair share of the credit. That week it had been announced in the *Manchester Evening News* that *Teleclub* – a monthly television programme for youngsters – was returning to screens and their March 22nd programme would feature Duncan Edwards giving soccer tips to 30 members of Beaver Road Youth Club of Didsbury. And, on the day of the Youth Cup game, Edwards was voted by readers of the same newspaper as one of the United players who would get in a combined 'best of' United and City team: "Edwards has already shown us he's got what it takes to become one of the finest in the country."

The attention wasn't showing any signs of slowing. On March 14th, Edwards was called into the England B team to face West Germany eight days later in Gelsenkirchen, and on March 20th he was back in the United first team, muscling out Cockburn, who had deputised for a boy 13 years his junior at Villa. Against Huddersfield in what was now unofficially becoming *his* number six shirt, Edwards had another match-defining influence, setting up what turned out to be the winning goal for Viollet.

England's next match, a 'B' international with West Germany on March 24th, was the first against them at any level since the war. Edwards, at 17, was by far the youngest player in a team with an average age of 25. Not for the first time, the youngest player on the pitch was the best player on the pitch – prompting German officials to question Winterbottom about the accuracy of his age. England won 4-0, with Fulham's Bedford Jezzard scoring a hat-trick, but even that could not steal the headlines from the dominant force of nature that was Duncan Edwards.

"Already man-sized and carrying a football brain to match, this Edwards is going to become the terror of the continent before he has even got down to serious shaving," wrote Desmond Hackett in the *Express*. "He was certainly the despair of the Germans."

In the *Evening Chronicle*, John Graydon ranked Edwards as "favourite" for the next full international against Scotland if he played well in United's next game against Arsenal, describing him as a "Sherman tank", and also noted: "In Germany, his tackling put the continentals completely off their game and when he cleared the ball, he hit it really hard and accurately to his colleagues."

At Highbury, United stormed into a second-minute lead against Arsenal. Whether it was a case of complacency creeping through the team, or Edwards just not being at the races, it was from his misplaced passes that the hosts scored two of their three second-half goals.

"I'm afraid that both Edwards and Byrne were below the form which has put them high on the international list this season," Tom Jackson observed in the *Manchester Evening News*, and Edwards' failure to make the full England squad was confirmed in the *Daily Herald* on March 29th: "Young Duncan Edwards certainly did not add to any laurels gained in the match in Germany last Wednesday."

It seemed as though he was desperate to play himself back into form and so Edwards dismissed the prospect of a midweek break to play in the Youth Cup semi-final first leg at West Brom. The *Birmingham Gazette* praised Edwards' "prominent" role in a 3-1 win for his team.

From the kids to legendary veterans – Edwards equipped himself well against Blackpool's Stanley Matthews, and in one challenge earned a round of applause from the entire Bloomfield Road crowd for a crunching but fair tackle; but United were otherwise uninspiring and lost 2-0.

The games were coming thick and fast with the conclusion of the season rapidly approaching. Two days after the Blackpool game,

Edwards was playing in the second leg of the Youth Cup semi-final and was desperate to get on the scoresheet. He unleashed a number of shots at poor Geoff Barnsley and was finally rewarded with a thunderous drive which almost ripped the netting to make it 3-0 in the 64th minute. The 4-0 win on the night made it 7-1 on aggregate and gave the holders another final with Wolves to look forward to.

Duncan was selected for the Young England XI trial which would take place at Highbury on April 30th, the night before the FA Cup final. He was, however, omitted from the 32-man England B tour squad – causing Bob Ferrier of the *Mirror* to complain. "Duncan Edwards is a youngster – but so was Cliff Bastin and Stanley Matthews and Tommy Lawton when their international careers started, and Edwards's career will surely stand on such pinnacles at the end," wrote Ferrier. "Manchester United's youth team, for which Edwards is still eligible, will play in Switzerland in May. If that prevents his selection, then how stupid that this minor event is allowed to cut across England's sporting prestige."

Edwards was back in the United first team for a 2-0 win over Charlton, but the game was dismissed as "guileless, soulless and almost hopeless" by one reporter. And then the criticism got personal, with one journalist saying Duncan was "distressingly inaccurate in his passing" despite his "immense work" in a 2-0 win over Portsmouth.

Perhaps sensing the counter-productive nature of such words when United's season was effectively over, Busby decided to recall Cockburn for the final two league games, leaving Edwards to concentrate on the FA Youth Cup final.

Colman and McGuinness had been exceptional as half-backs in the run and there was no need for Murphy to switch that around, so Edwards was back in at inside-right for Wolves' visit to Old Trafford on April 23rd.

United's demolition of Wolves a year earlier naturally encouraged the idea that this would be a walkover. But there were just two players in the Wolves team who had featured in the 7-1 defeat.

The feeling of complacency intensified when United landed the first blow, netting a fifth-minute goal through a thumping Edwards header. This was not, however, the meek Wolves of 12 months ago. Their swift response rocked United to their core. They stormed back to score three goals before half-time. No respite in the dressing room, however – Jimmy Murphy was at boiling point and had 11 young boys wishing they were already back out on the pitch. Murphy was renowned for his hesitance to be in the public eye. But he was no shrinking violet.

A collective pride was stung, with United's boys realising they were being given a runaround for the first time. It didn't feel good. Desperate times called for desperate measures. Murphy ordered Edwards to move to centre-forward and moved Charlton to inside-right. And the Welshman – famed for his fire and brimstone approach – caught his players off-guard. He praised them. He told them how good they were and how good they had been. How the tie was all to play for. The players knew they hadn't been good enough. But Murphy was reminding them of their standards. They dare not return at full-time without pride being restored.

Wolves were immediately panicked at the change. "With mighty Duncan Edwards bulldozing his way through the middle and David Pegg and Albert Scanlon teaming up perfectly on the left wing," Tom Jackson wrote in the *Manchester Evening News*, "United had the big-kicking Wolves defenders on tenterhooks."

Charlton's shot was handled. Pegg scored the penalty. Cometh the hour, Duncan Edwards equalised with a carbon copy of his earlier goal. He had taken the setback personally and, as well as his team-mates were doing to rouse themselves, it was Edwards storming forward, dominating the field. He would be the player passing the ball and then demanding it back. Even when Wolves hit back with a sucker punch to make it 3-4, Edwards pushed relentlessly for another equaliser, and through those endeavours

Pegg grabbed his own second to make it 4-4. Blushes were spared – everything was still to play for at Molineux.

Outside-right Tommy Littler described it as "probably the best (game) I ever played in".

"Jimmy and Bert encouraged us no end in the dressing room, told us how good we'd been," Littler told Steve Hobin and Tony Park in their *Sons of United* book. "In the second half we completely bombarded them. The ball seemed to keep coming back to me from Duncan, in fact so often that I was completely knackered after about an hour. We got a corner and I called Duncan over, I told him to give the ball to someone else for a few minutes so that I could get my breath back. He was playing them on his own at times, and winning too. There are times in football when you have to accept defeat, only nobody seemed to tell Duncan that was the case."

Edwards was back in his number eight shirt for the return three days later but started at centre-forward, as Murphy indulged in the sort of gamesmanship the Hungarians had done. 28,651 supporters turned up at Molineux hopeful that their youngsters could claim a famous scalp. As the home side tried to figure out where Duncan would be popping up, they quickly realised it didn't really matter; once he was on the pitch, he was everywhere, and unstoppable in any position he desired to occupy.

Just before the half-hour mark Wolves struck the inside of the post. Once more, the threat stung United into retaliation. From a United corner in the 34th minute, Edwards was challenged by John Timmins, who was deemed to have handled. A seemingly harsh decision, but Pegg was unforgiving with his strike from the spot, and so too were the United defence and midfield, who controlled the pace of the game masterfully from that point.

Tom Jackson's assessment was that Edwards "was once again the forager-in-chief in a tactical switch to centre-forward", but praise was liberally given to the other players whose reputations were all enhanced after this impressively professional victory. Pegg, who had scored the decisive goal on the night, did so on his last appearance in the competition as he would now be too old to compete – so, thanks to Duncan's generosity, he also had the opportunity to lift the trophy as outgoing captain.

Pegg did have one more official duty before his graduation, and that was to skipper Edwards and the other youngsters on their trip to Switzerland for the Blue Star tournament which some publications had described as "the World Youth Cup". Before that, however, Duncan may well have been flying to the Alps for different reasons.

On the eve of the first leg of the Youth Cup final he had learned that Bill Slater, the Wolves left-half, had suffered an injury so was possibly going to withdraw from selection for the forthcoming senior World Cup in Switzerland. Edwards and Roger Byrne were called into a 40-man squad which would be trimmed for the tournament. On April 30th, Duncan competed in a 'Young England' versus 'Old England' match which was billed as a trial, and came out on the losing side. "The opposing forward line of Matthews, Mannion, Lawton, Shackleton and Langton certainly gave us the run-around," Edwards later said of the 2-1 defeat, "but I really enjoyed playing against such great players."

Chapter 7
Crossing Borders

With the 1954 World Cup on the horizon, Duncan Edwards and Roger Byrne continued to train with the senior England squad but did not make the final selection. There was still some reward for the 17-year-old Edwards, as he was included in the England B team to face Switzerland in Basel on May 23rd. Duncan played the full 90 in a disappointing 2-0 defeat before flying back to Manchester to report to his club for the flight back to Switzerland, via London, on May 26th ahead of the Blue Star tournament. To show just how seriously the youth competition was being taken, Busby, Murphy and Whalley were all leading the tour, with Arthur Powell completing the coaching staff. United made their temporary home at the Stoller Hotel in Zurich, which would become their base as they became perennial competitors in the tournament.

The tournament took place just one day later on May 27th in a series of 30-minute games. Though most of the sides in the competition were Swiss, teams from Denmark, Germany and France were also present.

This was a significant moment in the history of Manchester United. Busby's dreams of taking on the cream of the crop from overseas were always apparent, as evidenced by the post-season exhibition tours he had led United on in 1950 and 1952. This was something different, though. This was competition, and serious enough for Busby to do away completely with the senior tour for this year. It was a priority statement which increased attention and expectation.

Technically speaking, the youngsters were still playing for Murphy and Whalley, but they knew Busby was watching every move. Shorter games make fair judgement a little harder but there was some suggestion that the 'Babes' were struggling in the spotlight. Perhaps the fact they were wearing white shirts and dark shorts made them feel even more out of sorts. Their first game against domestic side Young Fellows ended 0-0, and their next was won 2-0 against FC Bern. Against host side Blue Stars, United were controlling the game in midfield thanks to Edwards' faultless display at left-half, but could not find a killer touch – they were on the brink of elimination until Eddie Lewis scored in the last minute to take them into the semi-final.

Another single-goal victory followed in that game, with Billy Whelan's strike enough to see off MTV München. The final was against Red Star ZH. Murphy made a switch. United's goals had come in the second halves. They were feeling out their opposition and then taking the initiative, with Edwards comfortable at left-half. Colman and McGuinness could control the final – pushing Edwards further forward seemed like an obvious choice. It was a move which paid dividends, as Edwards scored a hat-trick in a 4-0 win which almost felt routine. The reward was United's first ever continental success at any level – the Hermes Cup.

The entertaining Manchester United boys had proven themselves sporting players and quickly made friends with their opponents, with some Swiss boys taking the Manchester lads out dancing in town. Eddie Colman was inseparable from Edwards, only taking breaks from his pal's side to snap pictures or to write postcards to send home. "The place is very clean," he told his parents, after also beaming about the "smashing" weather. "I could walk about in the same shirt all week."

"It was a wonderful experience!" Wilf McGuinness told reporters. "We gave 'em a real Busby-planned United burst in the second half of every game – and we had 'em knocking at the knees."

United's kids weren't finished there. Two days later the party travelled to Bienne to play against a Berne Select team in a 40 minutes-each-way game. There was a Wolves-esque shock as Berne scored twice in the opening minutes but Edwards and co quickly responded, registering a 3-2 lead at half-time. With Jimmy Murphy again insisting his boys be relentless, they struck six more goals without reply to win 9-2 – Edwards, at inside-forward, helping himself to one in the second half. The star of the show had been Billy Whelan, who scored five times. In attendance were the Brazilian national side, who were all impressed with United's prowess; some tried to convince Whelan that he should move to Brazil.

Before returning home, there was another game which was officially a friendly but certainly a serious one; 42,000 were in attendance to watch Switzerland play the Netherlands, but those who got in early were able to see this shorter match between United and the Swiss youth national team. Duncan netted the final goal in a resounding 4-0 win to end the tour on a hugely positive note.

There was in fact one more official duty before the youngsters could clock off for the season – a civic reception at Manchester Town Hall arranged in their honour. A marker of how seriously United's success had been received could be seen in journalist Arthur Brook's take: "Busby's bonny Babes, who did to the Swiss what all Britain hoped our Soccer maestros would do to the Hungarians, are home again. They have returned with the knowledge that the Continentals can be beaten – and heavily."

Matt Busby recorded his thoughts on the tour for the *Evening Chronicle*, writing: "'There is nothing wrong with the future of English football if this is a sample of your youth.' This remark was passed to me after the Manchester United youth team had beaten a Swiss selected youth team in Zurich… I need hardly say that the comment gave me nearly as much pleasure as the fact that United's youth team won six of their seven games… I am delighted. I am not usually given to boasting, but I can assure you that British prestige has taken a terrific leap through the wonderful football of the United youths... it has been a magnificent tour and I think I can honestly say that my young players have done much to restore continental confidence in the future of British football."

Eddie Colman took a bunch of personal photographs for his own memories and, of course, the press took a number upon United's return to Manchester. In almost all, Duncan could be seen at the back, almost embarrassed by the platitudes the team were receiving. In one photograph, he looks as if he is posing with the trophy against his will.

It could be argued that United's success was a hugely restorative step for English football after the embarrassment inflicted upon them by Hungary. That was the approach taken by Tom Jackson of the *Manchester Evening News* just before the final leg of United's Swiss adventure:

Matt Busby and his team of Manchester United youngsters left their hotel in Zurich, Switzerland for Interlaken with the cheers of the Swiss folk ringing in their ears for a brilliant display which has helped to heal the wounds of England's soccer debacle in Hungary. They finish their programme in Zurich, the city which has taken them to heart after what one Swiss soccer official told me was "a series of wonder games" against the Continent's crack youngsters. "They are the toast of Zurich just now," he said. "They are grand young fellows who celebrated their tournament success in lemonade when the champagne was there simply for the taking."

Matt Busby, the proudest man in Europe today, was hailed by soccer officials of many nationalities now gathering for the World Cup games after his boys had won the final match by defeating Red Star of Zurich 4-0. Duncan Edwards scored a hat-trick.

"This is the best tonic English football could have had" was their verdict.

Manager Busby... was really putting to further test his all-out policy of grooming promising boy footballers for first-class careers in the game. His Old Trafford 'nursery' is simply bristling with talented youngsters. It has now become such an efficient organisation that Matt Busby and Manchester United are the envy of managers and clubs throughout Great Britain. What makes a Busby boy? First the young footballer must have ability and determination. Secondly he must be ready to listen to the advice of the United manager and his coaches, Jimmy Murphy and Bert Whalley, and thirdly, he must be imbued with team and club spirit. There is something 'magical' in the name of Manchester United which has made all the difference between an outstanding boy throwing in his lot at Old Trafford and joining another League club.

The case of Duncan Edwards, already, at 17, on the brink of senior England honours came readily to mind. As captain of England boys he was trailed by dozens of League clubs on leaving school, but even though it meant leaving home and mum's cooking, he never hesitated about becoming a Busby boy.

The 6-3 Wembley defeat for England in November 1953 had been followed by an even harsher lesson in the pre-World Cup warm-ups, where Winterbottom's side went down by seven goals to one in Budapest. England's misery was complete when they were eliminated by Uruguay in the World Cup quarter-finals. As for the great Hungary and their own players? After defeating South Korea 9-0 and West Germany 8-3 in the group stages, they went on to face West Germany again in the final, where they lost controversially after taking a 2-0 lead. Despite missing out on the official title, Hungary's domination at international level continued for the next couple of years as they went unbeaten from the final in 1954 to February 1956. Most of their great stars played for Budapest Honved, whose chances of shining at European level were diminished, as soon as the club entered the European Cup, by the Hungarian Uprising of 1956, which forced many top players abroad. The synergy and seamless style of the national side was undermined and this helped to expedite the demise of one of the greatest teams in history.

Manchester United were England's greatest hope of creating the platform for a similar system. At the time, this was perceived as a potential rebirth of British football consistent with its own values. The reality was that United's approach was much closer to the Hungarian philosophy than anybody would give credit for. It would take some time for this to blossom; before then, a heavy burden was placed upon the considerable shoulders of Duncan Edwards to represent a new age for both club and country.

Chapter 8
Renewal

Where there is a catalyst for change or a defining moment – particularly in sport – there is a tendency to presume that change was immediate and improvement was instant. It simplifies the matter but makes it easier to comprehend. Manchester United's team of 1953/54 included appearances for the following players: Roger Byrne, Bill Foulkes, Jackie Blanchflower, Duncan Edwards, Johnny Berry, David Pegg, Tommy Taylor and Dennis Viollet. Eight players who would go on to taste much success.

So perhaps this period of time is best defined by the progression of Mark Jones. After three seasons making four, three and two appearances respectively, Jones spent the entire 53/54 campaign playing as centre-half in the Central League, as Matt Busby and Jimmy Murphy felt the Barnsley-born defender required more time getting accustomed to the physical demands at the highest level. With the reliable Byrne, John Aston, Foulkes and Blanchflower manning the first-team defence, it seemed United would soon have to make that call on Jones, especially with Aston's retirement that summer. Aston would be followed by record goalscorer Jack Rowley, who became player-manager of Plymouth Argyle in February 1955. Only goalkeeper Jack Crompton and half-back Allenby Chilton from the 1948 FA Cup-winning team remained, as Henry Cockburn was granted his transfer early in the season. On top of those, only Berry and Byrne could claim to have proper experience of being in the title-winning side of 1952.

Busby was two years into his claim of having the best young talent in the country. He had some vindication in their Youth Cup success and then their triumphant Switzerland expedition. It was no surprise that he was going to persevere with youth, but it was eye-catching when so much experience was permitted to leave without being replaced.

That his team had bested Wolves – who were following the United idea of rearing their own – in the Youth Cup gave Busby much confidence. United had finished fourth in the First Division in 1954, nine points behind Stan Cullis's champions.

Cullis invited Budapest Honved to Wolverhampton to play in a friendly in December 1954. Wolves had played a number of such midweek friendlies at Molineux under new floodlights which had cost £30,000; an inventive way of recouping some gate receipts and allowing supporters to witness exotic opponents. Glasgow Celtic had been beaten 2-0, Racing Club of Argentina succumbed 3-1, Maccabi Tel Aviv were obliterated 10-0, and it was a 4-0 win over Spartak Moscow which had seemingly caused Honved manager Jenő Kalmár to accept the invitation to test his great team, which included József Bozsik, Zoltán Czibor, Péter Kocsis and Ferenc Puskás.

Cullis was unapologetic about his team's long-ball style and had brushed off criticism for having the pitch heavily watered before kick-off. Honved were 2-0 up inside quarter of an hour. At half-time, faced with the embarrassment of the second half being shown live on BBC, Cullis doubled down, sending apprentice players on to pour more water over the turf. One of those youngsters was Ron Atkinson, a 15-year-old wing-half. "They were a sight," Atkinson says. "Short shorts, light shirts, lightweight boots. They went two goals up and played some brilliant stuff. Wolves looked light years behind, plodding around with heavy shirts and boots. So Cullis ordered me and the lads to go out and drench the pitch even more. They would have probably hit 10 past us. But they started to get weighed down by the mud."

Wolves, in front of a captive audience, turned the game around to win 3-2. The thrilling nature of the comeback captured the imagination. Cullis proclaimed his side to be the best in the world. This was, in his mind, evidence that the old English way still had life in it. To say there was disagreement would be putting it mildly. There was a sense that Wolves knew they could not win in a straight game of football so had tipped the odds in their favour. Journalist and author Willy Meisl was studying for his seminal book *Soccer Revolution*. He scoffed at the "quagmire" of a pitch and said that even if Cullis felt his triumph was worthy of the accolade, then Red Star Belgrade of Yugoslavia were similarly worthy considering their own recent victory over Budapest Honved.

Gabriel Hanot, the editor of French sports daily *L'Equipe*, suggested that Cullis' side should travel to Moscow and Budapest to play return games to make it fair, and that teams like AC Milan and Real Madrid should also be given the chance to play in such games. "A world club championship, or at least a European one should be launched," Hanot wrote. He then called a meeting in Paris which representatives of 15 clubs attended. A proposal to create a new competition was submitted to FIFA and they accepted so long as it was governed by UEFA (which itself had only been formed in June 1954).

The intent for this new competition was that all qualifying clubs would be champions of their domestic league, but with the invitations coming through the middle of the 1954/55 season, this wasn't possible. For instance, Hibernian of Scotland were not the champions, but they accepted the invitation. England's invitation did not go to Wolves, but to Chelsea, who were top of the table at the time. Watching this all unfold with a dream that his players could one day be a part of it was Manchester United manager Matt Busby.

It was clear they would have to mature quickly. Before the start of the campaign, it seemed there were senior players in the United squad now serving as understudies for much younger stars. "Youth is no sure passport to the United team," Tom Jackson wrote in the *Manchester Evening News*. "Hovering in the background as challengers to Edwards and Whitefoot in the middle line are experienced fellows such as Henry Cockburn and Don Gibson."

The same newspaper carried a word of caution the following day: "Many people thought towards the end of last season that prodigy Duncan Edwards was showing signs of constant big-match strain. His display at wing-half will be watched with particular interest now that he has had the benefit of a rest."

This seemed an unnecessarily harsh way to describe one or two below-par performances. It was unfortunate that the Arsenal game had occurred at a crucial time but Duncan's response to this had been strong, with influential performances in the Youth Cup and on the tour. On the other hand, it was a fair representation of the reputation he had developed – with those man-of-the-match displays at senior level at such a tender age, reports from rival managers that it was unfair that he played against them, and remarkable tributes paid from some of the biggest names in the game – an indication of what was expected with just 26 club games behind him.

Before the Youth Cup, Busby had relied on his team's performance in the 1948 FA Cup as the carrot for his scouts to dangle to young prospects around the country. In the early 1950s there was the sense that word of mouth was elevating the legend of what was being created at United, especially due to the lack of television footage from almost all matches. But once young players saw that United's system was very real and not just hype, it served as a greater lure. Surely they couldn't have scored more than 20 goals in one game? Well, they did, because it's there in the record books. Surely they didn't score seven past the next best youth team in the country? Well, that is a matter of fact, as that was how the first FA Youth Cup final went, and that is the performance which convinced the next best young thing, Wilf McGuinness, to sign. And when these statement scorelines registered around the country, they served as confirmation of all that was being said.

Despite the excitement, Busby stuck to the patient approach. There were no pre-season warm-up games due to the World Cup, and so United had only their annual 'Reds versus Blues' game at Old Trafford the week before the league season got underway.

Duncan had enjoyed a little more football in his pre-season. "Some players needed part-time jobs in the summer to top up their wages," recalls Tom Clare. "Eddie Colman and Bobby Charlton worked at Butlins at Pwllheli. They'd be Redcoats or help with the football coaching." Duncan and Gordon Clayton were just two other United lads who went too, but only on holiday – they would take part in the sessions organised by Colman.

Upon returning home to Stretford, Duncan and Bobby discovered they would need new digs. Mr Watson, their landlord, had been caught in an intimate position with somebody who was not Mrs Watson – it was deemed this was not an appropriate housing situation for teenage footballers. Duncan was eventually moved half a mile away into Mrs Dorman's home at 19 Gorse Avenue, where Billy Whelan was staying. However, in the short term, Duncan was housed with the Willey family on 2 Barlow Avenue, where he would stay for the entirety of this season. To maintain his fitness in the pre-season he would run to and from the city centre from his digs in Stretford.

The ascension of many of these boys into the first team had cemented them as heroes to the local boys. "Even though he wasn't local, Duncan might as well have been," remembers one of them, Tom Clare. "His broad Dudley accent was always very distinctive. We'd hang around his digs. He'd still give the autographs but now he seemed a little embarrassed by it. He always used the old ticket office behind the ground to get away but the kids got wise to it. He'd tie his bike up to the drainpipe outside the office with a piece of old string. He later had a car even though he couldn't drive and it was his pride and joy. He'd clean it and we'd just hang around the other side of the road, watching our hero from a distance. It was easy to feel attached to him. He was the most amiable lad and he treated the kids tremendously. There was no bigging it up. He'd have played on the streets if he could. He'd joke around with kids, even though they all wanted his autograph and that must have been frustrating for him sometimes. But he never let on."

Another impressionable youngster was Irish teenager Johnny Giles, who arrived in Manchester for summer trials. "I arrived in Manchester and stayed with Joe Armstrong in Stockport over the weekend," Giles remembers. "On Monday morning we went to Old Trafford for the first time. As we were walking down Stretford Road there was this big fella sitting on a post box. Just sitting there eating an apple, probably waiting for the bus. Joe said, 'John, this is Duncan Edwards.' He was a big lad. He was like a grown man. He said hello and then just carried on eating the apple."

If the players this youth system developed were already attaining cult status, then it stood to reason that a boy in Giles' position might expect the most extraordinary facilities where he could hone his skills. Not so. "Nowadays the facilities would be considered as ancient," he says. "Tom Curry would go out on to the Old Trafford pitch in a morning and you'd be lapping the pitch. That would be for about an hour on Mondays. After that, the boys would go around the back of the stand and have a big game. Tuesday was ball day. We might go to the Cliff, sometimes it would be Old Trafford again, and we'd get the ball out. They had a saying – "Don't let them have the ball during the week, because they'll be hungry for it on the Saturday." Wednesday and Thursday would be the same and Friday would be sprint morning.

"Now and again you might have a first team versus second team match. The kids didn't train with the ball with the first-team players but we ran together, so I was running alongside Duncan, Liam Whelan, all the Babes. It was unbelievable. There were so many players that when the first and second teams played against each other the rest of us would be standing around the pitch watching. I can remember standing next to Bobby Charlton on the touchline. He couldn't get a game!"

United's amenities may not have been revolutionary, but their philosophy was. "The Youth Cup was a big competition," Giles says. "It was the first time anything like this had ever happened. There were rules about how many young lads you could bring into the club, but Matt Busby would bring in youngsters and put them on the ground staff. So they'd be sweeping the terraces. Great young players, not officially footballers, sweeping the terraces. He could bring in as many ground staff as he liked. It wasn't breaking any rules. Busby was the first to even think of getting that many young players and then putting them in the first team. Nobody was doing that."

The kick-abouts in Pwllheli were not sufficient practice for these youngsters to prepare for the new season of First Division football. Underdogs Portsmouth stormed into a 3-0 lead at Old Trafford on the opening day, with Jack Rowley scoring a consolation. Two days later, United enjoyed a 4-2 win at Hillsborough, though Edwards conceded a penalty for a foul on Albert Quixall. That was followed by a win of the same score at Blackpool, a trip where Duncan was accompanied by Eddie Colman, who was travelling with the first team for the first time as 12th man.

Duncan's home life was not the only part of his usual routine to have been disturbed. United had sought advice from nutritionists and changed their pre-match meals. "Those nice, fat, juicy steaks now being tackled by Manchester United players BEFORE a match are just what the doctors order," wrote Tom Jackson in the *Manchester Evening News*. "It's all a question of timing, say the medical men. Apparently grilled beef steak three hours before helps players to replace tissues broken down during a game or by pre-match exercise. The smallest man in the side – Johnny Berry, 5ft 6in and 9st 5lb – thinks these steaks are wonderful. And so does that strapping young wing-half Duncan Edwards, whose big frame calls for 'big eats'."

The big eats were resulting in big performances after that first day disappointment. United swept away Sheffield Wednesday in the early return game and then won 3-1 against Charlton.

Up next was Tottenham away; United found an opponent committed to playing attacking football, and excelled in the space they were allowed as a result. Busby's side won 2-0 to top the table, but a draw at Bolton saw them lose first place. Seven days after visiting White Hart Lane, United hosted Spurs at Old Trafford. There was thrilling excitement from the opening exchanges – Rowley scored after five minutes, Spurs levelled on 14, but three minutes later, Viollet struck the winning goal which moved his team back to the summit. Tom Jackson's assessment was that United were "Top Again – Thanks to Mighty Duncan", adding: "Mr H. Shentall, chairman of the FA selection committee, must have been greatly impressed by this Edwards 'power' display."

George Follows, in the *Daily Herald*, described Edwards as "the star of the match", concluding: "He gave one of the best displays of wing-half play we have seen at Old Trafford for years. Everything he did was accomplished with the ease and grace of a seasoned player."

Shentall was at Old Trafford for the visit of Huddersfield a few days later. Edwards was once more on form, with Alf Clarke of the *Evening Chronicle* describing his performance as "outstanding". Two days later, Duncan was in the youth team which played a Liverpool County side at Anfield. He scored goals in the 16th and 21st minute as his team controlled a 3-0 win – and was described as "a grand leader" by the *Liverpool Echo*.

It seemed as though he was a certainty to be called into the England team which would face Northern Ireland in Belfast on October 2nd – the day after Duncan's 18th birthday. Bob Ferrier of the *Mirror* certainly appeared to think so: "The left half who most combines present skill and potential greatness is Duncan Edwards, of Manchester United."

It was reported that a call-up would place Edwards as the youngest ever debutant for the national side. This was not strictly true – James Prinsep, Thurston Rostron and Clement Mitchell were all younger when they made their debuts in the 19th century. If Walter Winterbottom and his committee had taken the gamble at the end of the prior season, then Edwards would have broken the all-time record at the World Cup. However, he would have to continue to wait, as 28-year-old left-half Ray Barlow of West Brom was given a chance to make his own England debut in the post-World Cup rebuild.

The disappointing news that Duncan would not receive his first cap compounded a miserable weekend. The day before, United had lost at Manchester City to end their eight-game unbeaten run, and Edwards – desperate to protect a positive result – had thrown a leg at a shot, only for it to divert into the net.

In the crowd at Maine Road was a City fan by the name of Molly Leach. She was just about the only home fan unhappy with that goal, as she had recently started courting the unfortunate chap wearing the red shirt with the number six on his back.

Duncan had attended a function at Manchester Ringway airport and was captivated by a dark-haired girl who had an energy and aura; she was as confident and well-spoken as she was beautiful. There was no need for an introduction for Molly – everyone knew who Duncan was. Molly, however, was not affected by his celebrity, nor the fact that he played for the team across town. They quickly became inseparable.

As was par for the course with other people receiving credit for things United were doing, City were inspired by 'The Revie Plan', in which nominal centre-forward Don Revie drew inspiration from the Hungarian's mischief-making to drop into deeper positions to confuse defenders. City had trialled this style in their reserve team the previous season, and were suitably convinced to go for it in the first team. As we know, Edwards himself had carried out a similar decoy plan in the Youth Cup.

There was no sleight of hand when United went to Molineux – the game Duncan would be playing while Foulkes and Byrne turned out for England (in these days, international fixtures would often be scheduled to clash with the league calendar, with the national team taking precedence with their pick of players). There were, however, two changes of position. The first was obvious from the start – he had a new shirt number, eight, and lined up at inside-forward.

Things started well. United – with two young players, Ian Greaves and Paddy Kennedy making their own debuts – took a lead into half-time thanks to Viollet's goal. Champions Wolves needed a huge stroke of luck to overcome the plucky Babes when Allenby Chilton, the half-back moonlighting at centre-half, had to come off injured in the second half. Edwards was moved back into defence and Wolves took advantage of a 10-man opponent. 1-0 down in the 70th minute, the hosts were 4-2 up by the 87th.

With a full complement, United bounced back with high-scoring wins in their next two games. Tommy Taylor hit a hat-trick against Cardiff in a 5-2 win, and it was Viollet's turn to notch a treble (with Taylor getting two) in a sensational 6-5 win at Chelsea. Edwards, according to Joe Hulme in *The People*, had a "grand game".

On October 19th, Duncan was named in an FA Youth XI side to play Wolves at Molineux on November 8th, and then on the 20th he represented a Football League side against an Irish League side at Anfield. This was played in front of some of the national selection committee, so it was another chance to state his case for a full cap. However, the English side suffered an embarrassing defeat, and for once, Edwards could feel the brunt of criticism. "Duncan Edwards must accept some of the blame for haphazard distribution," was the take of the *Daily Herald*, while Eric Butler discussed prospects for a full national team call-up in the *Daily Worker*: "At left-half, the choice rests between two. Duncan Edwards never really settled against the Irish. My preference here would be for the recall of the experienced Ray Barlow."

Edwards stood up to the hard words, playing well in a 2-2 draw against Newcastle. Busby then had a dilemma on October 30th. His first team were at Goodison Park to play Everton, and a few hours earlier, the youth team were across town at Anfield in the Youth Cup first round. The manager decided McGuinness and Colman could handle Liverpool and United eased through with a handsome 4-1 win.

At Everton, however, Duncan Edwards' afternoon could barely have been worse. Again, members of the England selection committee were present. A ding-dong start saw Rowley score in the 10th minute, Dave Hickson equalise in the 11th, and Taylor restore United's lead in the 20th. Chilton, at 34, was showing signs of his age catching up with him, while Don Gibson was also labouring.

Edwards, the third central figure in that back axis, was having to plug too many holes. The result was a loss of his trademark composure. In the 32nd minute, Chilton had been caught out and Edwards was forced into a lunging tackle. He was late. Everton scored the penalty. The hosts took a second-half lead and then, five minutes from the end, Edwards rounded off a dire 90 minutes when he was penalised for handball in the box. Tommy Jones, scorer of the first spot-kick, dispatched the second. In the *Evening News*, Tom Jackson felt Edwards' confidence had been hit by that first penalty award: "Not surprisingly, Duncan Edwards lost touch after conceding the first of two penalties."

The defensive issues meant that goals from Viollet and Taylor were necessary to keep United competitive. The defeat at Everton had taken United from first to fourth – and Viollet needed to score twice to get his team a win at home to Preston.

At Sheffield United in the league, Busby watched his team lose 3-0. If *Match of the Day* were a thing (it wouldn't be for another decade), one might imagine the 1954 version of Alan Hansen sneering that these kids would not win anything.

There was a theme developing – the senior team needed Edwards to perform the role of three players. And the Youth Cup team found it difficult to do anything but look for Duncan once he was back in the side, as he was for the important derby game against Manchester City in the second round at Maine Road. Edwards' importance was underlined by the number nine on his back as he played in the unfamiliar role of centre-forward. "This is the hardest position on the field in which to play," he would confess.

The tie had been rescheduled due to a waterlogged pitch, and it was in doubt again due to thick fog. The game did go ahead, though the 6,849 in attendance could barely see. City scored – it was 1-0 at half-time. Jimmy Murphy, unable to make a genuine comment on how his players had fared, simply admitted: "I believe you are a goal down."

As the players trotted out for the second half, Duncan paused as he was walking past Jimmy, and reassured him that he could make the difference.

"Don't worry son. I'll get a goal or two for you this half."

"And he did," Murphy said. "That's what I loved about that kid. He always called me 'son'!"

The *Daily Dispatch* reported of United's 2-1 win, with goals courtesy of Edwards: "It was practically impossible to see across the ground, but visibility was good enough to see that City were quicker on the ball than United, who, in spite of the tireless work of Edwards, were obviously surprised by the strength of the opposition... City held this lead until the 65th minute, when Edwards equalised. The United centre-forward won the match 20 minutes later with another splendid individual effort."

Willie Evans of the *Mirror* felt that United were over-dependent on their star name. "After watching this year's 'Busby Babes'... I am convinced that they will not be the powerful force they were in the past two seasons," Evans suggested. "United have not the same rhythm of the past, and rely too much on Duncan Edwards, whose winning goal in the last five minutes scraped them into the next round."

It was more youth duty at the weekend – Edwards was called into the England under-18 side to face Holland in Arnhem. His single appearance at this level was marred by defeat, with all the goals in the 2-3 game coming in the second half. At the same time, United played Arsenal, and won 2-1, with Freddie Goodwin – three years older than Duncan – deputising for him.

Leslie Nichols of the *Express* noted Duncan as one of the few to emerge with credit after the international setback. "Hurrah for Harry Middleton, Alan Woods, Duncan Edwards and Johnny Roach... the men who saved England's Youth from a first-class licking at Arnhem," he wrote. It was a similar account from David Williams of the *Daily Herald*: "Our main trouble was too much textbook football and not enough British Lion spirit. I must except the two wing-halves Duncan Edwards and Alan Woods, both of whom tried like trojans to get England moving."

Edwards' difficult spell in the first team continued on his return, as he was back in at wing-half at West Brom. Chasing a first-half deficit, Edwards once again found himself desperately defending. His performance at the Hawthorns was admirable, plugging those defensive holes and driving his team forward. However, once more, that desire to be everywhere came at a cost. In the 78th minute, an attempted block was deemed to be handball – the third spot-kick Edwards had given away already this season. It was converted, as United slumped to another defeat, though Busby dismissed it as a "harsh decision". Edwards, however, had harsh words himself. "How could I help the wind blowing the ball on my hand?" he complained.

"Duncan Edwards was the star of the United side," reported the *Birmingham Gazette*. "His ball distribution in the first half was dangerously good, but later he lay back more and more in defence."

Duncan reported unfit for the next game against Leicester with a boil on his ankle – and while he would have been unhappy to miss United's 3-1 win, it was probably for the best that he had a couple of weeks out of the spotlight to adjust to the numerous changes in his life. Now a bona fide Manchester United first-teamer, an England cap also seemed inevitable. It was clear he was an important part of United's team, with Busby pondering how to reduce his responsibilities in order to best utilise his strengths. It was evident that a large percentage of the work he was doing was compensatory.

Of course, not everyone agreed. Seeing Duncan concede three penalties and fail to assert his reputed influence in United's defeats had some wondering if he was as good as he was made out to be. Some even wondered if his new relationship had caused his eye to be taken off the ball. Duncan was his own biggest critic. He did not need to be told where he could improve. But he was also very headstrong, a stickler for fairness, so refuted the suggestion – even though he knew, in the early days, he was probably pushing things a little too close for comfort.

Ever the gentleman, Duncan would accompany Molly on the bus home to Timperley, and then get the bus back to Stretford. On one occasion he was spotted by Stan Orme, the local Labour politician. Orme was also of a red persuasion when it came to football, so when Duncan pleaded with him not to tell Mr Busby he was on a bus minutes before midnight on the Friday evening before a game, he promised he would keep his secret. Though he rejected any suggestion there was some form of distraction, Duncan resolved to once again prove how good he was with an extra-determined approach.

An injury to Tommy Taylor meant young striker Colin Webster was required for the first-team trip to Burnley, making the decision to draft Edwards in at centre-forward for the Youth Cup game at Barnsley on the same day a little easier. Webster scored a hat-trick in a 4-2 win – and Edwards notched two himself as the junior side won by the same score.

Barnsley had a 2-0 half-time lead, prompting Edwards to make the same promise to Murphy as he had in the prior round. This time his influence was even greater, as he scored twice and set up the other two. "We were glad Duncan was with us for that one," the relieved defender Alan Rhodes said.

Job done, Edwards was recalled into the first team for the trip to Portsmouth a week before Christmas. "For Manchester United nobody worked harder than left-half Duncan Edwards, the biggest 'Babe' in the business," read the report in *The People*. "This husky 18-year-old was effective in attack and defence, and not averse to trying a shot. This young man is well on the way to becoming that rarest of all gems – a real personality."

The *Daily Herald*, meanwhile, described the 0-0 draw thus: "The Busby Babes bogged down in the mire – all except the biggest, lustiest, huskiest of the lot, 18-year-old Duncan Edwards. What a babe! The boy with the Nordahl thighs and the Joe Louis shoulders treats his football as a gay romp, but behind all his courageous cavorting is the kind of ball control that makes other managers sigh in envy."

United lost close back-to-back games with Aston Villa on the 27th and 28th of December, with Edwards receiving much praise for his performance in the second of those matches. He was the man who came closest to getting his team a draw, with two long range shots that missed the target.

"Man of the match was United's Duncan Edwards," wrote Anthony Smith of the *Birmingham Gazette*. "His tackling, ball distribution and pace marked him as a future fellow of Manchester's colony of internationals. Edwards, who was moved to left-back for the last 20 minutes because he had a stitch, had previously sowed his seeds diligently and sent in three useful shots."

Clifford Webb in the *Daily Herald* praised Villa player Con

Martin for a certain bravery: "Most of the shooting was left to Duncan Edwards, who gave another of his fine all-action displays. One terrific shot from this chunky left-half sailed high over the bar after Con Martin had got his head to the ball. The big surprise was that Martin stayed on his feet when most expected him to be laid flat out."

At the turn of the year, United were down in seventh, but only two points behind leaders Sunderland. Those games against Villa illustrated Duncan's keenness to break his goalscoring duck. In his 48th game, that moment finally came. Blackpool visited Old Trafford on New Year's Day 1955 and United put on a show, scoring twice in the first half and then sealing the points with a goal that was worth the wait. In the 78th minute, the ball bounced invitingly for Edwards, whose connection was a "veritable detonation" according to Don Davies of *The Guardian*. The ball rose, and then dipped, flying into the top corner. "Edwards leaped and gambolled like a soul possessed until his adoring colleagues pinned him down with their embraces," Davies wrote.

Attentions turned to the Wembley trail. With his team 1-0 down against stubborn lower league Reading in the FA Cup, Matt Busby admitted: "I had given the game up." Busby was to learn just how influential Edwards could be. With United ponderous around goal, Duncan demanded possession.

"There is nothing in the laws that says that football has to be a silent game – as long as your shouting does not mislead the other side," Edwards said. "Then it is classed as unfair play."

This was a specific instruction from Jimmy Murphy drilled into the young player on weekday mornings. The coach insisted that Duncan should demand the ball and do it loudly. "Maybe there is a big crowd and a team-mate might not hear you," Murphy said, "so make it clear that you want it."

Here, he let his team-mates know by example what they should be doing, letting fly with numerous shots from range to emphasise the need to be direct. "Enter Edwards," sportswriter Sam Leitch reported, "living up to the high reputation which England manager Walter Winterbottom, who looked on, has of him. Four shots whizzed by, shots which emphasised the tip-tapping tenderness of United's attack."

His colleagues rescued a replay through a late Colin Webster goal. After the game, Edwards learned he had been called into the under-23 England team which would face Italy at Stamford Bridge on January 19th. In slightly less welcome news, now he had turned 18, he would probably have to participate in his national service from June. Duncan had heard his team-mates like Roger Byrne speak of their experiences in the Army and it was not something he was looking forward to. He was not alone. United's players remained hopeful that there would be a way to get out of it before the time came.

The performance of Reading danger man Wally Hinshelwood in the first game made Busby do something unusual in the replay. Hinshelwood would operate in the space between the full-back and centre-back, so the United boss asked Edwards to play a role that in modern times would effectively be the left centre-half. It was a sensible approach. "The Busby blueprint was designed to provide closer marking," Tom Jackson observed in the *Evening News*. "It involved Duncan Edwards lying so deep that he appeared to be an extra left-back. It all worked out so well, even on such a treacherous surface, that Reading were really beaten in the first half hour."

However, as relayed by Henry Rose of the *Express*, this did not mean Edwards shirked his attacking responsibilities. Once more he set the tone. "With the pitch like an ice-rink, and snow falling for much of the game, class football was impossible," Rose wrote. "Duncan Edwards set the pattern with two 25-yard drives. His colleagues took the hint and Dave Meeson pulled off save after save."

United struck goal after goal, too, notching four before the late concession of another penalty – and, again, this one was awarded against Duncan for handball.

One matter of retribution complete, Duncan joined up with the England youth team keen to right the wrongs of the 3-0 loss to Italy a year earlier, which had felt so underwhelming after the senior side's capitulation to Hungary. There was plenty of press scrutiny on this young group. So much so that even their hour-long practice match at Fulham the day before the game attracted press attention. Eric Butler of the *Daily Worker* described the half-back line of Edwards, Wolves' Ron Flowers, and Birmingham's Trevor Smith as "rich in promise", adding: "All three allied powerful defensive work with cultured use of the ball." Yet Clifford Webb of the *Herald* still managed to find something to criticise even in a glorified training session. "Duncan Edwards messed up several chances by blazing away into the clouds," Webb complained.

Desmond Hackett of the *Express* reported that there had been some confusion over the rules. The Italians had claimed they could include players born on or after January 1st, 1931, when all of England's were born on or after January 1st, 1932. It meant there were three older boys in the visiting team's line-up. They also had the incentive of a £50-a-man bonus to win the game – more than five times Duncan's weekly wage.

"But I think these gilded youths of Italy may be in for a shock because of the three wise young men who make up the half-back line: Ron Flowers, Trevor Smith and Duncan Edwards," Hackett predicted. "They are not likely to panic against the so artistic, so temperamental Italians."

Revenge was sweet for the junior Three Lions. Over 33,000 made their way to Stamford Bridge, an impressive turnout for a 2.15pm kick-off on a Wednesday in January. England's boys won 5-1.

"I played on the left-wing and Duncan played inside at left-half," Frank Blunstone recalls. "He was great to play with. Unfussy. Uncomplicated. He'd get the ball, give it you and let you get on with it. He was mature beyond his years. It was his power that tricked you. You couldn't have thought he was just 18."

The plaudits flowed, with Edwards receiving a generous proportion of them. "Our half-backs set the efficiency standard," Clifford Webb wrote, despite his barbs the prior day. "After a slightly shaky start, Ron Flowers, Trevor Smith and Duncan Edwards took absolute control."

The Times described Duncan as "the master of the midfield" while the Italian captain, Giuseppi Corradi, said: "Edwards was the best player on the field."

In his book *Soccer in the Fifties*, Geoffrey Green said: "Edwards – the master of the 40- or 50-yard pass – played like a tornado, attacking, defending, always wanting to be at the eye of the storm. He pounded forward on a solo run like a runaway tank to release a shell from the edge of the penalty area that would have penetrated a steel wall."

The future was finally beginning to appear rosy for England. At Manchester United, the present was still proving a little sticky. A 1-1 draw on a mud bath of an Old Trafford pitch against Bolton was followed by a trip to Manchester City in the FA Cup. Derek Wallis of the *Mirror* suggested that Edwards would be tasked with the job of following Revie around: "The Busby tactics this time? My guess is that left-half Duncan Edwards, whose power-play destroyed the Italians recently, will be detailed to shadow Revie. The speedy Edwards is just the player to disrupt Revie's scheme."

Edwards was outstanding but once more even his all-action display wasn't enough to push this United team to victory. In the first half he was called into defensive action to clear off the line twice. City scored in the 65th minute – Edwards' response was to storm through the home defence on a rampaging run. Just as he was about to unleash a shot, he was hauled down on the edge of the box. Two minutes later Chilton was sent off. Edwards was moved to centre-half again, and still came the closest to levelling things up with a header. Revie – free from the claustrophobic marking of the omnipresent teenager – scored in the last minute to seal the result. A return to Wembley would have to wait for Duncan.

The cup defeat was the final bow for star striker Jack Rowley, whose move to Plymouth followed soon after. So, with Taylor still injured, it meant Duncan being asked to fill in at inside-forward at Huddersfield. His energy elevated the front line, with United registering three goals in the first half – Duncan himself getting the second of them. "Edwards was here, there and everywhere," Alf Clarke wrote in the *Football Pink*. "His tremendous energy was certainly proving a great boon to the United attack."

Tom Jackson's take was that this was just another sign of over-reliance on the boy who was only making his first steps into first-team football a year earlier. "Matt Busby may be fortunate in having such an inspiring young footballer as Duncan Edwards to call on when things aren't working smoothly in attack," he wrote.

Duncan was called into the England under-23 team to play at Scotland. The night before the game he played in a practice match against Rangers at Ibrox that had to be abandoned due to heavy rain. There was a similarly difficult start at Shawfield Park the following evening. After just 30 seconds, young centre-forward Bobby Ayre fell to the ground with a dislocated elbow. After nine minutes of treatment, Ayre was substituted and his number nine shirt was given to Duncan, who moved up from left-half.

Chances came and went, and Edwards grew frustrated enough that inside-right John Atyeo switched positions with him at half-time. The consequences were devastating. "Atyeo switched with Edwards after the Manchester United man had missed three simple chances," wrote Bob Pennington in the *Express*. "There was no holding Young England now... Haynes gave Edwards the chance to restore his confidence with a defence-splitting pass for goal No. 3 (53 minutes). Hooper now to Edwards, who right-footed the ball inside the far post for No. 4 (61 minutes). Then Haynes again with exactly the same service to Edwards for No. 5 (62 minutes)."

The *Morning Star* described how Edwards "showed nothing more than a good positional sense in his unfamiliar position, but after he had missed three gilt-edged chances, he suddenly struck shooting form, adding England's third, fourth and fifth goals in the space of 20 minutes."

Through a series of circumstances that forced the hands of respective managers, more than it was a case of a player demanding to play the role, the idea of Duncan Edwards as a forward was suddenly a matter of consideration.

The *Manchester Evening News* led the campaign. "Edwards is a ready-made leader of dash and shooting power," argued Eric Thornton. "He employed his huge frame expertly for the late challenge, and picked the open spaces and scoring spots he wanted with glee and precision."

Alf Clarke in the *Football Pink* considered the issue. "The chief problem is where to play him. He is a brilliant wing-half, can also adapt himself to centre-half, and now both Manchester United and England realise his possibilities in the attack. That is where I think he should be played... We cannot escape from the fact that Duncan Edwards is the greatest young player of his age. I rank Edwards as the best player I have ever seen."

Busby was sufficiently tempted to give Edwards another go in the number 10 shirt. Sometimes what is lost can outweigh what is gained and that much was painfully evident as United's soft centre was exposed by Manchester City's fluid system. City won 5-0 at Old Trafford in another of those milestone moments which helped Busby blow the wind of change through his team. Busby, though, was not a knee-jerk man. Having invested in the idea of Edwards as an inside-forward, that was where he would remain for the rest of the season.

In fact, Edwards could consider himself fortunate that Busby was not often prone to impulse; on the evening of the derby defeat, Duncan was stopped by a policeman who saw him riding his bicycle unsteadily on the way back to his digs from the city centre. The officer told Duncan that he would receive a fine for riding without a light. The teenager accepted, and hurried home. Busby found out, and told Duncan in no uncertain terms that he was not impressed. Remarkably, the case went before Sale Magistrates Court, and Duncan was fined the equivalent of £1. His punishment from United was more significant – a fine of two weeks' wages for bringing the club into disrepute.

The defensive frailties continued to reveal themselves. On February 24th, Wolves came to an icy Old Trafford on a pitch so poor the markings had to be traced with red dye. United were 2-1 up at half-time thanks to a drilled effort from Edwards, but the visitors scored three times late on to win 4-2. "I give full marks to Taylor and Edwards, who did much to try and infuse pep into a reshuffled line," concluded a sympathetic Tom Jackson.

The disarray at the back finally prompted Busby to make one big decision – Allenby Chilton's first-team career was over. Mark Jones, who had impressed in the Central League, now had his big promotion. He played against Cardiff, but it was too much to ask him to solve United's issues from the start. With Gibson and Whitefoot as his half-backs, the team was still missing the protective presence of Edwards further back, and the three goals scored by the Welsh side were no surprise.

Tom Jackson again showed sympathy: "It's often said that to be the manager of a successful soccer club one must have many sleepless nights before things begin to click in your favour. I'm not suggesting that Matt Busby now has any urgent reason to burn the midnight oil, but three successive defeats for his youngsters have certainly queered the pitch so far as that title ambition is concerned. And let us say immediately there was so much to admire in the display of the side as a whole, that the Busby rebuilding plan must continue to be founded on youngsters possessing such potential ability. The Cardiff folk complimented United on copybook methods under treacherous ground conditions, but they couldn't hand out any laurels for shooting. That is United's biggest let-down. Duncan Edwards and Tommy Taylor worked hard to try and supply the missing link, but there was not sufficient all-round strength in the line."

Compassion for United's transitional issues was all well and good. But three years after Busby's claims of a rosy future, there was nothing tangible to show for it – his Babes would have to start to realise their potential to show they were worthy of the generous platitudes they had so far received.

Chapter 9
Infant Hercules

Three consecutive defeats in February 1955 meant Manchester United dropped to eighth in the table. There was still only a five-point gap between them and leaders Wolves, but Matt Busby decided that further changes would be needed. There were promising players coming through, not least Eddie Colman at half-back who seemed destined to eventually succeed Don Gibson. But Colman's small size meant he had been understudy to Gibson and Jeff Whitefoot, and it was only in this period when the Salford lad finally started to get some serious Central League action.

After pushing his defensive options as far as he reasonably could, Busby shuffled the attack. Out went Viollet and Pegg – the latter spent the rest of the season in the reserves – and in came Berry and Scanlon for the visit of Burnley. Duncan Edwards retained his place at inside-forward.

It was a laborious afternoon for all in attendance. "Just as the game seemed about to enter on its last, desultory, featureless, wearisome half hour, Edwards did himself and his colleagues an unexpected kindness by leaping to head the winning goal," wrote Don Davies in the *Manchester Guardian*. "Edwards so far had been anything but a success as an inside-left. Yet how the crowd rose to this infant Hercules when, with one mighty swing of his monstrous left leg, he launched the missile from which McDonald fashioned the last of his many breathtaking saves."

In the *Evening News*, Tom Jackson's view was that "even with

Tommy Taylor and Duncan Edwards a little below their usual form, the line was much more virile and full of shooting ideas."

It would take another 21 years before yellow and red cards were brought into the British game. Before then, a player would be sent from the field or 'booked' – ie their name was taken in the referee's notepad – if they had committed a serious enough misdemeanour. So if the man in charge stopped the game to talk to a player, it was deemed a serious enough moment to bring into question a player's dedication to fair play. One Burnley player complained to the referee that the United teenager had gone in for a tackle with brute force, prompting the official to check Duncan's studs. Duncan was aghast that his sportsmanship should be questioned. The referee found nothing untoward, but even the act of the Burnley player was memorable enough to place the thought in the mind of others.

United might have been eliminated from the FA Cup but they were still in the Youth Cup. The fifth-round tie meant a swift return to Old Trafford for Jack Rowley as Plymouth manager. It was a weekend where Busby's long-term planning could be seen again. He had arranged a friendly at Lincoln, where Duncan's room-mate Bill Whelan played in the number 10 shirt. Could he be ready for a call-up? Duncan didn't play at inside-forward against Plymouth. Nor – with Colman and McGuinness undroppable at wing-half – did he play in his regular position. Busby and Murphy decided to test Edwards as the centre-back behind his friends, to see how the combination would work. It was possibly the first and only time a team has ever been bold enough to go with a 'false 5'. The selection was made easier as regular defender Peter Jones was injured.

United won 9-0. "Charlton and Brennan both got hat-tricks in United's runaway victory," reported Tom Jackson, "but a big feature was the brilliant work of the half-backs, Colman, Edwards and McGuinness... generally Edwards was the master in the middle."

So beleaguered were the southerners that Edwards was able

to charge through from the back to net his team's ninth goal. Plymouth captain Reg Mitchell admitted they had been blown away. "We'd never seen anything like it," he said. "It was as if they had come from another planet."

Duncan was called into another English League representative side, this time to face the Scottish League in Glasgow on March 16th. Scotland won 3-2 in a disappointing game for the visitors. One of the goals for the hosts came from the penalty spot for, you guessed it, handball by Duncan Edwards.

"There was really little to enthuse over in the Football League side," read one report. "Frank Blunstone worked hard, but, generally, the forwards lacked inspiration. Wing-halves Ken Armstrong and Duncan Edwards strove manfully to bring poise and threat to a disappointing side."

Douglas Ritchie of the *Daily Herald* wrote Edwards "missed the merit list because he had his name taken midway through the second half." This was the second incident in a matter of weeks that Edwards had been talked to by an official – this time it was probably earned, as his tackle on Gordon Smith was late – and it caused the Football Association to write to Duncan warning him about his conduct.

"Big, bulldozing Duncan Edwards comes back into Manchester United's attack at inside-left, after taking time out to help the Youth team at centre half, for tomorrow's return League game with Everton at Old Trafford," wrote Tom Jackson on March 18th.

The ages of the 1-11 for that game were, respectively: Wood 23, Foulkes 23, Byrne 26, Gibson 25, Jones 21, Whitefoot 21, Berry 28, Taylor 23, Webster 22, Edwards 18, and Scanlon 19. That made for an average age of 22.6 (which for comparison's sake was two years younger than the average age of the 'Fergie Fledglings' team which won the league and FA Cup double in 1996). They delivered what might have been expected – a vibrant start without the professional experience to see out the game. Scanlon scored on 14 minutes, but the Toffees scored sucker-punch goals either side of the break to take the win.

Duncan remained in the national set-up. He was named in the England B team to face Scotland at Ibrox on March 2nd, but the match had been called off in the morning due to ice and snow. There were no such weather concerns for the next scheduled B match, against West Germany at Hillsborough on March 23rd. The game ended 1-1, with Duncan's performance under particular scrutiny, and he was either a cert to make it into the full national team – one report reading "Edwards was a young colossus' – or, as far away as as he had ever been, with another summary of his performance reading that he put on "a rather poor showing and did nothing to claim a place in the full England side to face Scotland in April."

Duncan would only have to wait until March 27th to find out if the selection committee were of the former or latter opinion. He put on a solid display at Preston – a game in which Whelan made his debut, taking the average age of the side down further still. "It was the left wing of Duncan Edwards and Albert Scanlon which really took the eye," the *Manchester Evening News* reported of United's 2-0 win. "Edwards got through a tremendous amount of foraging."

Tom Jackson had the pleasure of confirming the news Duncan had been waiting to hear: "Within three years of captaining England schoolboys against Scotland at Wembley, Edwards returns to the big scene as the youngest-ever to play for England in a senior international against the Scots. For Edwards it is the realisation of a boyhood dream, and for Matt Busby the fulfilment of a prophecy he made to Duncan's father in May 1952, when his boy signed as an amateur for United."

Chapter 10
Lion

It had not been a perfectly smooth season for Duncan – the hand-balls, the cautions, his inconsistent place in the team – but there could be no doubt that since the start of 1955, there was a growing sense of his importance to whatever team he played in. The debate about his best position would take some time to resolve (if it ever was) but it was widely accepted that he wouldn't be a striker. He did not have the natural instinct for that, and yet, was still an accomplished enough finisher to make it a worthwhile conversation. United were working out how they would best benefit from his talent. Busby had the luxury of over 40 first-team games and a dozen or so youth and cup team matches to try out. Walter Winterbottom did not. So, for his international debut, Duncan was named in his familiar number six shirt at left-half. If this was an attempt to ease the teenager in, then it was apparently unnecessary.

"People said to me before my first international that as a youngster I would feel the mental strain, that I would not be able to play my natural game," Edwards said. "Nothing of the sort happened. Apart from feeling that I was going to try harder, my main impression was one of enjoyment at playing in the highest class of football."

Duncan joined up with his national team colleagues and played a couple of practice sessions – first against Charlton on March 28th, and then against Arsenal at Highbury on the 29th. Both games were won 2-1. But even in practice matches things can go wrong – as Len Phillips found out. The veteran Portsmouth wing-half was injured in the game at Charlton, meaning that Duncan was one of three debutants, as Ken Armstrong of Chelsea was called up to play at right-half. Armstrong was 30, but had no experience at this level, so both he and Edwards were fortunate to be guided by the most-capped player in England history, Wolves and national team captain Billy Wright, at centre-half.

Edwards had the benefit of familiar faces around him. At left-back was Roger Byrne, making his 10th appearance, and at outside-left was Frank Blunstone, playing his second game for the England team after spending time with Duncan in the junior sides. It was clear, though, that big things were expected from the teenager, even accounting for his inexperience.

"He was such a nice person, he was so modest about things," Walter Winterbottom said. "You were always pleased to see him because he had this strength and power… he was a lovely boy, so cheerful."

There seemed to be a relaxed mood in the England camp, although Duncan confessed to only a slight amount of anxiety. "During the week leading up to the match, I never really gave it much thought," he said. "On the Friday, however, I was a little nervous. By lunchtime on Saturday I really had butterflies. Once I got to Wembley itself and into the dressing rooms, there were good luck telegrams to read and I began to feel better. All the players wished me luck and just before we went out Billy Wright said, 'If any of us shout at you out there, take it with a pinch of salt, it will be for your own good'."

For the first time since the Hungary humblings it looked as though England were turning a corner. They scored after just 45 seconds through Dennis Wilshaw and never really stopped all afternoon. Wilshaw added three more and England were 7-1 up before Tommy Docherty struck a fine free-kick in consolation. The resounding win was enough to earn England the Home Championship.

Docherty's main memory, though, was how impressive his direct competitor had been. "Just as it was hard to believe that Stanley Matthews was 40 and able to play this well," Docherty said, "so too was it almost incomprehensible that Duncan could only be 18 and play like such a powerhouse. He was already noticeably more mature than in the league games I'd played against him."

The *Glasgow Herald* reported of Edwards: "He played with the confidence of a 30-year-old and was the driving force of the team, continually powering into the opposition half."

Sportswriter John Arlott could hardly have been more effusive. "Although he looked a dominating player in league football, it would have been understandable if he had been overawed in such a match," Arlott wrote. "On the contrary, there were times at Wembley when he looked almost too good for his contemporaries. Time and again he snatched a marginal ball in his stride, and then, as the Scottish defence fell back, he casually flicked a square cross the complete width of the pitch, precisely to the feet of Matthews at outside-right. The perfect cross-field pass is hard to deliver. Yet here was this lad executing it with complete mastery. Edwards, however, is the complete all-round footballer. Equipped with natural ball-sense, he is so perfectly two-footed as to be utterly indifferent as to which foot he uses, and is master of all the basic skills. This is the modern Continental patter, the technical completeness which makes a footballer more than a one-position specialist but − like Edwards and John Charles, of Leeds − capable of an adequate performance anywhere on the field."

Duncan's new team-mate Don Revie was also generous with his description − it was clear that it was a memorable debut. "You don't hear many professionals talk lightly of greatness because it is so rare, but that is what I saw in Duncan Edwards the first time I set eyes on him," the City player said. "He reached the same fabulous standard at left-half, centre-half, inside-left and centre-forward. He is the kind of player managers dream about."

Roger Byrne commented on his club-mate's international bow in his *Evening News* column. "Duncan Edwards, only 18 and yet the proud possessor of a full cap, with the prospect of many more. He can play anywhere, and yet it never seems to affect his style. In fact, one could say that Mr Busby has yet to find his best position. We can't imagine what a player he will be when he matures."

Tom Jackson, also in the *Evening News*, felt that Duncan could only improve. "Edwards, always as strong as a horse, is going to benefit considerably from playing alongside such an experienced campaigner as Billy Wright," he said.

Byrne and Jackson were right. In fact, Edwards would make a point of seeking out his captain before pulling on an England shirt. "Before an international match I always have a talk with Billy Wright about players in the other side," Duncan later said. "Wright will brief me on their tricks, their strengths and oddities. Tips of this sort make my job so much easier." And yet it was obvious by all the praise, that Duncan's own presence would make the job of his new international colleagues easier too. It was a sensational start to life in an England shirt.

In an article for *Football Forum* magazine that year, Duncan was asked to explain the differences between playing for the under-23s and the full team. His response was compelling.

My answer can be summed up in two words – speed and positioning. When I played against young Italy at Bologna in January last year my team-mates were footballers who, like myself, had been picked for the promise they had shown in club games, rather than for any particular achievements. Against the precise passing of the Italians, who had been blending into a fast-moving combination in a series of practice matches, I found it hard to think and act in unison with my colleagues. We were not accustomed to one another's style of play and the ideas we had successfully exploited in our club teams did not work out. Though I thoroughly enjoyed the experience of playing on the Continent, I felt that with more time to 'tune in' to the ideas of the rest of the side better results would be forthcoming.

Soon after the Bologna trip I was chosen to play for England in a B team international in Germany. There I had the advantage of playing in front of my club colleague, Roger Byrne. He kept me on my toes, was always urging me into the tackle, and for me the game was made much easier because there was always someone waiting in the open spaces for a quick through-pass. I say it was an easier experience not because there was anything simple about the way we defeated the Germans, but because it was more like playing with my club side… whatever the grade of football, physical fitness and willingness to learn from those able to teach the finer points of the game are important essentials. It all helps to foster team spirit and brings that extra enjoyment and real kick in life which soccer has always provided me with right from my schoolboy days.

Team spirit was something that would feature heavily on Duncan's mind over the next couple of years. And of course that was something he would know all about due to his involvement with the Busby Babes. The kids went all out to entertain at a rowdy Roker Park on Good Friday. Edwards was inspirational in his forward role. He scored in the 16th minute to give United the lead and then netted a 52nd-minute equaliser to make it 3-3. However, Sunderland netted late on to snatch both points. Easter weekends were traditionally as busy as the Christmas programme, so 24 hours later, Duncan was lining up at Leicester. The hosts won a bad-tempered game 1-0, with the new international coming in for some rough treatment from the Foxes players and barracking from the crowd.

On Easter Monday, Duncan passed a late fitness test to face Sunderland who made the journey to Old Trafford. The game ended 2-2 and with hopes of a title challenge now over, Duncan's presence was required in the FA Youth Cup side.

"Dennis Viollet, Manchester United's top scorer with 19 goal until Duncan Edwards was switched from the left-half position to replace him at inside-left, gets his place back against West Bromwich Albion at Old Trafford today," reported Rex Bellamy in the *Birmingham Gazette* on April 16th. "They have pulled Edwards out of the first team so that he can play at Chelsea in the first leg of the Youth Cup semi-final."

Chapter 11
A Duncan Complex

It had been argued that United's Youth Cup team had become progressively poorer over the three years of the competition. But the 1955 semi-finalists had plenty of quality. They did not need Duncan Edwards to score seven past Sheffield Wednesday in the fourth round. With Colman and McGuinness looking a certainty to be a strong pairing at half-back at senior level, with Shay Brennan starring as an inside-forward, and with Bobby Charlton scoring in unstoppable fashion, there was still an embarrassing amount of promise bubbling away.

So it was not with the intention of adding another story to the growing legend of Duncan Edwards that Jimmy Murphy relayed a new message to his players before the first leg at Stamford Bridge. "He said to us all, whilst Duncan was sitting there, that we were not to have a 'Duncan Edwards complex'," recalls Wilf McGuinness. "Duncan had just played for England and was a first-team regular. Jimmy told us that was there for us to accomplish too. That we were good enough too. So we should not always look for him to get us out of trouble, we should rely on ourselves to make it happen. He said, 'Go and tear them apart like I know you can do.'"

Bobby Charlton remembered it vividly too: "'Try to put more pressure on your own ability,' he told us. 'There may be days when Dunc isn't around. Sometimes you have to solve your own problems.'"

If those United kids had played as Murphy believed they could, then his team-talk may well have gone down in history. But

Chelsea were a good team: taking heed of what was happening in Manchester, they were hoovering up the local talent. They gave a polished display in the first half and took a lead in at the break. United, meanwhile, looked disjointed. Kenny Morgans was struggling at outside-right, and Brennan looked uncomfortable at centre-forward. Edwards and Charlton had been on the periphery of the game as inside-forward and outside-left. Murphy needed his two stars to exert their own influence.

"At half-time Jimmy was a bit quiet, and we were all thinking he was going to blow," McGuinness said. "And just before we went back out, he said, 'Remember I told you not to always pass to Duncan? Forget that. Give him the fucking ball whenever you can.'"

Edwards was moved to centre-forward, and Charlton to inside-forward, with Murphy hoping some blunt force would do the trick. Within 10 minutes, his team were ahead. It took less than 60 seconds of the restart for Edwards to restore parity, shrugging off two challenges to fire home from the edge of the box. Then, in the 55th minute, Duncan struck one of his trademark goals; receiving the ball in the Chelsea half, two home defenders launched into tackles but literally bounced off him, such was Edwards' upper body power. From 25 yards he unleashed a right-footed drive which flew past Brian Pickett.

The final score was 2-1 – a slender lead, but an advantage nonetheless, and it was Chelsea's turn to have a complex now they knew what was in store for them. Murphy made it clear from the start, putting Edwards in the number nine shirt for the second leg. "I always liked him as a forward, as you knew you could always play the ball up to him, and he'd either get you out of trouble or create something special," McGuinness says, and while that much is true, it is also worth remembering that McGuinness was the left-half in this side, so possibly had his own reasons for wanting Edwards elsewhere on the field.

Early in the first half of the second leg, United were awarded a penalty. Charlton deferred to Edwards, who smashed in to give his side a 3-1 advantage. However, for a moment, it seemed as though the script was flipped – Chelsea looked inspired in the second period, and scored early on. Could they do to United what United had done to them three days earlier? The answer was no, because United had Duncan Edwards, and almost as soon as Chelsea had rediscovered some hope, it was lost again. United won a corner, and Charlton strolled over to take it. He remembered Murphy's words of the first leg. Look for Duncan. Of course, Duncan always stood out, and there he was, the beacon on the edge of the penalty box, just waiting for the delivery to be perfect.

It was. Edwards did not disappoint, thundering home the header which settled this tense tie once and for all. 'What more can he do, what more can be said? It's just bloody sensational,' Charlton remembered thinking as his team-mate celebrated, although he could probably have afforded to take some of the credit himself.

Edwards was boosted by the news he would be included in England's post-season tour for games in France, Spain and Portugal. He was also rumoured to be getting a recall to the United first team to face Arsenal due to an injury to Jeff Whitefoot – ultimately, Duncan picked up a knock too, and Freddie Goodwin made the team. While in the capital preparing for the game at Highbury, Matt Busby was offended by the topic of one conversation he held with a friend.

"A London friend told me Manchester United were 'not playing fair' in their Youth Cup competition progress by including Duncan Edwards," Busby wrote in the *Manchester Pink*, continuing that it was suggested at a referee's meeting that United should not be allowed to include him. "So that's what some people think. It annoys me! Duncan is eligible to participate... and is keen to play. He is no keeper of cups and medals, but he is just as anxious as any other United young player to have the United name inscribed on the Cup for the third successive season... he may be 'outsize' in juniors, but he will probably tell you that he has to work just as hard – if not harder – in the Youth Cup competition as in senior football.

"He is 'football daft'. He dreams football and loves to talk about it and is eager to learn everything he can from the game. Duncan Edwards has not become a great footballer by bulldozer tactics. He is undoubtedly one of the greatest examples we have ever had of a footballer maturing at an early age. Here is an 18-year-old whose example can be a lesson to every soccer-thinking youth. I am happy to think that Duncan is getting so many honours from the game. I am glad to know that he remains as keen a player in junior soccer circles as in representative games. But to suggest that because of his exceptional talent he should not play in Youth games is ridiculous."

The fact of the matter was that fair or not, Edwards could only take part in the final against West Brom anyway, as he would be ineligible the following season due to age. And Murphy was not about to leave out his star player just to make other people happy. So Edwards started as the number nine, but it was McGuinness and Colman who were the influential figures of the first leg. Still, Edwards did leave his mark on the occasion scoring the fourth in a 4-1 win – a "fantastic goal" according to the *Daily Mail*.

The second leg was a scrappy affair. More or less a formality, West Brom could not get the first leg out of their system, and were too anxious in possession. It also meant United took their own time to settle – in fact, it took them 71 minutes to break the deadlock, but once they did, two more goals followed, as United strolled towards their third FA Youth Cup in succession. After the game, the team posed with the trophy and had a photograph taken. "We're all there with the cup," Charlton recalled, "and he was standing there at the side of us like a man who had come into the picture by accident. He was enormous."

"He was the Kohinoor diamond against our crown jewels," Jimmy Murphy said of Edwards. "Even when he had won his first full England cap, he used to love turning out at youth level. And most important, he never changed. He remained an unspoiled boy to the end. He just loved to play anywhere and with anyone."

Edwards had played, and starred, for the United youth team in each of the three years he had been at the club. There could be no question that his contribution elevated the status of the new Youth Cup competition so that nobody could be in any doubt about the prestige it held, or the quality required to win it. Without him, Manchester United were going to have to prove that their own proud tradition was not reliant on the Dudley boy.

Edwards himself could see this as a transitional period, as despite only having 62 senior appearances under his belt, he could now consider himself a full-time first-team player. He celebrated that status with a new contract, dated April 25th, that had an increased weekly salary of £15 in the season and £12 in the summer, and he registered his address at Barlow Road. For the next couple of years, he would find himself all over the place.

Chapter 12
Iron Man

The 1954/55 club season was over, yet Duncan Edwards still managed to fit in another five games between May 6th and 22nd. While most of his youth team-mates at Old Trafford travelled to Switzerland to compete in the Blue Star tournament again, Duncan was part of the senior United squad that flew to Denmark for a post-season tour.

Manchester United had finished fifth in the league, five points behind first-time champions Chelsea. The Stamford Bridge club were invited to participate in the European Cup, but the FA barred them from entering.

Matt Busby had dreams of these continental visits being competitive, and so the prospect of playing in the European Cup sharpened his ambition to win the First Division again. If they could, he would have no problem butting heads with the FA about their reluctance to allow their teams to take part.

"The Danes gave Matt Busby and his boys a tremendous welcome on their arrival by air in Copenhagen," reported Tom Jackson in the May 3rd edition of the *Manchester Evening News*. "Many offers of hospitality had to be turned down, but everywhere the players went they were besieged by autograph hunters. The player everyone wants to meet is Duncan Edwards. Manchester United's 18-year-old has really set the Danes talking. Mr Busby, however, has decided to rest Edwards from tonight's opening match at Aarhus stadium. The United manager feels that Edwards has been fully taxed in recent first-team and Youth Cup matches, and he is reserving him for the two bigger tests this week against the pick of Copenhagen."

Duncan missed that first game against Jutland, but played two of United's three games in Denmark, against a Copenhagen XI and then a 'Copenhagen Combination'. However these sides were put together, neither were good enough to beat United, with Busby's side winning 1-0 and 3-1. Duncan was the most popular player, with many of the 15,600 who attended the first game, and the 11,500 who were at the second, desperate to try and get an autograph from him afterwards.

One day after that second game on May 8th, Edwards and Roger Byrne left the party to join up with the England team in London before they travelled to France. On the day of their game in Paris, Edwards was described in the *People* as "Manchester United's Iron Man" in reference to his durability.

The nickname was repeated by sportswriter Roy Peskett. "Not since blue-chinned Wilf Copping have England had a top-class 'Iron Man' half-back… at least not until the arrival of Duncan Edwards," he wrote. "Now into the International arena has stepped a new Colossus – the 18-year-old Edwards, of the ultra-short shorts, massive thighs, the phlegmatic temperament, and the ankle-high cutaway boots. Edwards can look back on perhaps the most astonishingly successful season any player has ever had. This boy, who puts every ounce of his 13 1/2st into a tackle and who, while on the wrong foot, can hit a ball straight as a bullet for 40 yards, has an astonishing record… Nothing seems to worry young Duncan. Not for a long while will I forget his introduction to international football, at Bologna, Italy in the under-23s match in January of last year. The boy, then only three months over 17, was affected by his first air trip and, on the ice-bound Bologna ground, had a shocking first half against the lively Italians. Then, out for the second half came Edwards, his sleeves rolled up and his shorts hitched even higher. He was the outstanding player in the second half, and a new international star had been born."

Duncan gave a decent account of himself against the French (Bob Pennington of the *Express* writing that in the second half "Edwards came surging through with his old confidence") but otherwise his second international was a disappointment, as France won 1-0 and their man-marking of Stanley Matthews eliminated much of the visitors' attacking threat.

Some 125,000 supporters packed into the Santiago Bernabéu stadium on Wednesday May 18th hoping to watch Spain and England compete in a football match. They were, however, treated to a physical encounter more associated with a sport with an oval ball. England took the lead before being pegged back. The game ended 1-1, with one report describing Duncan as being "impressive as the heartbeat". He certainly showed heart to finish the game after picking up a heavy ankle knock.

In his column in the *Manchester Evening News* on May 20th, Don Revie reported from Spain that some of his team-mates were missing the northern weather: "This was my first visit to France and Paris. The weather was enough to gladden the eye of any Mancunian – brilliant sunshine. The United boys Roger Byrne and Duncan Edwards are rather missing the rain, but have hopefully brought our raincoats. We seem to have been transported quickly from muddy grounds to turf baked hard by the hot sun. Observing these grounds it is not difficult to understand why these Continental boys have to be excellent ball players."

Duncan's 1954/55 season finally concluded with a 3-1 defeat to Portugal in Oporto on May 22nd. It was clear that this was still an England team in transition, so their defeat was hardly a great surprise.

Journalist Geoffrey Green picked up his own injury, at the hands of Duncan. "The England team had an afternoon off to watch a bull fight in Madrid," he remembered. "Afterwards Edwards pretended to be a bull: I played the part of the matador.

As I was still waving my handkerchief as if it were the cape, the 'bull' struck me amidships like some tornado. Sent flying, I broke a finger and to this day the swollen joint reminds me of that splendid young-spirited young man."

Young-spirited he may have been, but Duncan was not best pleased at the length of his summer holiday – or, rather, the lack of it. His national service was due to start on June 1st, which meant little over a week to spend with Molly and no time to go home to see his parents. He was given a little reprieve when the Associated Society of Locomotive Engineers and Firemen announced a strike, so he would not have to report for duty until June 9th.

The strike was still continuing a week later. Duncan Edwards and Bill Foulkes travelled to the station, hoping to be told of a further delay: "Duncan Edwards and I were ordered to report to a station in Piccadilly, Manchester, where there was momentary hope of a reprieve because of a rail strike," Foulkes recalled. "Unfortunately for us a truck ride was soon organised. The truck took us to Birmingham. From there they put us in a minibus. I was sent to Aldershot and Duncan was packed off to Woolwich Barracks. As he got off the truck he had tears rolling down his cheeks. But he got through it."

In fact, Duncan described his readjustment period as "not too bad", although he never enjoyed the long travelling or the hours where he was forced to do things other than play football. After his training, Duncan was stationed at Nesscliffe Central Ammunition Depot where he served as an ammunition storeman. Front-line duty could be considered a reasonable prospect if conflict broke out, most likely in the Far East.

Thankfully for Duncan, there was also an understanding reached that the enlisted footballers should continue to train – so footballers from various clubs would often be stationed together, and would practise together. One of those was Jimmy Armfield, who had only just broken into the Blackpool first team.

"I first met Duncan when he was doing his national service in the Royal Army Ordnance Corps," Armfield recalled. "He played for the Western Command team and the British Army team from 1954-56 when we were team-mates. He was an outgoing type; he dressed well and could easily manage, even at his early age, the fame and adulation that showered upon him. He was a marvellous footballer and a very nice young man."

On their first day training together, Armfield's boot lace snapped, so he had to find a replacement. As he searched, he caught a glimpse of Duncan on the training pitch. "I watched him through the Army hut window for a while and was amazed to see what a superb touch he had," Armfield recalled. "He was actually bouncing it with the sole of his foot on the ground and must have repeated it 20 or 30 times."

This was a trick Duncan had mastered since his youth. "He was always doing that," his cousin, Laurence Brownhill recalls. "You would watch and wonder how he was able to do it."

Frank Blunstone, who had appeared with Duncan at international level, likened Army duty to being away with the national side. "I was stationed in Aldershot," he said. "We would get called up into the Army team from our different camps and travelled to wherever the games were played. It was a little bit like playing for England – the difference was that we had to stay in Army units, no hotels! I worked in the sergeant's mess on the latrines. We couldn't have jobs where we would be required to fight because we were away so much playing football. If we were called to play a game, we'd only meet the day before, and then we were off again back to our units."

The number of games Duncan went on to play over the next two years has almost become as legendary as his talent itself. Some went unrecorded simply because they were deemed as friendly matches. Take, for example, the soldiers stationed eight miles along the London-Holyhead Trunk Road down in Copthorne. "I served in Copthorne Barracks and I knew Duncan from the team at Nesscliffe," remembers Derek Thorpe. "We played against them regularly, and I remember those games, especially Duncan with his skills. He was excellent. I didn't see him a lot off the pitch, only once when I was injured and I was put in the medical centre at Nesscliffe. Bobby and Duncan came in one day to see one of their mates I presume, and they recognised me and came across to ask if I was okay. It was very nice, though I wasn't surprised as they were a great bunch of lads.

"I remember one match very well, and it might be the first time Duncan played. I thought I was pretty nippy, but he tackled me and I felt it. I thought to myself, 'Right, I'll have you mister'. I went in again and finished two yards further over the touchline than I did the first time! He came across and asked me if I was okay. I tried to steer clear of him for the rest of the match! His skills, his ball control and passing was… oh. When he hit a ball, you wouldn't want to be in front of it. It wasn't very pleasant."

In mid-July Matt Busby expressed his wish that he would still be able to call upon his young star for league football. "I am hoping both Edwards and Foulkes will be available during the season," he said. "All things considered, United have every reason to anticipate a good season. We still have a young side, but the players are now more mature…"

The closest Edwards got to a pre-season with United was a single practice match on August 9th. A Great Britain select team were preparing to face a Rest Of Europe XI in Belfast, and were facing off against United on the University Athletic Grounds in Fallowfield. "A surprise inclusion at left-half was Duncan Edwards, who had got short leave from his military depot at Shrewsbury," reported the *Manchester Evening News*, though it did not help the United team who lost 6-2.

That week, Tom Jackson offered his thoughts on where Duncan might play: "It's anybody's guess just how often right-back Bill Foulkes and left-half Duncan Edwards will be given leave from the forces to assist United in the new season... Edwards had a long spell at inside-left last term, but whenever this 18-year-old powerhouse gets a leave ticket I think we shall see him at left-half."

Nesscliffe was closer to Birmingham than Manchester so the release of Foulkes and Edwards for the opening game of the season at St Andrew's was straightforward. Edwards was in at left-half, with Mark Jones and Jeff Whitefoot completing the defensive core.

United looked as though they had snatched a late winner when Dennis Viollet got his second in the 82nd minute – but three minutes later, the hosts snatched a point when a header was deflected in off the unfortunate Edwards. "I had it covered perfectly," goalkeeper Ray Wood complained to the *Birmingham Gazette*, "then at the last moment Duncan Edwards popped up and in a flash the ball had slipped off him."

"I'm so sad," Edwards said, "I just could not get out of the way."

The *Sports Argus*, though, praised Edwards' performance as influential in ensuring United came away with anything at all: "It was fortunate for the visitors that they had burly Duncan Edwards, primarily detailed as a defensive half-back. He was not so much a personality in this role as in his customary attacking flair, but United needed him to keep those Blues at bay."

On the eve of United's first home game of the season, club captain Roger Byrne had some interesting thoughts on the campaign to come. "We have now the youngest staff ever at Old Trafford and so a new era has been born," Byrne said. "The football we intend to play this season may take some time to develop to the best Continental standards. But we are always learning. It may take us three years to reach a level where we 'click'. It may take even longer.

"What is our system? It's simply 'What we have we hold.' Football has been likened to draughts, a game in which you generally move in one direction. But the way we intend to play bears little or no resemblance to draughts. We intend to pass the ball forward, sideways, and yes, even backwards, until we can create a position where we can move into attack without much danger of losing the ball. Basically a soccer team with five forwards and six defenders. The way we play, we may find Jeff Whitefoot wearing a number four jersey alongside centre-forward Tommy Taylor, and perhaps Duncan Edwards playing in front of Jackie Blanchflower, wearing a number eight shirt. For at Old Trafford we know we have the players. All we need is confidence in our own abilities."

Some confidence would have come from United coming from 2-1 down to get a point against Spurs, although the low turnout of 25,406 did not suggest the Old Trafford faithful shared Byrne's optimism.

The rude health of Midlands football meant plenty of reunions for Duncan. That was the case again when West Brom came to Old Trafford. Their centre-forward Derek Kevan recalled his first impression of meeting Duncan the previous year. "My first meeting against Duncan was when he was playing for United against us at the Hawthorns," he said. "Before the kick-off I looked across at their team and saw him. 'Oh hell,' I thought. 'Look at the build of that man.'"

On this occasion, Kevan scored – but it was Edwards once more leaving the impression as United won 3-1. "Manchester United, with an average age of 21, gave a brilliant display of virile and assured football," reported Alan Williams in the *Sports Argus*. "Nicholls and Carter slogged away earnestly but never looked like deceiving the mighty Duncan Edwards or the tireless Whitefoot."

Edwards was making the most of his time with United, be it the freshness of a new season or the escape from daily duties in the Army. There was no middle ground with the national service these footballers were undertaking and there was no special treatment for special players. While Duncan Edwards was on national service, he was not training with Manchester United.

"On a typical week we would never see them," Johnny Giles says. "When they were in the Army they were gone. The players would come back for the matches and then they'd be gone again."

Giles, though, had spent enough time with Duncan to know the difference – if any – between the reality and the legend. "He was as good as everyone said he was," he says. "He was physically mature. You would get a lot of lads who were talented but didn't grow into it until they were 19 or 20. And then you had lads who maybe had some physicality but not the talent. Duncan had both from the age of 16 and that's what made him so exceptional. He had the ability of an experienced professional. He was two-footed, could distribute the ball, could win the ball, could score goals. He established himself straight away and he was pretty much in the team all the time. That is a sign of just how exceptional he was. This was a special group of players but even Bobby Charlton didn't become what you'd call a proper first-team player until much later. Duncan was in and he stayed in."

United's next game is one of those that has gone down in Duncan Edwards lore thanks to a tale told by Wilf McGuinness. Duncan excelled for certain, with the *Daily Herald* reporting that he "gave Spurs a lesson in marksmanship with crack-shot goals in the second and 40th minutes" which were "two power drives to give United a slick 2-1 win."

The first goal came as Spurs failed to clear a corner, and the second was a shot from distance, assisted by Eddie Lewis. However, this is McGuinness' long-standing recollection of this goal:

"I remember Bobby Smith going by a couple of players. He was about to put the ball into the empty net, but big Dunc put his foot there, and the ball stayed still – Bobby went flying into the net. Duncan looked up – he played the ball to Eddie Colman, who swivelled his hips like he was prone to do, sending their players the wrong way. He back-heeled the ball to Duncan. Duncan hit this ball and it must have been 50 yards, below head height, all the way across to David Pegg on the left wing. He played it to Bobby Charlton, who let it run through his legs and then curled a pass into the Spurs half. Who should be there running to collect the ball? Duncan. Chased by some Spurs players,

others in front. He dribbled delicately past the first. Smashed through the second. The third got out of the way. From 30 yards he let rip a roaring drive of thunderous power. Everybody cheered the great Duncan Edwards."

The issue is that United's team-sheet of the day did not include Pegg, while Eddie Colman and Bobby Charlton hadn't even made their debuts yet. It's entirely possible that Whitefoot was Colman, Scanlon was Pegg and Lewis was Charlton. But in McGuinness' recollection, the story always takes place at White Hart Lane, and these were the only goals Edwards scored there – so, if it was indeed the second goal on this day, and there is nothing to suggest it wasn't except a corroborative report, the absence of one doesn't mean it did not happen exactly as described; but, in a book where the aim is to strip away the legend and allow the reader to determine the truth based on facts, it is nonetheless an important point.

United aimed to keep their strong start to the season going with a positive result in the Manchester derby. Previewing it for the *Manchester Evening News*, Eric Thornton believed the result could be determined by the performance of one of the youngest players. "Of course, there's that boy Duncan Edwards with as fine a pair of tree-trunk thighs any wing half has possessed," Thornton wrote. "Some believe he still needs experience to gain the final polish. But he can well shape the final result of the game. It could be a thriller. The name of Edwards may be the one imprinted on the game."

Edwards, who had been so impressive at left-half, was moved to inside-forward at the last minute after Dennis Viollet reported unfit. Once more, two facts revealed themselves – that Edwards could be trusted to be United's best player in any position, but, when he wasn't at left-half, United just did not look the same. After conceding a first-half goal, United pushed for an equaliser without success.

Don Davies, for the *Manchester Guardian*, felt that United deserved credit for the style in which they played even in defeat. "They passed the ball with a fluency and a rhythm so smooth that one could almost imagine M. Busby training his young charges to play by metronome, with short crisp passes marking every beat," he wrote. "To add to United's rosy prospects of victory in this period was the trustfulness of Edwards as substitute inside-left for Viollet – a hint of positional versatility which may yet place this active young man among the Careys and the Crabtrees of the game… when more foolish dithering gave Scanlon scope to race away and centre to Edwards closing in on the right, a terrific volley, dead on the mark, pointed to the one decisive factor which was to tip the scale in City's favour – the superb goalkeeping of Bert Trautmann. Edwards stood, hands on hips, a picture of open-mouthed frustration… Edwards contrived to make one last low venomous thrust which would have beaten nine goalkeepers out of 10 and purloined a belated equaliser. But not Trautmann."

Edwards held Trautmann in particularly high esteem. "I have noticed that he seems to know what is going to happen before the man in possession of the ball does," he said. "Some of his cat-like saves from seemingly impossible positions are uncanny."

It was a significant learning curve for Duncan on an afternoon of temporary frustration. He would never again taste defeat in a Manchester derby.

Education featured so strongly in Duncan's life. Whether it was in the respect he always showed his old schoolteachers, or the professional intelligence that seemed to be developing month by month, he always seemed conscious of its presence. Indeed, in September 1955, he wrote an article with the headline 'Nine months after quitting the classroom I made my Football League debut'. In it, he gave a summary of how he saw his career so far:

"All footballers have one ambition – to play at the wonder Wembley Stadium. That lovely turf, huge crowds, put a match into a setting unequalled elsewhere. I played there twice before I was 15… After that, the thought of making my football League debut was not terrifying. It was still a thrill,

however, for it came only nine months after I had packed away my school books for the last time. On leaving school I did not face the difficulty of most youngsters – finding a job. Football was my future; I had no lack of prospective employers. Schoolboy internationals are always noted by the League clubs. I chose to go to Manchester United. I thought my future would be better away from the Midlands. And United had a great reputation for giving plenty of opportunities to young players and treating them in the best possible manner.

"To return to my League debut. It came in the remarkable 1953 season when I won a medal with the club's under-18 team, and also turned out with the seniors. I went to the ground one Friday morning and was called to Matt Busby's office. He quietly told me I was selected for the first team. All I could think about was letting my mother and father know.

"There are stories told of experienced players getting jealous of a youngster succeeding them. I have never come across this. Whatever teams I have played with – club, FA under 23, Football League or England – I have been accepted on level terms by my colleagues. My youth has meant nothing. So long as I do my job satisfactorily no-one cares whether I am 17 or 70."

More headlines followed as Duncan starred in United's 2-1 home win over Everton. Edwards was again at inside-left and was credited with his team's equaliser in the 60th minute – though the visiting defenders insisted the ball had not crossed the line after hitting the crossbar. They were incensed when the draw was turned to defeat by Jackie Blanchflower's late goal.

"Manchester United have played much better (and yet failed to win) than they did when scrambling to victory over Everton at Old Trafford in a match which revealed the Reds' below-strength forward line in modest light," Tom Jackson wrote. "Duncan Edwards deserved his goal for the tremendous way in which he tried to give the United line the vital thrust missing from so many moves."

It seemed impossible that anything could wear this big lad down but perhaps the long days of physical work, long journeys up and down the country and highly intense football matches were beginning to take their toll – Duncan started to feel unwell, and he missed the game with Sheffield United on September 10th with suspected flu. He reported back to training the day after the 1-0 defeat to the Blades but he was soon ordered back to bed rest. On Monday 16th, his condition had worsened significantly enough for him to be taken to Davyhulme Park Hospital. Journalists tried to find out information about how ill he was – the *Manchester Evening News* reported that he was "comfortable". Peter Lorenzo of the *Daily Herald* asked the hospital, and was told: "We can't tell you what is the matter with Edwards. But there is no change in his condition." Lorenzo did get a line from Walter Crickmer, who was keen to calm everything down. "You know when you have just recovered from flu you're prone to catch anything," Crickmer said. "But we don't think there's anything seriously wrong with Edwards."

However, as it transpired, Duncan was suffering from severe influenza. The complications were so significant that doctors were concerned he had caught pneumonia. Despite being unwell, Duncan was conscious of his loud, harsh cough, and kept apologising to the gentleman in the next bed. They struck up a friendship – the man had suffered a motorcycle accident and Duncan was worried he was disturbing his rest. On September 23rd, Duncan was finally released, but ordered to rest at home before returning to the Army.

He was able to spend time with Molly, and, desperate to avoid the glare of the press, went to extreme lengths – almost every night was spent in the cinema watching films such as *Blackboard Jungle*, the movie which was pioneering the 'rock and roll revolution'. It was just about the only film that fell into a neutral genre considering Molly was a fan of romantic stories and Duncan liked the old-fashioned Westerns.

Duncan, like his team-mates, had often joked that Mark Jones was a grandfather of the team, but he too was of an older sensibility, and although he didn't mind the new wave of music, he was more a fan of the classics. This had something to do with his awkwardly large frame – while some of Duncan's team-mates became obsessed with the latest fashion trends, Duncan was conscious that the clothes would not suit him.

On the occasions that Molly would convince Duncan to go out dancing, it was usually Eddie Colman who'd end up on the floor with her for the faster songs. Molly and Duncan also spent evenings at Manchester Ringway, where they had met, just watching the planes land and take off. They made friends with others doing the same. Duncan befriended a young boy, Robin, who seemed obsessed with planes. The young boy would later travel the world with his brothers Barry and Maurice Gibb.

Duncan was a celebrity himself now of course, and, despite his discomfort with the profile, accepted that he should take advantage of some of the financial incentives on offer for endorsing products. The first advertisements he accepted were for Service Sports Watches and could be found all over newspapers that autumn. These ran in late September in the *Daily Express* with the tagline *"Never been known to miss!" – Duncan Edwards knows the values of accurate timing... in tackling, passing... and the watch he wears.*

Later, Duncan would also famously advertise Dextrosol, a glucose supplement claiming to give you extra energy. "I remember seeing it and thinking, there's our Duncan," recalls Laurence Brownhill, a paper boy at the time. "And then I thought, what's Dextrosol?!"

Duncan was conscious on this front and even opened up to the journalist Frank Taylor. "It's nice to be cheered," he said, "but you can't live forever on cheers. It's what you have in the bank when you have finished with the game that cheers a footballer most of all."

In the short term, those watches would have come in handy for Duncan, who was rushed into action before he'd even properly recovered. The games were coming thick and fast, and he was required to report back to Nesscliffe after spending his birthday with Molly, so his time-management skills had to be on-point.

On October 4th, he was called into the Army football team for the first time in organised competition, as the Western Command faced Shrewsbury Town on October 6th. A report in the *Manchester Evening News* on October 10th, though, claimed he had not even resumed training yet – that finally happened on the 12th of the month, so in the end his Army bow would have to wait.

Duncan was well enough to sit with the coaches on the bench at Villa Park to watch his team-mates play out an entertaining 4-4 draw. Sitting right behind the bench was a Villa fan who could not believe his eyes. George Nicholls had played for Cannock District Schoolboys in a game against a combined Dudley and Brierley Hill Schools side which featured a young Duncan Edwards. "I remember the manager saying there was a player on the other side who was going to be the next big thing," Nicholls recalled. "You could tell he was a bit special. He was full of confidence and carried a bit more weight than I did… At Villa Park I was sat right in the corner where the teams came out. He was not playing that day because he had the flu. He was sat there with his overcoat on and scarf and I began talking to him about the match in general. I mentioned how I had played against him when I was younger. He was an affable man."

On October 18th, Duncan put in a great performance in what was billed as a 'private game' between United and England B at Old Trafford. United won 6-0. His club were also able to call on Duncan for a friendly against Clyde the following day, which finished 2-1 to the hosts in Glasgow.

On his return to league action at left-half against Huddersfield on the 22nd, Duncan was phenomenal, inspiring his team to a 3-0 win. His understudy, Wilf McGuinness, had done a commendable job, but Duncan's performance as always was notable. He starred again as United won 1-0 at Cardiff to go top of the league. Scottie Hall of the *Herald* noted a line he'd been told by Matt Busby. "A half-back in a thousand," Busby had said of Edwards, "and a thousand half-backs in one."

Duncan was then finally given his 'proper' Army team bow

as they faced Rangers at Ibrox on November 2nd. Edwards was going to be centre-forward in the number nine shirt – but he was, according to the *Mirror*, "completely blotted out by George Young", the experienced defender, in a 1-0 defeat. After the game, he and his team-mates went to the cinema, before retiring to the hotel where he wrote to Molly, excusing the quality of his handwriting because the hotel had no lined paper. "We have just been to the pictures to see Dean Martin and Jerry Lewis in *You're Never Too Young*," he wrote. "Well I think I'll turn in, good night. I received your letter on Wednesday morning, also I will be in Manchester on Thursday if you like I will see you at the traffic lights in Stretford at 7 o'clock. Well I think that's all till I see you hope you can make it. Lots of love, Duncan." He signed off with nine kisses.

Duncan remained with the Western Command team to play against an FA XI at Newcastle on November 9th, and again for the Army against Worcester City under the floodlights at St George's Lane a day later. He was also notified of his squad selection for the national team against Spain at Wembley on November 30th. Before all that, he had to play for United against Arsenal at Old Trafford on November 5th.

"Midfield play was the order towards the interval when no goals had been scored," Alf Clarke reported in the *Evening Chronicle*. "One of United's successes was undoubtedly Edwards, and the selectors must have been impressed. In the second half, United started briskly, and Edwards had a terrific shot beaten down."

"United's best work came from David Pegg, the most progressive forward; Taylor, who was always striving to keep the line together, and Duncan Edwards, who was a forceful personality in defence and attack," wrote Tom Jackson after the 1-1 draw. Jackson continued: "Edwards is having treatment for a damaged ankle. He returned to his unit at Shrewsbury over the weekend and was having a final test there. So far United have not been advised whether he is fit to take his place in the Army side."

At this moment in time it seemed less of a consideration about whether he was actually fit or whether or not he could walk. If he could walk, then he could play, and so he did. It was back to the north west − Bolton, to be precise − to play in a 3-1 defeat at Burnden Park which was more notable for the debut of Eddie Colman, just 19, at right-half.

It was United's first defeat in nine games, and with champions Chelsea the next visitors to Old Trafford, Duncan might have hoped for an easier week. It turned out to be busier than ever. On the 17th, his Army game against an Aston Villa team was in danger of being called off. The match was being played at the Army stadium at Aldershot and heavy fog had caused the Villa team bus to get lost. However, instead of cancelling the game, the Army coaches decided to hastily arrange another match against a team of men attending a football coaching course at Aldershot and who just happened to be at the stadium. So a game of two 15-minute halves was played, and it ended 1-0, with Duncan scoring the only goal. By the time of the final whistle, the Villa team had arrived − and they were not going to go back home without playing, so an hour after the original kick-off time, Duncan played another match with two 30-minute halves. Villa won 1-0, with Alan Williams of the *Birmingham Gazette* reporting: "Duncan Edwards sent up some lovely balls."

The *Daily Worker* suggested that the remarkable double duty would mean Edwards would not be able to play against Chelsea. But he was never going to miss the opportunity to line up alongside Colman at Old Trafford for the first team in a league game − a sign of confidence from manager Busby. Home fans were excited too, as match reports of the defeat to Bolton had featured lines marvelling over Colman's "snakehip" body swerve which had embarrassed Nat Lofthouse of all people. Champions Chelsea had their own reputation for youth, with their players dubbed 'Drake's Ducklings' − and their younger players had first-hand experience of what Edwards could do to them.

It was a landmark victory for Busby's side. In a combative first half, Edwards' direct opponent, the veteran Ken Armstrong, went in hard on United's number six. Edwards reacted angrily, grabbing Armstrong by the throat. The referee ordered both to calm down, or risk being sent off. In the second half United flew out of the traps, scoring early and eventually winning 3-0.

"United's attack had a more dangerous look than Chelsea could muster," reported Tom Jackson. "But much of the credit must go to the half-back line, in which Mark Jones was always sound in the middle, and the wing-halves Duncan Edwards and Eddie Colman kept a tight grip on the champions' inside-forwards."

It seemed as though the unity Busby and his staff had worked so hard to create within the squad was thriving in testing conditions. It also seemed they had grown out of their over-reliance on Duncan Edwards. Still, Edwards remained the most influential figure, and it was he who came closest to breaking the stubborn resistance of the hosts in a top-of-the-table clash at Blackpool on November 26th. "Edwards was working like a Trojan," wrote Alf Clarke in the *Evening News*, "and he beat man after man, trying to force his way through, only to be upended 25 yards from goal." Blackpool smothered Roger Byrne's resultant free-kick on the way to a smothering 0-0 draw.

What many recognised as progression, others saw as developmental issues. Those sportswriters closer at hand were able to give a fairer assessment of what they saw every week, while others who did not always cover Manchester United formed their opinion on what they read. And those reports often came with descriptions of Duncan's physical edge, such as the confrontation with Ken Armstrong, and even if Duncan was not the instigator, his involvement was frowned upon. So when it came to being considered for the national team's game against Spain, some felt Edwards was still a little raw. Eric Butler included Duncan in his mentions when he said "not one who enhanced his reputation" in the friendly against

Spain in May. Maurice Smith of the *People* saw it differently. "No cold feet from England selectors today, please," he implored as the team was named on the 27th. "Duncan Edwards must go in. Even though he is only 19. He is an English John Charles."

But Duncan was named 'in reserve for the match' and sat it out as an unused substitute, with the experienced Jimmy Dickinson – famously never cautioned – preferred. England won 4-1. It meant Duncan had the luxury of a rare rest before facing Sunderland for United at Old Trafford. The 2-1 win kept United level with Blackpool at the summit, though the Seasiders retained a lead on goal average.

On December 7th, Duncan was in the Army side which played against Scotland again at Shawfield Park. It was a quick reunion with George Young. "I hope we both have a good game," Duncan said.

And they did – although it would depend on who you read to assess how Duncan fared. The tribal *Glasgow Herald* deemed the rematch another Young victory, considering the 3-1 win of the hosts: "The young centre-forward had an extremely poor night against George Young. He roved both right and left wings, leaving Young complete control in defence."

The equally partisan *Birmingham Gazette* fought their boy's corner. "Edwards was star of Army Eleven" insisted their headline, with the article reading: "In defence the Scots were sound, and their most serious trouble came from stemming the thrustful approaches of Edwards, the most accomplished player on the field. It was the big left-half who helped the Army to their only goal in the 62nd minute, when he disorganised the defence and Dunmore had only to nod the ball home."

Another report stated: "The outstanding player was Duncan Edwards, who was magnificent and frequently became a sixth forward."

One feature of the last two games had been the aggressive tackling Duncan had to face and that was no different in the next game at Portsmouth. Edwards passed a late fitness test but there was no mercy from Pompey, keen to help their man Jimmy Dickinson come out on top in a battle for the England number six shirt. Over 88 minutes Edwards bossed the match, with United looking set to claim a 2-1 win. In the last minute, Dickinson grabbed an equaliser, and then in injury time, Mark Jones's block diverted the ball past Wood and into his own goal.

"If ever a team lost a match they had done almost everything to win, it was Manchester United at Portsmouth," wrote Tom Jackson. "With only 90 seconds left and two points virtually in the bag they conceded two scrambled goals – and bang went everything they had previously worked so hard to achieve... individual criticism would be harsh, because until that fatal patch United had played streamlined football, with perhaps only their finishing amiss."

Jackson also gave a brief insight into the busy life of United's main man two days later. "Just a few days in the soccer life of Private Duncan Edwards, Manchester United's 19-year-old soldier boy and England international of the massive frame and willing heart – but they read like the pages from a travel book. Look at the Edwards story this week and spare a thought for a player who will do almost anything and go anywhere to get a game – and still enjoy every minute of it. Edwards was United's left-half at Portsmouth on Saturday, a trip involving the team in over 500 miles of wearisome train travel. Today, following a night trip north, he was turning out at Carlisle for his Army unit and on Wednesday he is due to play in an Army cup-tie at Perth. All told, Edwards, who was also engaged in a representative match in Scotland last week, will have added well over 1,000 miles to his soccer logbook when he turns out for United against Birmingham City at Old Trafford on Saturday."

The game at Perth was played on South Inch, a public park – and in torrential rain, Duncan's side lost 5-2 to Depot Black Watch. Once more Duncan had found himself the target of the opposition. It was beginning to grate. "Despite all his attributes, he was a steady, down-to-earth lad," Bill Foulkes said. "I think he knew he was special and he carried a certain quiet confidence, but there wasn't an ounce of conceit about him… the only time I ever saw him shaken was during his national service, when he was in the Army team which I captained. He didn't like the regimentation, what he saw as the petty discipline, of life in the forces and he railed against it in private. Because of who he was, there was always someone trying to make life difficult for him, and he told me, 'I'll be bloody glad to get out of this, the sooner the better!'"

Better fortune awaited against Birmingham. United had taken a lead through Viollet and were coasting to the point of complacency. Then Brum equalised through Eddie Brown and struck again with a goal they thought had given them the lead. "Edwards and Colman got in each other's way and the ball sliced away to leave Brown with a simple opening," wrote Alan Williams in the *Birmingham Gazette*. The referee, though, had himself become confused in the mix-up, and deemed Brown offside. Immediately, United won a corner that their visitors contested. When Mark Jones scored the winner from it, Birmingham were even more annoyed.

The Busby boys followed this contentious win with two victories more befitting their reputation. Foulkes and Edwards had recently been joined by Eddie Colman in the Army – and all three were granted leave to face West Brom on Christmas Eve. Buoyed by the idea that he could be near family at Christmas, Duncan was inspired to help his colleagues put on a show. United played their best half of the season, obliterating the Baggies with a 3-0 first-half lead. The final score was 4-1, and it could have been five if Byrne had scored his penalty. He made up for that by netting from the spot in United's next game, a 5-1 win the day after Boxing Day over Charlton which now gave them a lead of three points over Blackpool, albeit having played a game more. It was a lead they maintained despite losing 3-0 to Charlton a day later – a game in which Jimmy Gauld gave Duncan "the biggest runaround of a brilliant career" according to Bob Pennington of the *Express*.

The successful season so far inspired a post-war record crowd of 60,956 to turn out at Old Trafford on New Year's Eve for the derby against City. United were on the way to a turnaround 2-1 victory when Duncan tried to usher the ball out for a goal kick. City player Billy Spurdle swung his leg at Duncan. He was strong enough to withstand the physicality but was incensed when the linesman awarded a City corner. Edwards grabbed the ball and threw it to the ground as he remonstrated with the officials. It earned him a booking – and some playful ribbing from Molly later that evening. Duncan could console himself with the victory but felt aggrieved at the unfairness.

The kicks from Spurdle, and others, had resulted in ankle and knee swelling. This was one reason cited for Edwards' absence from the team against Bristol Rovers in the FA Cup, though other reports also described it as a "recurrence of boil trouble". United still had a strong enough team that should have been expected to beat Bristol with comfort. Rovers triumphed with a remarkable 4-0 scoreline, netting early and scoring at crucial times when United threw men forward. Despite the victory, some Bristol players would later admit they would have accepted losing if it meant they could have played against Duncan.

The one positive consequence of cup elimination was a slightly less congested fixture list. Matt Busby was not a man to accept defeat in any competition but it was no secret that this season he was desperate to win the league. The prospect was more favourable with an opportunity to rest players, especially considering the extra obligations placed on them due to their Army commitments.

On January 11th, a 'special correspondent' wrote about United's chances, and the evolution of the Busby style, in the *Manchester Guardian*:

Manchester United's being at the top of the First Division table of the Football League at the turn of the year is yet one more proof of the outstanding quality of the club's post-war team-building... The extreme youth and ease in ball-play of many of those who now join Busby's club, and the large proportion of them to emerge as capable players, suggest that they are selected largely on the premise that the boy who has developed true ball skill by his early teens is usually ripe for expert development. For all the emphasis upon mastery of the elementary skills, there has been no move towards any form of stereotyped 'Manchester United' football. Each player has been encouraged to develop his particular gifts to the advantage of the team, so that the dash of one, the shooting power of another, the speed of a third, the long passing of a fourth have been exploited in harness with the ranging of a fifth, the mobility of a sixth, the plodding steadiness of a seventh. Variety has been achieved without loss of balance, through mutual understanding of the game's problems, upon which the players are encouraged to think for themselves. Most of the successful teams of post-war football have employed a particular style of play, such as the long-ball and straight wing-running of Wolverhampton Wanderers, the quick clearing and wedge forward-formation of Newcastle United... There is, however, no characteristic Manchester United style. Aiming to produce players of all-round ability, the club's planners have sought to place in the team the varied skills necessary to defeat every type of play with which they may be faced.

There was some proof of this development in the next couple of games for United. Edwards was in good form as his team won 4-1 against Sheffield United. By now, it seemed as though Busby had settled on him at left-half – when Johnny Berry and Tommy Taylor missed the trip to Preston with injury, Duncan stayed in position. On this occasion, United's lack of firepower cost them, as they went down 3-1 to a North End team inspired by new signing Eddie Lewis.

With United out of the cup, a friendly game was arranged at Leeds on January 28th – Busby not quite ready to give his players a week off just yet. Edwards was thankful, as he struck two magnificent goals in a 4-1 win, his first club goals since the contentious strike against Everton in September.

Two days later he was on duty for his Army team against East Fife. His team were 1-0 down at half-time – he switched from left-half to inside-left, and inspired one of those turnaround victories, scoring in the 59th minute. The game was more memorable, though, for another one of those infamous stories of legend. With 15 minutes remaining, Edwards struck a shot that was so powerful it knocked the goalkeeper, Steedman, unconscious after catching him flush in the face.

Another busy week followed as Duncan was informed he had been selected to play in an England under-23 match against Scotland on February 8th. Edwards was again at left-half for an impressive 2-0 win at Burnley on the 4th, and after joining up with his international colleagues, he played a 20-minute each-way practice game at Sheffield United on the 7th. That game was lost 3-1 – but England won by the same score 24 hours later at Hillsborough.

Busby was informed that he would not be able to select Duncan for his team's trip to Luton on the 11th, due to the fact that the player was required to play in an Army match against Belgian troops in Brussels on the 12th in a competition called the Kentish Cup. The journey was made by ferry, but it was a tumultuous crossing on turbulent waters. Duncan was violently sick in his cabin. The game was postponed due to the inclement weather, and an uneasy Duncan was soon back on the boat for the return journey.

A crucial run of fixtures followed for United. Wolves away, Villa at home and Chelsea away. Their strong form since defeating the reigning champions in November had given them a six-point lead at the top of the table, albeit having played a game more.

In that first game of this mini-run, United took a 30th-minute lead through Tommy Taylor. A few minutes later, Wolves were awarded a penalty – given for handball by Edwards. He was furious, feeling it was completely accidental, but his complaints fell on deaf ears. Thankfully for him, Johnny Hancocks fired over the bar, and Taylor made sure of the points with another strike in the 71st minute.

"I felt justified in my protest to the referee, for it was an unintentional affair," Edwards complained after the match. "Still, the improbable thing happened for Johnny missed the kick."

It had been an impressive performance. "Matt Busby's team of young stars would be a credit to the title of league champions on this form, but Wolves' followers will probably be haunted by the memory of that penalty kick almost sailing into the roof of the stand," Arthur Satchwell wrote in the *Birmingham Gazette*.

A week later, Billy Whelan's goal earned a 1-0 win over Villa, and one week after that it was time for that return game with Chelsea. There was no chance of the reigning champions retaining, but just as they had done at Old Trafford, they were going to put up a physical fight. They went 2-0 up after 22 minutes. Pegg responded instantly. The scene was set for an iconic second half, if United could get their act together. There had already been many a story in Duncan's short career of how conversations in the dressing room had altered the destiny of football matches. At least one of those had happened against Chelsea before. Now, however, it was the talk of the Chelsea players which would prove to be their undoing.

Before the match, Ken Armstrong had vowed to get his revenge on Edwards. Chelsea youth team player Brian Dellar had listened in awe as Armstrong had said he would be the player to put Edwards in his place. Early in the second half, the two came together.

"After a thigh-high tackle on Duncan, Ken bounced off him," Dellar recalled. "He'd hurt his own foot. Duncan just stood over him and grinned."

Chelsea were rattled. United sensed their lack of composure and grew immediately – scoring in the 60th and 69th minute through Viollet to turn the game on its head. Taylor hit a fourth goal to put some gloss on the scoreline, a definite divide of quality between the two sides. The Busby Babes had made a statement – the title was theirs to lose.

Chapter 13
Boom Boom

Duncan was back in the United team to face Cardiff at Old Trafford after playing for the Army against the Royal Navy on March 7th, 1956. The Welsh side were more formidable opposition than champions Chelsea had been, and it required one of those Herculean Edwards efforts to take something from the game. Just after half-time, Cardiff attacked, searching for an opener. Duncan – who had caught the attention with an effort from fully 40 yards in the first half – was once more a roadblock at the other end, winning the ball and stopping it going out for a corner. From there he hit a raking cross-field pass for Viollet, who surged into the box and was hauled down. Byrne scored from the spot, but this was a flat afternoon after the intensity of the previous three victories, and Cardiff scored a late equaliser to get a point.

It was another man-of-the-match display a few days later as Edwards inspired a fightback for his Army team against Worcester City in a benefit match for former Worcester player Eddie Wilcox. "Slow to start, the Army side gradually improved under the energetic marshalling of Duncan Edwards," read one match report.

Another draw followed at Arsenal for United on the 17th. Duncan travelled from London to North Wales to play in a rescheduled Army match against his own club side in Rhyl on March 20th. From there, he travelled to the south coast, to meet up with his England B colleagues, having been selected to play in a game against Switzerland that was due to take place at the Dell on

March 21st. Remarkably, he arrived in time to play in a 40-minute practice match against Portsmouth at Fratton Park on the evening of the 20th – and scored, in a game that ended 1-1.

Against Switzerland, Edwards made another case for his recall to the national team, starring in a 4-1 win and setting up the first goal of a Tommy Taylor hat-trick (the others were created by David Pegg). "Duncan Edwards silenced those cries of 'Stop fiddling, England' by sweeping a perfect centre from the touchline, Taylor hurtled through the air to head England into the lead," reported Bob Pennington in the *Express*.

Back-to-back games at Old Trafford were navigated comfortably. The in-form Taylor scored the only goal in a win over Bolton, and then again to give his team the lead against Newcastle. That strike settled down a nervous Busby side, who had conceded an earlier equaliser which Edwards would later receive some criticism for. But nobody was really upset with the United team after this result, as they ran riot to score three goals in nine minutes to win 5-2. Nobody, that is, except for maybe Jackie Milburn. As the teams were in the tunnel preparing to come out, Duncan glanced across to see the famous Newcastle striker standing tall. They locked eyes. Perhaps with the memory of Ken Armstrong fresh, the United midfielder decided to make a pre-emptive statement. "I'm a big admirer of yours," Duncan told Milburn, reaching out a hand, "but reputations mean nothing to me. If I get any bother from you, I'll boot you over the stand. Alright, chief?" Milburn was taken aback by the confidence of the boy – and could only admire as Edwards' actions spoke louder than his bold words.

"No opponent was too big or too famous for Duncan," Matt Busby said. "When he went into the tackle he seldom came away without the ball. He was as fair as he was powerful. But opponents would bounce off him. He was as good with the delicacies of the short pass as with the space-consuming long pass."

Tommy Taylor was at the double in a 2-0 win at Huddersfield, registering his 99th and 100th goals for the club in just three years.

Duncan came the closest to scoring in a 0-0 draw in the return league game with Newcastle, but the result came with a positive consequence – should United defeat Blackpool at home in their next game they would win the league title. Their preparation for this important match was, ironically, a few days in Blackpool. The entourage was led by Jimmy Murphy and Bert Whalley, as Matt Busby had travelled to Scotland with his wife Jean, as her mother had passed away.

It was fitting, in a way, that Murphy would have this moment. Eight of the lads starting the game in outfield positions were players he had mentored. Greaves, Byrne, Colman, Jones, Edwards, Doherty, Viollet and Pegg. Ironically, it was the two outfield players bought in by Busby – Berry and Taylor – who would deliver the second-half goals which turned around a second-minute deficit, and in doing so, delivered the league title to Manchester United. Once again, though, it was Edwards who earned the most praise for his omnipresent performance. Occasionally, his desire to be everywhere and do everything had come with some negative consequences. Not today. "Duncan was majestic, playing like three men," recalled Ian Greaves.

This was not, as it seemed in 1952, the conclusion of a journey. It was the start of one. Don Revie had watched United's reserve team – with Bent, Whitefoot, Cope, McGuinness, Whelan, Charlton and Scanlon – sweep aside City with a 3-0 win on New Year's Eve. "If he isn't the happiest manager in Britain he ought to be," Revie said of Busby. "His first team (most in their twenties) top the First Division and are already being hailed as the team of the season. Yet his reserve team are so good that I wouldn't back the so-called first team to beat them. It's quite true. For 20 minutes I saw this reserve team roll the ball around with the slick precision passing I thought was the copyright of the Hungarians."

Well, it may well have been, but it now bore the additional hallmark of football taught by Matt Busby. And even the great Hungarians could not boast this firepower in reserve. Duncan may have been missing from the Youth Cup team but players like Bobby Charlton had stepped up to accept the responsibility, winning the competition again in 1956. The reserve team was so strong that it had scored seven times on four different occasions. The future Busby and Murphy had been planning for was here.

The important business over, United's season concluded with a 2-2 draw at Sunderland – Edwards didn't play, and Busby wasn't present again (more on this in a moment) – and a 1-0 win over Portsmouth, which was preceded by a reception at Manchester Town Hall held by the Mayor and members of the council. Busby was introduced as "the wizard of the whole business" and said his side were "a great young team with a wonderful future ahead." Byrne and Taylor stepped forward to say that their wonderful supporters had, "more or less", got them where they were.

So, to the game Duncan missed. This was no rare weekend off – Edwards was recalled to the England team to face Scotland at Hampden Park, in front of 132,817. The game ended 1-1, with England snatching a last-minute equaliser. Edwards had begun to influence the game after England fell behind on the hour-mark.

Tom Finney had been missing from Duncan's first few internationals, but was impressed by how well he had settled in. "He was an outstanding prospect from the word go," said Finney. "He was extremely big for his age, he could pass, he had a good shot on him. He scored many outstanding goals. He was a bit special. He had a good temperament as well, as though he'd played there all his life. He wasn't at all nervous. He went about his job as though it was just an ordinary league game."

It was surely clear that Edwards had more than proved his worth to be a full international. This totemic midfielder was the one opponents had gravitated towards. Older professionals had looked at the teenager and it seemed they were offended by his status in the game. How could it be that he was showered with accolades that some players took a full career to earn? They looked to bring him down to size, only to realise they would come off worse for daring to try. He had grown supremely confident, as his clashes with Armstrong and Milburn proved. He read the newspapers. He knew what was being said. He knew that he could take it with a pinch of salt – and yet could not help but feel motivated by the power that came with being the best player in the best team in the land at the age of just 19.

Edwards also knew his best position. He would describe himself as a wing-half, and described those players as "the men who make or break a side... before a ball is kicked or a tackle made, the keynote of this position is stamina. The wing-half is never still. The main part of his defensive job is to keep a check on those inside-forwards. Yet he cannot do it through close marking. Rather he has to rely on his own speed to get him back in defence once his own side has been suddenly robbed of the initiative. His dominance of midfield is the deciding factor in any match. The wing-half needs all the defensive skill, power of recovery and hardness of tackle of the full-back, yet he must ally these to the enterprise of the inside-forward. Two-footed he must be, for every reason under the sun. He must have the initiative and confidence to burst through the middle suddenly when everybody on the other side is waiting for the pass. Styles of wing-half differ greatly. Some play a delicate, probing type of football like Tottenham's Danny Blanchflower, while others, like myself, recognise their strength and rely on power. My own idea of the top class wing-half is that he should defend and attack with equal competence, and that he should always remember that he is the nearest thing to perpetual motion the game will ever see. It is a position that will sap a man's strength both physically and mentally. Yet it is infinitely satisfying."

The man of many positions and many nicknames could now add 'league champion' to the list. But his description when it came to the Football League team that travelled to face an Irish League side in Belfast on April 25th was 'travelling reserve'. It was a decision which provoked derisory remarks from journalists. What was the point? England's senior side was due to face Brazil and Germany in a few weeks. Either rest him, or play him. "Instead of putting the probable England team on view they left out men like Billy Wright, Duncan Edwards and Jimmy Dickinson to make pointless experiments in defence," Bob Pennington blasted after the English side lost 5-2. "The result was a shambles."

Duncan played his last Army game of the season on April 28th against the French Army at Dulwich Hamlet. He was at inside-forward and scored his team's equaliser, though they went on to lose 3-1. French international striker Just Fontaine also scored, and criticised the style of the opponents. "The British, they try hard," he said, "and have plenty of shots, but they don't shoot straight."

This perception of English players being limited in skill as opposed to their foreign counterparts was still evident for the first ever match between England and Brazil at Wembley on May 9th. In his preview of the game, *Mirror* writer Frank McGhee described Edwards as "as yet too impetuous" and insisted he was one of the apparent weaknesses "riddling" the England team. What some admired as fearlessness, others clearly felt was a lack of professional maturity.

In truth, McGhee wasn't completely wrong. There was some of the petulance in Duncan's performance; on one occasion, he shrugged off a challenge with his physical power, before stopping to confront his opponent. By this point, however, Edwards had already shown that he had the skill to match that strength.

"Edwards always used his powerful frame to good effect," wrote Alan Williams in the *Birmingham Gazette*. "England's first goal came after two minutes. Edwards sent Matthews away and after drawing

Nilton the winger pushed the ball across for Haynes to touch on and leave Taylor with a chance to smash the ball home."

McGhee was forced to admit he had been hasty. "Before the echoes of the kick-off whistle had died away, centre-forward Tommy Taylor – how cruelly I underrated him – had hurtled through to fire over the bar. Not much more than a minute later we were ahead. Duncan Edwards, the Manchester United left-half who played all through with every ounce of mind and muscle, slammed the ball out to the right wing. Matthews fastened on to it with that wonderful slither that starts you cheering without knowing why."

England were 2-0 up in four minutes, and even though Brazil levelled in the second half, Winterbottom's side scored twice more to claim a famous win. For Stanley Matthews, the man of the match, it was vindication. In the build-up he had to face talk that Nilton Santos was the best in the world. At the final whistle, Nilton approached Matthews and said, "You are the king."

And one Manchester United midfielder was the future. "The forceful Duncan Edwards, a modern Wilf Copping, has assuredly come to stay," claimed Tom Duckworth in the *Sports Argus*.

England left for their post-season tour which would take in games against Sweden and Finland before the headline clash with West Germany. Sweden manager Gustaf Kock named Edwards as "outstanding in attack and in defence" in the build-up – but was left criticising Duncan's contribution after a handball in the box was fortunately waved away. England escaped too, with a 0-0 draw they scarcely deserved. "Duncan Edwards will never be luckier than he was in the 17th minute," reported George Follows. "He overran a centre from the left wing and flicked the ball to safety with his left hand. Referee Leo Horn waved play on. The Swedes whistled derisively."

In his defence, Edwards resolved to become England's strongest player, coming closest to making a breakthrough at the right end with a few charges with the ball up the field. That ambition had more penetration in England's next game, with Edwards setting up the first two and playing a big part in the third of five goals against Finland. "Edwards tore the Finns apart with a 30 yards pass and Wilshaw's shot slapped in off the far post," wrote Follows. "The second was by Haynes two minutes later. Again the pass was from Edwards." In the *Mirror*, Archie Ledbrooke decreed that Edwards "was the star of the game".

The mood was good in the England camp ahead of the game against West Germany in Berlin. Duncan was clearly missing home, though, and decided to write to Molly. "I thought it would be nicer if I wrote to you by letter than postcard," he wrote. "Well pet we had a grand flight over here, we arrived here in Berlin around 4 o'clock so far the rain has kept off."

There was a task at hand, though, and Duncan was a fully committed member of his team. The win over Brazil in particular had been a big boost as the Three Lions continued this redemption journey. West Germany were the world champions. Victory here would surely make that journey complete. Winterbottom's side started with plenty of confidence. In the 26th minute, they got the goal their play deserved. Duncan Edwards showed fine anticipation to take control of a loose ball and spin towards goal, displaying all of the grace taught to him by Stella Cook back in Wolverhampton Street School. In fact, one might describe the move as impossible.

For a player who has so few moments captured on tape, one might watch this back and be confused that this is the Duncan Edwards of legend. He is so light on his feet and yet in possession of this most extraordinary upper body strength. Karl Mai and Hans Schafer quickly sensed Edwards' intentions and tried to form a human wall. Another player would have tried to go around them. Edwards continued to charge forward. They couldn't get near him. Their challenge had at least been close enough to force Duncan to take a heavy touch to get it away from them. That touch tempted Heinz Wewers; the centre-half thought Edwards was not quick enough to get there. He was. Wewers was nowhere near as Duncan shaped to shoot from 25 yards. It was magnificent. 1-0.

"In the 25th minute the goal their early play deserved duly arrived, and what a cracker it was!" reported Mike Payne. "As the ball ran loose... Duncan Edwards pounced, and with that characteristic power, he swept past three tackles with consummate ease before crashing an unstoppable shot past Herkenrath's right hand. The youngster, in that one moment, demonstrated to the world what an awesome sight he is when he is in full flight."

George Follows was similarly impressed. "Duncan Edwards went through like a tank in the 25th minute, destroyed four tackles, and bashed in the goal he had been threatening to bash in all through the tour. Ninety-thousand Germans shuddered every time Duncan got the ball after this."

The People's Maurice Smith was the next to pay tribute. "I was never more proud to be an Englishman," Smith gushed. "Never more delighted to be able to point to an England soccer team and say 'This is ours.' For this evening in the rain-soaked Olympic Stadium here I saw English football come into its own again... If I were asked to describe England's victory in one short sentence, I'd say it was a triumph of grit. Good old British guts as personified by tough, bustling never-give-in Duncan Edwards, 20-year-old prodigy from Manchester United. Edwards was magnificent. Under his inspiration the boys fought like bulldogs, got their teeth in and never let go... I'll give Duncan Edwards the D.S.C., the Iron Cross and even Charing Cross for the goal which set England on the road to victory. He deserves the lot. He made 30 yards of ground and beat three men in a great mazy, weaving run. That effort took him five yards inside the penalty area, and from there Mr Edwards cracked the ball hard, low and true into a heart-warming position at the back of the net."

To be perfectly accurate, Duncan was still only 19, and it was three men, not four, though that did not make his goal less

Sweet sixteen: He was so good, so young, he was pulling on a Manchester United jersey for the first team at the age of just 16

Happy together: Duncan with his fiancée, Molly Leech

Picking pals: Duncan (back, left) on a hop-picking trip in Ledbury with friends in 1951

Stand-out pupil: A 1948 school team photo shows a 12-year-old Duncan towering over most of his team-mates

Tomlinson Trophy winners: Manchester United youth team players (back row, l-r) Billy Whelan, Eddie Colman, John Doherty, Gordon Clayton, Bryce Fulton, Paddy Kennedy, Duncan Edwards. Front row: Noel McFarlane, Eddie Lewis, Ronnie Cope, David Pegg, and Albert Scanlon

Table manners: Duncan sits down with team-mates in 1953 at the house in Birch Avenue, near Old Trafford, where he boarded. With him are Tommy Taylor, Bobby Charlton, Bill Whelan, Jackie Blanchflower, Mark Jones, Gordon Clayton and Alan Rhodes

First of many: Duncan darts from the pitch after making his debut in 1953 against Cardiff City at Old Trafford – the 16-year-old was congratulated after the game by Jimmy Murphy (left), one of the most influential people in his career

Right place at the right time: This clearance against Scotland in 1957 was immortalised in a statue that stands in Duncan's home town of Dudley

Air time: Duncan joins David Pegg, Ronnie Clayton, Alan Hodgkinson, Johnny Haynes and England manager Walter Winterbottom on a journey to Romania in 1957 that turned out to be rather eventful

National heroes: Duncan benefits from training with England legends Stanley Matthews and Billy Wright at Highbury in 1957

Keeping the Wolves at bay: Duncan and goalkeeper Ray Wood leap to clear the ball in a match played in snowy conditions at Wolves in 1956

United legends: A team photo from December 1957 including (back row, l-r) Duncan Edwards, Bill Foulkes, Mark Jones, Ray Wood, Eddie Colman, David Pegg, plus (front row) Johnny Berry, Bill Whelan, Roger Byrne, Tommy Taylor and Dennis Viollet

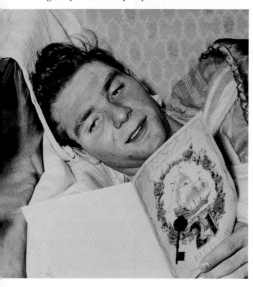

Under the weather: Duncan raises a smile as he recovers from flu on his 21st birthday in October 1957 – but he did miss a European Cup match against Shamrock Rovers. The following month, he's trying on a new tracksuit with Matt Busby and Roger Byrne

New digs: Duncan moved to Gorse Avenue, where Mrs Dorman looked after several young United stars

European adventures: The lads needed to look the part if they were to take on the cream of Europe. Here they are in 1957 as they left Manchester Ringway airport to take on Real Madrid in the European Cup semi-final first leg

'State funeral': A huge crowd gathered outside St Francis' Church in Dudley in February 1958 to pay their respects to one of the area's favourite sons and a footballing great

Reunited: Duncan was buried with his sister Carol Anne at Dudley Cemetery

Honoured: Sir Bobby Charlton unveils a plaque at Duncan's old school on the Priory Estate in Dudley

impressive. England, inspired by this pivotal moment, went on to win 3-1.

"We were all a little trembling about the match," Walter Winterbottom admitted. "So many of our soldiers were there. And then Duncan picked the ball up and dribbled along, through the team. 'All the way Duncan,' I could hear the players shout. He did, and scored from outside the area. We never looked back after that. He had this tremendous power in his shooting. We had tests of power shooting by using a slow-motion camera, putting sticks in a line and seeing who had the strongest kick. Duncan came out top. The supreme confidence he had in himself carried through the England team."

It was a seminal goal in a seminal match. "Duncan tackled like a lion, attacked at every opportunity and topped it off with a cracker of a goal," captain Billy Wright said of his "phenomenal" colleague. "He was still only 19, but already a world-class player."

In his *Express* column that week, Wright gave even more praise. "As captain, I am very proud of a young side whose unlimited enthusiasm and drive are typical of the present-day youngsters," he said. "They 'live' the game and never stop talking about how they can improve. On and off the field, these young men are striving for perfection. Take Johnny Haynes and Duncan Edwards. They are their own biggest critics. When they do badly, these fine young players are the first to criticise themselves. That is why they are always improving."

His pals back home were just as happy for him. Jimmy Armfield, who had spent much time with Duncan at Nesscliffe and in the Army team, was one of many to put on record the reverence he held his team-mate in. "Such was my admiration that I named my eldest son Duncan," he said in 1983. "My abiding memory of Dunc was his size. Big thighs, strong shoulders and even at 18 always appearing to be a man amongst boys. When I saw him stalking the dressing room before a match I always thought, 'I'm glad he's playing for us.' Once he was out on the pitch he was afraid of nothing. He was a natural winner because he never contemplated anything else.

"Duncan Edwards had absolutely everything one looked for in the perfect footballer. He was good in the air; he had two good feet; he had a most powerful shot; he was firm and fair in the tackle; exceptionally strong physically and never less than fully fit. He could also apply the deft touches. To top it all he was a total inspiration to all who played with him. At 18 he was an automatic choice for England. Duncan destroyed the West Germans in Berlin with his immense power. He scored a goal that day that even had the Germans shrieking acclaim."

The tour had been a resounding success with a big statement for England. The German press dubbed Duncan 'Boom Boom' for the power of his shots. The evening after the game, Duncan celebrated as the centre of attention with his England team-mates. Normally teetotal, this was one occasion he allowed himself a drink. "I was drinking some pretty strong German wine with Tom Finney, Roger Byrne, Dennis Wilshaw and Duncan," Nat Lofthouse recalled. "I told Duncan to go easy as it was a bit more potent than anything we were used to. Duncan said, 'Oh, I'll be alright' but we finished up having to take him to the lavatory. He was in a bad way but we all reckoned he had earned his little celebration."

While most of the England party returned home for the summer, Duncan remained in Germany to play in some Army games. In early June, they played against the holders of the West Berlin Cup, Spandauer SV, in the Berlin Olympic Stadium. After an hour, the Army team had a 2-1 lead – the first goal scored by Duncan – but the game was abandoned because of a heavy thunderstorm. That was how Duncan's season finally ended – but it was not reflective of his achievements over the last two months. If the 1954/55 season had been the "most astonishingly successful season any player has ever had", then Edwards had even surpassed himself in 55/56.

Chapter 14
Battleship

There was a platform upon which Manchester United and Duncan Edwards could demonstrate their skill and talent, and this had the potential to make the 1956/57 campaign better than anything they'd experienced before. Better than anything British football had ever experienced, come to that.

Matt Busby had achieved his ambition of winning another First Division title, but he was mistaken if he thought it would be straightforward to convince the Football League that United should be allowed to compete in the European Cup. Busby, however, was more resilient than Chelsea had been the previous year. He expected Football League secretary Alan Hardaker's letter forbidding United to take part, so he travelled directly to the FA in London to discuss the matter with its secretary, Sir Stanley Rous. Busby knew that Rous had ambitions of becoming FIFA president, and so English clubs supporting continental competition may well help his chances. The United manager asked if there was anything within the Association's rules which would prevent his club from entering the competition. He was assured there was not.

Busby then discussed the matter with the board of directors. They had initially been reluctant to go toe-to-toe with the league, but Busby made a proposition. Games would have to be played in midweek to avoid clashing with the league calendar, and Old Trafford did not have floodlights. Busby suggested that the club could ask Manchester City if they could use Maine Road, which did have floodlights, and arrange a gate receipt split which would prove so beneficial for all parties that United would be able to afford to install their own floodlights for the following season.

"United are an exceptional club," Busby said, "and that is why my directors and I felt we were doing the right thing to pursue our international ambitions. We possess the finest reservoir of reserve talent in the game. I had no fears about United's ability to fulfil all commitments."

For Duncan, the off-season was spent between Nesscliffe and Dudley. His parents had switched homes to move to 34 Elm Road – just across the street – and Duncan would return there whenever he was permitted. He still would admit that his favourite escape from football was even more football, but even Duncan needed some down time. "My main relaxation is fishing," he said. "Quietly I collect my sandwiches and Thermos flask and sneak off to a river to sit there in peace and quiet with never a thought for the bustling world of professional football... a day or two away from the game occasionally is very refreshing. I find my game is so much sharper when I return to it."

There was little escape from football when Bobby Charlton arrived at Nesscliffe to report for his national service. Not that Duncan minded in the slightest. Charlton was just as shy in new surroundings as he was when he arrived in Manchester.

"Duncan was a year older than I was and he took charge of me the moment I arrived at the Army camp," Charlton recalled. "He had my billet arranged and everything. When he showed me to the billet, he noticed there was a spring sticking out of the bed, and said, 'We can't have that'. It was a great big iron bed, but he hoisted it over his shoulder – mattress, frame and all – and went off in search of a better one for me."

Duncan would take Bobby to Dudley on their rare time off. "Duncan would always tell us how brilliant Manchester was," Laurence Brownhill says, "but then when Bobby came down he said that Duncan was always saying how brilliant Dudley was!" Duncan's returns home would attract the attention from all of the neighbours, with kids hero-worshipping on the doorstep keen for their local lad to come outside and have a kick of the ball with them. Often, he obliged.

In Manchester, Duncan was now settled with the Dormans and Billy Whelan at 19 Gorse Avenue. They received a new housemate over the summer. "I'd just left school and he'd been living there for a little while with Bill Whelan," David Gaskell, a promising goalkeeper says. "I was introduced to them as someone who was coming to live in the digs with them. I was a naive boy from Wigan who'd never been very far away from home. Duncan was already a first-team player and already an England international."

So Edwards was preceded by his reputation, though United's number six quickly made a personal impression on the young Gaskell. "I'd never even seen Manchester United play before I joined them," he admits. "I had seen Duncan play for England because in those days they would play on afternoons because there weren't floodlights. I remember wagging off school with some friends to watch Duncan play for England on the television and even then he stood out like a colossus. When I joined I was supposed to learn a trade. I would see Duncan in the morning, before we both went off for our day, and then at tea time. I'd then go off to the Cliff to train. But my job wasn't working out, so the club put me on the ground staff. I'd walk to the ground with Duncan every morning. I'd be in the dressing room doing the odd jobs, cleaning boots and putting the kit away.

"Duncan was a gentleman. He was just an ordinary sort of chap. A little bit old-fashioned. But he was so very helpful. Duncan and I would go and play billiards and snooker. He was a quiet housemate. Unassuming. But then again I was in awe of them, both him and Bill. These were international stars and I was a schoolkid from Wigan. The landlord and landlady adored him. He was big and strong but not aggressive. He was the sort of bloke that if he said to do something, you would do exactly as he said. He wasn't threatening, but he was so powerful. It was strange because I would describe him as a gentle giant, but once he was on the field of play you could see that opponents viewed him very differently. It was like they sensed his power."

Busby's championship winning team started the season in remarkable fashion. A 2-2 home draw with Birmingham gave one sportswriter the opportunity to write of Edwards' performance that he was "combining the power of a battleship with the manoeuvrability of a destroyer". United really kicked into gear on matchday two, hitting three goals past Preston. They scored three more against West Brom, another three against Preston in the return, and three again against Portsmouth at Old Trafford. Of those 14 goals, seven had been scored by Viollet, three by Taylor and two by Whelan. There was some seriously impressive firepower in the team but they were able to shine on a platform created for them by the faultless partnership of Colman and Edwards at half-back.

"Duncan and Eddie had other dimensions," Charlton recalled. "They could lift the game on to another plane and you could hear the effect they had on the terraces, which for youth matches were amazingly well filled with crowds touching 30,000 and sometimes more. That was the hard evidence of the magic Matt Busby was creating in the public mind. Make excitement, create colour, he told his young players and you only had to listen to the noise of the crowd, the expectant buzz when Duncan or Eddie got on the ball and the huge roars when those moments of promise were beautifully fulfilled, to know that his demands were being met quite perfectly. If Busby wanted United to be a work of art, Duncan was supplying the wonderfully bold brush strokes and Eddie was performing a series of inspired squiggles."

The artistry continued with the first big win of the campaign. Roger Byrne was still the club captain but Duncan Edwards would be the player following Busby's diplomacy and Murphy's politically incorrect barb with a missive of his own. "Before a match," Busby recalled, "after we'd done our last talking before the players went out, big Duncan used to say, 'Go on boys. We haven't come here for nuffin'. This was always his favourite saying."

They went home with everything. Whelan scored four minutes from time at Stamford Bridge, but the win was more convincing than the scoreline suggested. United's prowess caused *The Times* to question whether the current team was even better than the 1948 FA Cup winners. "This is especially true at half-back, where Edwards is a giant both in thrusting attack after attack and covering Byrne in any emergencies."

Desmond Hackett of the *Express* gave a glowing report of what was possibly Edwards' most accomplished league performance yet (though again referred to him as 20 when he was 19): "Big-Boy Duncan Edwards, the 20-year-old with a veteran's confidence, saved the League champions from being reduced to leaving a point at Chelsea. The rest of this highly talented bunch were happy to be big show-offs and repeat their party pieces without getting down to the serious business of scoring. Edwards, having completed the task of keeping the Chelsea right-wing in order, kept going forward determined to force the winning goal. And he did. In the last four minutes Edwards stroked a chance down to inside-right Billy Whelan and Whelan, four yards from goal, was almost impudent in the way he picked his spot."

David Williams of the *Herald* felt this was an ominous performance. "Count your blessings, Chelsea," he wrote. "First, that United were in exhibition mood; second, that goalkeeper Bill Robertson was in top form. Otherwise there would have been a grandfather of a hiding for the Chelsea kids... I felt sorry for these Chelsea fledglings, the way they tore all over the place without getting anywhere, while United's defence, studded with international class, seldom got out of an amble. Maybe United felt sorry for the youngsters, too – about as sorry as a cat with a mouse under its paw."

Williams felt that Chelsea daring to score only expedited their downfall. "This forced United out of their exhibitionism. Net result… a draughtboard goal as good as any that Matt Busby has ever dreamed. The ball was worked upfield from Roger Byrne to Duncan Edwards and then square to Eddie Colman. Colman transferred to Tommy Taylor, who sent Johnny Berry tearing away, and there was Taylor in the middle, waiting as though it had all been planned beforehand, to head home. It was as simple as that. United should have 'declared' there. It would have been kinder to Chelsea. But the punishment went on."

It was a frightening and exhilarating Wednesday evening. Frightening for the league that United could win against the most recently-dethroned champions at such a canter. Exhilarating for Busby that his rookie side could play like this against one of the best teams.

Three days later they went to Newcastle. Jackie Milburn was on guard after Edwards' previous warning. Just before half-time, the pair were involved in an altercation where the United midfielder did indeed 'upend' the legendary Magpies forward. Edwards was spoken to by the referee. A few months ago Duncan may well have remonstrated with the official. Not today. Moments later, he struck the post with a ferocious effort. On this occasion, Milburn had the last laugh, scoring a late equaliser after Whelan's 65th-minute goal. It was feared that in the tussle with Milburn, Edwards had chipped a bone in his right foot.

While it would not be quite as serious as that, it was significant enough to rule him out of United's first ever game in European football. Viollet and Taylor – who else – scored goals without reply to earn the English side a 2-0 win in Anderlecht in the first leg of the preliminary round. Archie Ledbrooke of the *Mirror* travelled to Brussels. He was told by League secretary Fred Howarth: "We believe this competition should be played out of season. United may have to play up to 10 matches and that may mean fielding weak teams in league games. We did not interfere with this tie because they had started selling tickets for the return game in Manchester."

Duncan returned to the team for the visit of Sheffield Wednesday on September 15th. Here, Busby gave the prodigy the responsibility of following 'Golden Boy' Albert Quixall around the pitch. Quixall was highly-rated, and at Old Trafford too – Bert Whalley had seen the boy playing as a teenager on Blackpool beach and asked if he had a club. Unfortunately he was already taken – and United's admiration meant he required special attention. The game was over by the 32nd minute, with Viollet, Whelan and Berry scoring. Edwards' man-marking job was so effective that it earned the headline "Quixall Held Fast In Edwards Grip", although the Owls forward did evade attention for long enough to score a consolation before Taylor grabbed his customary goal near the end.

Edwards then represented the Football League in a 3-3 draw with a League of Ireland XI. He may as well have been the only one who turned up on his side. "Credit big boy Duncan Edwards with a world-class show, a one-man victory drive," beamed Desmond Hackett in the *Express*.

Manchester City were the next visitors to Old Trafford for what would be Duncan's 100th league appearance. There were still eight days remaining of his teenage years. To put this in perspective, David Pegg – Duncan's team-mate through the various sides at club and international level – made 36 league appearances as a teenager. Pegg, like Edwards, was one of the most highly-rated prospects in the country. Pegg's journey was normal in the context of the Busby Babes and accelerated in the context of English football. Edwards' own development was almost three times as advanced.

United dismissed City with the same sort of routine ease that Chelsea had felt. Viollet's first-half strike was followed by a Whelan goal in the second. The proficiency of the strikers had suddenly become exponential. Yes, that was in no small part due to their development playing alongside each other. But it owed much to the delivery of Berry and Pegg and also the peerless transitional play of Colman and Edwards in the middle.

"Edwards is truly a young giant," *The Times* reported of his colossal display against City. "He covered all of the field in defence, dominating everyone in the air. Some 30-yard passes whistled out to Pegg... Yet for all his size he can stroke the most delicate pass even when going at full tilt."

Don Revie had warned of these days. They'd arrived very quickly. "There is not a better pair of wing-halves in the country than Edwards and Colman," he confessed.

They were keen to prove that it was the same case on the continent, too. Some 43,635 packed into Maine Road for the second leg against Anderlecht – none of them officials represent-ing the Football League. They missed a historic night. It was a Manchester night. Rain soaked the pitch before kick-off.

If ever there was a 90 minutes to showcase everything Matt Busby and Jimmy Murphy had been working towards for a decade, this was it. And it's important to mention that, because this was the product of a decade's work. This is how long it took.

Bang, Tommy Taylor on eight minutes.

That was Busby and Murphy, slipping through the Barnsley roads in the dead of night, doing everything to get their man.

Bang, Taylor again, 20 minutes.

That was Busby, brave enough to replace the record goalscorer at the club and give a young boy burdened with a £29,999 price tag the responsibility of replacing him.

Dennis Viollet. 26 minutes.

This was Crickmer, Rocca and Gibson, determined that the best local boys should play for Manchester United.

Viollet, 39 minutes.

This was Busby, able to convince one of the best local boys, more than three years before the inception of the Youth Cup, that he would give them a chance in the first team.

Viollet, 40 minutes.

Busby's spirit of play. His desire for the working class folk of Manchester to be entertained.

Taylor in the 54th minute.

There's Jimmy Murphy's unerring eye for talent, scolding Gordon Clayton for conceding a goal to Taylor in the Central League, only to smile on the bus back to Old Trafford knowing he was going to tip Busby off about the next great striker.

Billy Whelan in the 63rd minute.

United's network of scouts, and the eyes of all the connections to the scouts, deployed all over the British and Irish Isles.

Viollet in the 75th.

Joe Armstrong in the north east or on the south coast trailing talent. In the living room of parents telling them Manchester United will look after their boy. Picking the boys up from the train station and settling them into their digs.

Berry in the 78th.

Busby having the expert nous to know just how and when to supplement this homegrown talent with great players from other clubs.

Whelan, making it 10-0 in the 89th minute.

Jimmy Murphy in the dressing room at half-time against Nantwich in the Youth Cup, screaming that 10 wasn't enough.

Tonight it was. It was the record win in the history of Manchester United, the clean sheet making it better than the 10-1 win over Wolves in October 1892, when the club were still known as Newton Heath. The *Halifax Courier* described the match as "a tonic" for English football and "the best possible answer to the Football League's earlier request that they would withdraw".

Don Davies in *The Guardian* reckoned that the visitors had been deflated by the fact that Edwards replaced Blanchflower, one of the first game's best players. How could United improve on what they already had? "(It) must have had a profound psychological effect on the Belgian players."

"In spite of that cricket score, I can still see young Colman running to collect the ball for a throw-in with only two or three minutes left, as if we were losing and his whole life depended on it," Busby later said. "That epitomised the keenness of the side that night."

The manager would describe it as "the greatest thrill in a lifetime of soccer. It was the finest display of teamwork I have ever seen from any team – club or international. It was as near perfect football as anyone could wish to see." And, also, a little later, "I do not exaggerate when I say my youngsters provided the large crowd, willingly braving torrential rain, with a display of football which has never been bettered by a British club side."

In the *Lancashire Evening Post*, Bernard Joy paid tribute to the long game Busby had played to achieve the near-perfection he spoke of.

"Matt Busby started off after the war with a great side and they set a standard for successors," Joy wrote. "In the weekly practice game, the established 'stars' play alongside the youngsters and teach them correct methods. Mr Busby bloods the players early, if only for three or four matches at a time, with the result that Mr Johnny Carey, the Blackburn manager and former United captain, can comment, 'They are young in years but old in experience.' Coaches Jimmy Murphy and Bert Whalley organise the biggest search for top-class schoolboy talent and then put these boys through the finest 'finishing school' in the country."

Twenty-four hours after conquering Anderlecht on the Wednesday, Duncan was in the Army team playing in a cup tie. He was then down to London, to face Arsenal with United at Highbury, on the Saturday. The 2-1 win was the 10th victory from 12 unbeaten games to start the season. "Edwards the courageous, doing two men's work," wrote Alf Clarke in the *Evening Chronicle*. "You would not think that this was his fourth game in a week, judging by his brilliance."

Busby's recollection was similar. In the team at Highbury for the first time was Ronnie Cope. "I remember saying to Duncan...

'keep an eye on Ronnie Cope. He might need a lift,'" Busby said. "Duncan kept an eye on Ronnie and did about half a dozen other jobs besides. A wing-half, he could have been a great centre-half or a great forward striker. He would have been one of the great leaders with his sheer inspiration. He inspired by his sheer presence, by his sheer enthusiasm. If there was ever a player who could be called a one-man team, that man was Duncan Edwards."

So far, Duncan had not notched a single goal from the average of three a game his team-mates were getting. Dennis Viollet, who was averaging one of those three himself, made it clear how important the left-half was to the supremacy of the Busby Babes. "What can anyone say about Duncan that has not already been said? Duncan was out of this world, one of the best players I've ever seen, and one of the fittest. There wasn't an ounce of fat on him and he was so powerful when he ran, his muscles stood out on him. He was so wonderfully talented in so many ways but to me his outstanding ability was in his ball control. He could control the ball with any part of his body, head, shoulder, chest, thigh. Duncan was something special."

The game at Arsenal was Duncan's last as a teenager. His first in his twenties was for England (not counting the 45-minute practice match he played against Birmingham on his birthday after joining up with the national team or the loss to Wolves at Lilleshall two days later). He was named in Winterbottom's team to face Northern Ireland in Belfast on October 6th.

"England's spirits are higher than I can recall before any international in recent years," Bob Pennington reported in the *Express*. "The confident youngsters like Duncan Edwards are playing schoolboy practical jokes. Veterans like Matthews are only too proud to be in a team that has found a heart, and above all, a great sense of humour."

Taylor and Byrne were alongside Edwards, and they found the harsh reality of the different styles alongside them difficult to adjust to after the seamless way United had been playing. Wright and Wilshaw were wonderful Wolves players, as was Don Revie for City (that year's FA Cup winners), but all three clubs had distinctly different styles of playing, and it did not result in a cohesive performance for England. They took a 1-1 draw, but, according to George Follows, Duncan played "by far his worst international". It was a comment that stuck with the United midfielder for some time.

There was some general criticism that followed his club and Army form, too. Duncan missed the home game with Charlton Athletic because of the clash with the England game, but played in a chastening Army defeat by Aston Villa four days later. The League side won 7-1. "There were six internationals in the Army team," reported the *Herald*, "but they played as if they were tired of seeing a ball. It was four matches in eight days for most of them."

Duncan played his part in a routine 3-1 win at Sunderland. United, who had won the previous season's league with a record 11 point gap, were three points ahead of Tottenham and five ahead of third-placed Blackpool.

On October 16th, Edwards lined up alongside Bobby Charlton and Gordon Clayton in a Western Command team *against* Manchester United. He was listed in the match programme with the description: "Needs no introduction. Has played for the Army and England many times."

None of this was any help to the preparation for United's next European Cup game, 24 hours later in Manchester against Borussia Dortmund of Germany (though the Army did give Edwards special leave to play in the Charity Shield against Manchester City instead of playing for the Western Command against Northern Ireland on the same day and a similar reprieve was given to him from the Football League's game with the Irish League XI on October 31st).

The first sign of new problems at United appeared against Dortmund. When they took a 3-0 lead in the 30th minute, the fans at Maine Road were expecting another avalanche. But the ease in which they were taking their opponents apart led to complacency, and the Germans took advantage, scoring two late goals.

It did not affect the tributes placed upon them by Archie Ledbrooke and Frank McGhee in the following morning's *Mirror*. "GREATEST TEAM IN THE WORLD" was the eye-catching headline of a story that continued: "Manchester United are the greatest team and the greatest club in the world. THEY are the reigning champions of English soccer. THEY are a model for every other club in the League. THEY are unbeaten in 26 successive League games, stretching back to last January. THEY haven't been beaten at home since March 1955. Their supporters have forgotten what defeat tastes like. And last night they beat Borussia Dortmund, the German champions, 3-2 in the European Cup."

The writers asked Busby how good United could be at their peak. "As good as they were two weeks ago when they beat the Belgian champions Anderlecht 10-0," replied the manager. "That was the greatest display of football I have ever seen. They had all the skill in the world, all the confidence in the world, all the ruthlessness in the world. They played as I've always dreamed they could... I want them to be confident. I want them to be arrogant. I want them to tell themselves that they are better than anyone else. Because they are, you know."

However, Frank Taylor in the *Evening Chronicle* gave a more critical evaluation of this game, feeling that United had appeared at times to be a little too arrogant, with Edwards and Colman receiving a telling-off for not controlling the game. In *The Guardian*, Don Davies tried to take a balanced look. "No doubt United's display against Anderlecht must be considered the zenith of their performances so far," he wrote. "We shall probably not see the like again. But tonight's exhibition in certain respects was not far below it."

Bobby Charlton had made his first-team debut in the game Edwards had missed against Charlton Athletic, and scored twice;

the pair played alongside each other in the first team for the first time at Goodison Park. Charlton scored early, but Everton responded to take a 3-1 lead at half-time. Edwards had already had to leave the field for treatment, during which time the hosts scored their second. And when he was back on, Everton scored a third. United responded with a goal from Whelan, but as they chased an equaliser late on, conceded two more for their first league defeat since January.

There was a good game for United to use to retaliate – the Charity Shield. It would be two more years before the fixture would be moved to the start of the season, so in these days it carried more of a serious air. On this occasion it pitted together league champions Manchester United and FA Cup holders Manchester City.

Duncan, who had played many different positions for United already, now added goalkeeper to the list when Ray Wood had to come off injured. The incident sparked a strange set of events.

"I got home from the ground after my day's work and Bill and Duncan had already gone to the game," recalls David Gaskell. "I was having my tea and still undecided whether I would go to the game. I couldn't drive and it would be a case of getting two buses. The landlord was going to watch it on the television and I was going to watch it with him, but decided at the last minute to go to Maine Road. A few minutes into the game, Ray Wood got injured. Before I knew it, Bert Whalley appeared on the touchline in front of me and said that I was wanted in the dressing room. As I got there I was getting kitted out in a goalkeeper's kit. There were at least four goalkeepers in front of me at the time. There were no substitutes but they'd agreed that I could come on. I was ushered down to our goal and who should I see there but Duncan! He'd been playing there since Ray was injured. 'What the fucking hell are you doing here?' he exclaimed. I was still stunned and said I thought I was there to play in goal. 'Get on with it,' he said. I played well and we won the game 1-0. Later I was told the commentator thought Ray had gone back in goal and was praising him, saying he was worth his place in the England team!"

After the match, Duncan's sporting spirit and team spirit were both on show. "I was given a winner's medal after the game," Gaskell says. "I was a bit embarrassed and when I got back to the dressing room I saw Ray looking all forlorn so I gave the medal to him. Duncan came up to me and said, 'No, that's fucking yours, son.' I didn't go back to Ray but a few minutes later Duncan came to me and gave me a medal. I don't know if it was Ray's. I didn't really know what to do as the rest of the lads were getting dressed in their club blazers and I just had the old t-shirt I'd come to the game in.

"I resisted their invitations to go out because I wasn't old enough to have a drink so I went out to the bus stop just outside Maine Road. The team coach pulled out onto the road and Bill and Duncan saw me waiting for the bus. They got out and pulled me on the coach. They were insistent that I should go on with them to celebrate but I said again about not being old enough so I got dropped off back in Stretford. The landlord was chuffed as hell because he was a big United fan but he hadn't spotted that it was me and not Ray who'd gone back in goal. I went up to my room to go to bed. When Duncan and Bill came back later on they called me downstairs, where they made this big song and dance about it. The next morning Duncan made sure I called my father to tell him. We didn't have a telephone in the digs. My father didn't have a phone either! But Duncan took me to the telephone box and stood with me to make sure I called somebody on our street so that they could tell my father and get him to talk to me."

Gaskell was considered too green to play in Wood's stead so one of those more senior goalkeepers, Tony Hawksworth, was called into the team to play at Blackpool. The hosts looked to have won it when Stanley Matthews tricked Duncan and got a cross in for Mudie to score – but, with 30 seconds on the clock, Taylor snatched a dramatic equaliser.

Duncan may have felt grateful for the Football League giving him a day off, but the Army took advantage and fielded him in a game at Norwich on the night he would have been in Ireland. It was a 1-0 win for Duncan's side, with one report reading: "The Army, with Bobby Charlton conspicuous at inside-left, generally held the advantage… with great support from Duncan Edwards."

The relatively indifferent fortnight (by his standards) was ignored by the international selectors, who named Duncan in the team to face Wales at Wembley later that month. United appeared to have their groove back judging by the comfort with which Wolves were taken apart at Old Trafford on November 3rd. And Duncan was in the Army team again for a game against an FA XI at Maine Road on the 7th. The FA team contained the likes of Tom Finney and triumphed 7-3, with Duncan unfortunately scoring an own goal.

"The Army, even with the aid of Manchester United's star 'babes' Eddie Colman, Duncan Edwards and Bobby Charlton, just could not match their more experienced rivals," read the *Herald*'s report. Don Davies, in the *Manchester Guardian*, did however claim the highlight of the game came from the Army side. "To the delight of the local onlookers, it was engineered by two of the bright characters from the Busby nursery – Edwards and Charlton," Davies said. "It was a masterpiece of split-second judgement and execution. First Edwards sent a long through pass scudding across the ground, with a peremptory cry to 'Bob!' as though 'Bob' (Charlton) needed telling that he was about to smack home the chance of a lifetime. How beautifully that boy slipped the ball past the goalkeeper on one side, as he swerved away past the other."

So that was the highlight of the game, but not the most entertaining moment – Charlton scored another of his team's consolation goals, but the FA side claimed foul play, as they said they had become distracted when a stray dog ran on to the pitch.

Chapter 15
Atomic

Back to serious business, Edwards was put in a bad mood by a 2-0 loss at Bolton towards the end of November 1956. Doug Holden, who had scored the opening goal, had gone in a little too aggressively on the United number six. A leg injury forced Duncan to play wide on the left, and although he saw the game through in left-half after treatment at half-time, it was a subdued struggle for the normally imposing figure. With 20 minutes to go, he let fly with a powerful shot, which aggravated his leg injury and also hurt his foot. Despite this, he insisted that he was hopeful of playing against Wales.

Busby was not optimistic. "Duncan's right ankle is badly swollen," he said. "It is too bad for him even to try it out on the pitch." Following further tests, United masseur Ted Dalton confirmed that there was no way Duncan could make the game.

Duncan was privately concerned that the injury might have been exacerbated by the fact he was now wearing lightweight boots, provided to him by Adidas. The boot-makers had earned a positive reputation after the German players had worn their products in the 1954 World Cup win over Hungary. "The modern boot is a vast improvement on the old thick leather type that encase the foot and ankle as if in steel," Edwards said. "The present boots allow you to feel the ball through leather, and thus make for better ball control." They also – as Edwards found out to his cost – offered less protection for the body against the old hammer boots.

He missed the win over Leeds, but was back for the crucial game in Dortmund. Viollet was injured, so Busby made the bold choice of asking Edwards to control the game from inside-forward, calling up McGuinness to play the half-back line with Colman that had been supremely effective in the youth side. A frozen pitch was waiting for them in Germany, and boots were once again on the agenda.

"Somewhere on the journey to Dortmund, the rubber studs for the boots had gone missing," remembers Tom Clare. "Tom Curry, the trainer, couldn't find them anywhere, and couldn't find any in Germany in the sports shops. So the players played on an icy pitch with no studs and they were like Bambi on ice. Wilf played in left-half, with Duncan moving to inside-left. It was one of the best performances I've ever seen from a Manchester United player. He played up front and then dropped into a midfield role where he broke a lot of the play up. His control was immaculate. I remember seeing him hit a drive from 35 yards. It never got off the ground but it nearly uprooted the goalposts…

"Everyone always says he was a mammoth of a man. He wasn't, really. He was only 5ft 11in. But he was solid. He was like a brick wall. He was broad. For a lad of that size he was so quick. He had complete mastery of all the skills of the game. I've seen so many descriptions of him as a gentle giant. They make me laugh. He was anything but a gentle giant. He would destroy you. He'd go through you. He would set tackles up like tank traps. That's where he got his nickname from. When he hit you, you knew it. If he wanted that ball he was going to get it."

United drew 0-0 – a composed performance when it mattered, with Edwards creating the best opening with a flashed cross across the face of goal. Aside from that, it had been a war of tactical attrition. Duncan was no particular fan of the continental tactics. "Probably the least likeable form of defence is the offside game," he said. "Defenders constantly move forward to put an attack offside and the game degenerates into a series of free-kicks and drives the crowd to distraction. I know just how they feel, too, for no player likes to be involved in this sort of match. Football was meant to be an attacking game, full of excitement, power and grace. So keep it that way."

Edwards was again at number 10 for the trip to Spurs. It was the most eagerly anticipated game at White Hart Lane for years. "We've never known anything like it," a ticket office employee told Frank McGhee. "No, not even for a cup tie. We've had to return thousands of cash applications for tickets. It is bound to be our biggest gate of the season."

McGhee rated the players on both teams. Two players got 5/5 – Danny Blanchflower, Spurs right-half, and Duncan Edwards, who was, in McGhee's words: "A human dynamo. Still only 20 years old and already internationally famous for his strength and shot."

It was a game worthy of the hype. Spurs stormed into a 2-0 lead after seven minutes. Busby and Murphy worked their half-time magic. Berry scored early on. United threw everything, including a Duncan Edwards-sized kitchen sink, at getting the equaliser. It worked two minutes from time.

"As mighty Duncan Edwards chipped a low centre across goal," reported Peter Lorenzo in the *Daily Herald*, "down in a heap went Spurs centre-half Harry Clarke, goalkeeper Ted Ditchburn and United's Tommy Taylor and Colman." Colman struck to get a point. "I was the first one up," he said of his first-ever goal, "so I just had to tap it in."

On November 28th, England faced Yugoslavia at Wembley. Walter Winterbottom kept faith with Dickinson at left-half and kept Edwards in reserve. Bill Holden of the *Mirror* suggested Edwards could play further forward: "Edwards is a giant England cannot ignore – and he would add ferocious firepower to the attack."

Midway through the first half, Johnny Haynes was injured. Edwards stripped off his tracksuit to come on, but Winterbottom called Tommy Taylor into action instead. Taylor scored twice to secure a 3-0 win. "As soon as I realised Haynes was not fit to return, I told Taylor to go on at centre-forward," Winterbottom said. "He was the reserve forward. There was no question of Edwards going on. He was the reserve half-back."

Edwards seemed strangely intent on proving his worth as a forward. In the number 10 shirt, he struck a magnificent left foot shot from 25 yards to get United on their way at Luton after just four minutes. Taylor and Pegg added goals in a 3-1 win, but it was Edwards' constant shooting from range which was the feature of the game. One journalist asked "Does England Need Duncan Edwards' Rocket Specials?" as though it would be better not to have them. "Yesterday he seemed to be trying to show the selectors that he's the guy to get goals. He turned out at inside-left and within four minutes rocketed one into the net. Not only that, he continued firing these rockets throughout the afternoon. Shoot when you see the whites of their eyes is a good way of going about scoring goals. But not, Duncan, when your colleagues are in a better position."

Wilf McGuinness, usually Edwards' understudy, was loving playing alongside his pal. He was proving something of a lucky charm himself, having remained unbeaten in his first eight appearances. "He had everything," Wilf said. "I describe him as the complete all-rounder. When he had the ball he was our best attacker – he could hit short passes and long passes. He could dribble. He was so nippy on his feet for such a big guy. He was tremendous in the air. The ball would come in and he'd control it with his chest. When the ball was lost, he was always the first to get it back. I never saw anybody give him a chasing. Ever. It didn't happen."

The temptation was too great for Winterbottom to at least not try it out – England had another match right away, against Denmark at Molineux on December 5th, and Edwards was called into play in the number 10 shirt, as Bill Holden of the *Mirror* reported:

Duncan's selection is the biggest shock of the lot – but it's right. It's a shock because Walter Winterbottom did not think of him as an inside-forward when he was included in the list of players from which the side was chosen yesterday. It's right because the power of Edwards and Taylor between Matthews and Finney means a glut of goals against tepid opposition. When the next England team is chosen, I'm certain he will be left-half again – just as he will be left-half for Manchester United on Saturday. "I'm not surprised that Edwards is in," Busby told me. "He has only to play three or four games in any one of several positions – and he's so good he can make it his own." Edwards took his selection calmly. "I can play anywhere," he said.

The Danes were not optimistic. Danish Football Combination secretary Vilhelm Skousen had been in England for a week studying the players. "Our defence cannot hope to hold your attack," he said. "I have seen Duncan Edwards. He is so big we cannot stop him."

They gave it a go. Though Tommy Taylor had scored a hat-trick, the Danes had scored twice themselves through Nielsen. When he got his second in the 73rd minute (assisted, unwittingly, by Edwards) they hoped for a great finale. Enter Duncan Edwards to make amends.

"What a fright these amazingly fast part-timers gave us before England's superior stamina produced a power finish with burly Edwards making the kill," wrote Bob Pennington. "Now Duncan Edwards took over. He had four good shots stopped before he made one mistake – a bad pass which let Nielsen through for his second goal. But Edwards was irrepressible. Three minutes later he cracked a glorious goal from 20 yards. 4-2. Edwards snapped England's fifth goal (77 minutes) when another left-foot power drive was deflected into the net."

A hat-trick could have been his, too, if the goalpost had not been able to divert a powerful free-kick. But it was the first goal which took the breath away of everyone in Molineux. He turned sharply at the end of the box and fired in a shot that was so powerful that the goalkeeper, Drensgaard, was still on his way to ground as the ball was spinning in the back of the net.

Despite this feat, Busby was true to his word when he said Edwards would be back at left-half for United on the Saturday. Viollet was back in the attack and scored in a 3-1 win at Aston Villa. Their next trip to the Midlands, a week later, was not quite so profitable.

Birmingham caught the champions cold with an early goal and then scored two more to get a lead that even Busby's side couldn't recover. This shock defeat meant United's lead was cut from five to three points.

From there, Duncan travelled to play an Army game against Glasgow Rangers on December 18th, then to Nesscliffe, and, via a brief pre-Christmas stop to his parents, back to Manchester for the Boxing Day visit of Cardiff. The Bluebirds had got the memo about rewards for starting quickly, and scored after just two minutes. United, on this occasion, were too strong, coming out on top 3-1. The crowd was staggeringly low, at just 28,607, and yet, it was – even more staggeringly – the highest football crowd of the day.

Tommy Taylor had picked up an injury after scoring against Cardiff so ahead of the next fixture, Busby bowed to recent news-paper letters demanding that Edwards be given a chance up front.

"Now Busby makes atomic Duncan lead the attack" was Frank McGhee's headline in the *Mirror*. "Look out, Portsmouth! Duncan Edwards, Manchester United's 20-year-old wonder wing-half with the atomic shot, is switched to centre-forward tomorrow in place of the injured Tommy Taylor," he wrote. "And the reason is just another illustration of the far-sighted planning of manager Matt 'I want to be on top for the next 10 years' Busby. For weeks he has been insisting that, even with 36 professionals on the Old Trafford staff, he still hasn't enough players. And that is why Edwards has been brought into the centre-forward position. It would have been simple to choose young Bobby Charlton, who has always deputised successfully for Taylor. But Charlton is being groomed for the reserves for an inside-forward job in an ambitious Busby scheme to build up a complete shadow side so that no reshuffle will be necessary if a first-team regular is not available."

From "atomic" to, as Henry Rose of the *Express* said, a "torpedo": Edwards recovered from a handful of first-half misses to score the goal that put his team in front, after a first-half deficit. The champions eventually won 3-1, and Bob Pennington – who still didn't rate Edwards as a centre-forward – believed that Busby's decade-long desires may well be proven correct. "Of course you can't win the European Cup, the FA Cup, and the League championship in one season," he wrote. "Of course it is impossible. But you still left Portsmouth believing that Matt Busby's dream of this triple triumph can be achieved. Here are Manchester United with enough talent to keep them happy for the next 10 seasons."

Pennington pointed out Byrne as the weak spot in the team due to his petulance – and that Busby should give him one last warning. "Then this Manchester United will be as near to the perfect soccer machine as maybe we will ever get in Britain."

Jack Mackenzie of *The People* was impressed as United wrapped up their 1956 in style: "What about Busby's Bambinos? They plastered Portsmouth 3-1 with England left-half Duncan Edwards at centre-forward. This husky he-man hammered in a goal and laid on a sweet pass for another. What a year it has been for Manchester United."

The first game of 1957 came on the first day. And they didn't come much bigger than Chelsea at Old Trafford. One of their rookies was given the task of dealing with United's main man, back at number six – who was still younger than him. "Derek Gibb, 21, started well enough at inside-right," wrote Henry Rose, "but was soon in the grip of Duncan Edwards." United were 2-0 up at half-time and killed the game off four minutes after the break, with Taylor and Whelan netting the goals.

It was a sign of Busby's ambition that he took a full first team to Third Division (North) team Hartlepool in the third round of the FA Cup. United had suffered embarrassment in the cup in the previous seasons, and this squad of Busby Babes had come nowhere near following the 1948 side with a famous day at Wembley. Now, though, they seemed to want it.

"Duncan was outstanding," Tom Clare remembers. But United had a few hair-raising moments despite going 3-0 up in the 30th minute. The hosts equalised, and then bombarded United looking for a winner – the ambition ultimately cost them, as Bill Whelan struck a heartbreaking goal late on.

A much easier task awaited United at Old Trafford. Newcastle were the visitors, but Busby's side coasted, scoring three goals in each half to win 6-1, conserving their energy in the second half; it was a needed breather, as United were off to Spain to face Athletic Bilbao in the next chapter of their European Cup adventure.

Real Madrid are the Spanish side everyone associates with the competition of these early years; however, their dominance of it did not necessarily mean they were similarly invincible in domestic competition. Bilbao had won La Liga in 1956 so Madrid had qualified by virtue of being holders, after winning the first ever final against Reims in Paris.

Bilbao had experienced an eventful journey in the competition. After defeating Porto in the first round, they were drawn against Budapest Honved. However, the tie coincided with the Hungarian Uprising; after losing the first leg away 3-2, Honved had to play the home game in Belgium, and drew that match 3-3. How Busby and Murphy would have relished a clash with Bozsik, Czibor and Puskás, and a meeting of the minds with coach Béla Guttmann. But it was Bilbao that awaited instead.

The journey was eventful. Bill Foulkes fell asleep almost immediately on the plane – and he kicked a lever which turned the heating system off. The plane stopped in Bordeaux to refuel.

Chairman Harold Hardman had complained that the cold on the first leg of the journey was making him feel unwell, so the heater was turned to full power on the journey from France to Spain. Journalist Frank Taylor, with the travelling party, noticed that Duncan was now feeling unwell.

Taylor asked him what was wrong.

"Too hot for me. I shall be airsick," he said.

"Turn the heater off, man," Taylor said.

"No, the chairman has been feeling the cold. Leave me alone. I'll be alright."

Once they had arrived in Spain, Taylor noted that Duncan was looking much worse for wear. "Do you think you'll be fit to play on Wednesday, Duncan?"

"Miss the match?" came the reply. "What do you take me for? A sissy?"

An incidental note to this story – Hardman's chill developed into pneumonia, and he was taken to hospital as soon as the plane landed. He said that he would only fly again if it was unavoidable.

United had been expecting warmer climes. They arrived to worse weather than they'd left back in Manchester. "'Travel to Sunny Spain', we are entreated by the holiday posters, but nothing could have been more cheerless than the industrial town of Bilbao," Matt Busby moaned. "There had been days of torrential rain, turning the playing pitch into a quagmire, huge flakes of snow were falling and a blizzard looked like developing."

United were equally ill-prepared for the tempo of the home team. Bilbao were 3-0 up at half-time and Busby confessed he felt his side were "virtually eliminated". Their best chance had come at 0-0 – Edwards put Viollet through, but Jesús Garay unceremoniously charged the striker off the ball. There was a fear that they'd be intimidated out of the match. As they had done before, though, they staged a fight-back. Taylor and Viollet scored. But Bilbao responded with two more of their own. With minutes to go, Whelan struck a magnificent solo goal – "A goal in a thousand" as Busby called it – to make it 5-3, and make the second leg much less daunting than 5-2 would have made it seem.

In the *Express*, Henry Rose felt there was plenty to be optimistic about. "British hearts are high here tonight, and the man responsible is that broth of a boy from Dublin, 21-year-old Bill Whelan," he said. "Oh yes, Bilbao won 5-3. But after seeing this eight-goal thriller I'm quite sure the league champions will scrub out the two-goal margin in the second leg at Manchester on February 6th and go into the semi-final of the European Cup. The wing-half play of Eddie Colman and Duncan Edwards was a joy to see... Manchester United might have gone ahead in a spell in which Colman and Edwards kept pushing the ball through to the inside-forwards."

Even Spanish outlet *Marca* felt that United's half-back line had been the most impressive feature of a first leg that really should have been all about Bilbao. "Manchester's success had many reasons, but one of the main ones was its midfield, which was superior to the two Bilbao players they were in charge of," reported Antonio Valencia (yes, that's not a typo – the namesake of a player who would, some 60 years later, run the right-wing at Old Trafford for a decade). "Thus, both Colman and Edwards, this robust young man, did not only attend to the marking of Merodio and Marcaida, they also dominated in front of them."

All eyes were on the return leg. A loss at Sheffield Wednesday wasn't the end of the world. United had rushed to return to England through difficult conditions – the club staff, players and travelling supporters were all given brooms to clear snow and ice from the frosty wings of the plane. "I could well imagine the repercussions if we failed to turn up at Hillsborough," Busby said.

Victory over Wrexham in the FA Cup was straightforward,

with Edwards' performance referred to as "a magnificent exhibition of hard constructive play". Even a derby at Maine Road – welcome though the win was, with Edwards taking the last goal of a 4-2 win – did not get the tastebuds flowing like the game that would be played there four days later.

Chapter 16
Greatest Game

"Atmosphere is something which can never be guaranteed in sport," said Manchester United manager Matt Busby. "Even the FA Cup final at Wembley, or the Men's singles final at Wimbledon, or the last round of an Open Golf Championship, may prove a flop, but when the electric tension does occasionally reveal itself in football, it is an experience to be remembered for a lifetime."

All of the ingredients to create a powder keg of an atmosphere were perfectly introduced at the right time into Manchester United's return game with Athletic Bilbao. The game started with the two-goal deficit from the first leg, encouraging supporters to get behind them from the get-go. Edwards and Colman were in full-blooded mood from the first whistle. No complacency tonight. This was not a game they could afford to just control. They had to push the tempo.

Try as they might, United couldn't score – until just before half-time, when Viollet found space in the box. Edwards let rip with a powerful shot, but it hit a Bilbao man, and the ball spun loose. Viollet fired home high into the net; the power of the shot inspiring adrenalin into the waving arms of the supporters.

Two disallowed goals early in the second half elevated the atmosphere to fever pitch. Edwards was putting on an all-action display to better anything the United fans had seen before. "Against Bilbao at Maine Road he was outstanding," recalls Tom Clare. "The way he marshalled the defence was remarkable. There were times he broke up attacks in a way that seemed impossible. Roger Byrne hit a short back-pass that left Ray Wood stranded. Duncan came from nowhere and got the ball clear just before it crossed the line. He would dominate people with the power of his performance."

With United in a good place at half-time, Busby had urged them to be calm. "You can win this match in the last minutes," he said.

"And so they did," wrote George Follows in the *Herald*. "They did not do it with a classic exposition of soccer's airs and graces right out of the Busby book. This was football red of tooth and claw. It was bull-ring football, with the red shirts of Manchester the tormenting capes of matadors and the Basques the braced, but bewildered, bulls. All 11 were heroes, though Ray Wood had little need for heroics, so magnificent were the men in front of him. Duncan Edwards was the dreadnought. He obliterated his inside-forward but still found time and place to charge up into the firing line. It was an Edwards whizzbang, cannoning off Garay, that gave Dennis Viollet that first 42nd-minute goal."

Frank Taylor described it as "a screaming drive speeding towards the net, till Garay stuck out a despairing foot. The ball flew to Dennis Viollet – and United now needed only two goals to win the tie."

Tommy Taylor marked his stellar display with a goal and then, with five minutes to go, Berry hit the decisive goal in the tie from an Edwards cross, sending United into the semi-final of the European Cup.

"Damn silly isn't it," Jimmy Murphy wept, after the match. "Damn silly after all these years in the game. But this is my greatest game of football."

Even the sportswriters felt emotional. "My hands are still trembling as I write," Henry Rose penned in the *Express*. "My heart still pounds. I saw the greatest soccer victory in history. I have never seen anything like it, and believe me, I'm not sure that I would welcome the experience again. It was almost just too much to bear."

Celtic manager Jimmy McGrory was at Maine Road. As he left, he told Rose, "Phew. That's enough to last a lifetime."

Spanish newspaper *Marca* congratulated United, observing: "This attack by the Manchester midfield was constant throughout the game. It never ceased. The Bilbao midfielders were, in turn, cornered in their area by the game that came from Colman and Edwards. The pace was channelled magnificently; fast, relentless and always thrown forward."

While defender Jesús Garay complained about some physical treatment at the hands of the "tough" United players, the Bilbao president, Señor Enrique Guzmán, had a little more grace. "The difference was Duncan Edwards," he conceded.

In attendance was Ronnie Clayton, who had played with Duncan at international level and had become close with him. "He was a human dynamo in defence and attack – here, there and everywhere," he said. "One instant this all-action wing-half was robbing an attacking opponent, the next he was surging through with the ball himself to carry the attack to the enemy. This was a great game, played by great players. And for me Dunc was the greatest that night."

As for Duncan, this was an evening of particular vindication. He had noted the presence of George Follows and was remembering the criticism of the game against Ireland. "Criticise me and I will go all the harder to make you eat your words. It stings my pride, and once I consider I have made an adequate reply in the shape of a good performance, I lose any animosity towards the writer," Edwards said. "What I feel is disappointment in myself that I left myself open to the charge that I played badly. A typical case occurred when George Follows attended one of our matches. On the Monday morning he gave me a most glowing write-up… in effect he said that I was the world's greatest. I glowed with pride. The following Saturday I had a dreadful game and, as always, I knew it. George Follows was among those who saw it, and the following Monday he wrote that he had decided to take back everything he had said about Duncan Edwards. I was running pretty well for the title of the world's worst wing-half. A few weeks later as I went into the ground I saw placards outside proclaiming that Mr Follows was present again. I thought, 'I'll show him something. He will never have seen the likes of this.' So I went out and played probably the best game I have ever played in my life. After that I was content again."

One of the most difficult things to do in football, after a pulsating evening like the one United had experienced, is to avoid a flat performance next time out. A huge crowd of 60,384 turned up to Old Trafford to show their appreciation. It seemed momentarily as though Arsenal might take advantage of that 'morning after' feeling; David Herd scoring inside two minutes. But United responded magnificently, hitting six goals in front of their real 'home' fans. Edwards got the game's decisive goal, and while for some people the exception to their goal tallies might be the blasters from the edge of the box, for Duncan it was the type of goal he scored here – a tap-in from right in front of goal. The 6-2 win gave Busby's side a six-point lead at the top.

Next up was Everton in the FA Cup. Initially, Duncan was not granted leave from the Army. They were playing their own cup semi-final just a few days before. The story was told in *Charles Buchan's Football Monthly*: "He chose this as the psychological moment to ask his Commanding Officer for leave to play for Manchester United against Everton in a fifth round cup tie some days later. 'You can have your leave if we get in the final,' said the CO. In spite of this incentive, Edwards' unit was losing 4-2 in the second half. Thinking of the FA Cup tie, this determined young man strayed to the touchline, asked permission to switch from left-half to inside-left. Fifteen minutes later his side were winning 7-4. Edwards had scored five goals. He got that leave!"

If any team could stop United's momentum in the FA Cup, it would be the Toffees, who had scored nine goals in the last two league games against them. United were still riding the crest of a wave, though, and might have scored nine goals themselves in one game if Albert Dunlop didn't have the match of his life.

"Just as it seemed that United would never score, up came Edwards to drive home a daisy-cutter from 20 yards," reported *The People*'s Harry Peterson in one of those rare moments where the feat was in fact understated. Peterson's colleague, Jack Mackenzie, was a little more complimentary: "Favourites Manchester United can thank that chunk of young English manhood, Duncan Edwards, for seeing them through against outclassed Everton. He hammered in their only goal."

"Everton were a bit of a bogey side," Tom Clare recalls. "It looked as though it would go that way again. They hit the cross-bar. Albert Dunlop in goal had a blinder. All of a sudden, Duncan won the ball in the middle of the pitch. He beat two men. He let fly from about 30 yards. The ball never got off the ground. Dunlop dived but he had no chance."

Edwards would label it his "finest ever goal". "It seemed the old Everton jinx was with us," he said. "We had attacked and attacked... then I hit a low shot through a crowded goalmouth near the end, and it finally beat Dunlop to put us through."

In the *News Of The World*, Frank Taylor described the identity of the match winner as "fitting". "The big left-half was a one man powerhouse," he wrote. "His golden goal capped four previous worthy scoring efforts."

United were through to the quarter final – now, alongside their league position and semi-final place in the European Cup, the treble that was described as impossible at the turn of the year now looked, well... possible. This much was underlined when Edwards was among the injured party for the trip to Charlton – and United still scored five.

"Manchester United may have had three regulars – Bill Foulkes, Duncan Edwards and Dennis Viollet – out with injury," reported

Frank McGhee, "but they still looked the finest, fightingest foot-balling outfit in the country."

Duncan accepted that this strength in depth was crucial if United wanted to realise their dreams. "The first essential of any team is a strong reserve side. This is not always easy," he said. "But if two teams can be built up the effort is worthwhile. With reserves striving for recognition, you will find that your first team will keep an edge on its play. At Old Trafford we have the best reserves in the country. That is one of the reasons for our successes. We in the first team cannot afford to lose interest in our game or show signs of being jaded, because once you go out of United's first team you are liable to be out for a long time."

From no Edwards to two Edwards' – or at least that's how one reporter called it, as he "played like two men" against Blackpool at Old Trafford. This was the flat afternoon that had been threatening to come since Bilbao. There was a drop in the crowd to 42,602, and Blackpool put in their best performance of the season, knowing that anything less than a win would more or less make the rest of the season a procession for the current champions.

The game was summed up, as ever, by the combative presence of Stanley Matthews and Duncan Edwards. "Stainless Stan Matthews was penalised for a FOUL on big Duncan Edwards," wrote Jack Mackenzie in *The People*. "Stan hurt his knee in the process! It slowed up the old Maestro. Oozing mud must take its toll at 42."

The visitors earned their win with two second-half goals, and though Duncan felt he had scored a late consolation, the referee insisted it had not crossed the line.

If the great Stanley Matthews now had to resort to fouling Duncan, then what chance a clogger? We were about to find out. United had been drawn against Bournemouth in the FA Cup. The Division Three South team had knocked out Tottenham in the last round, and Ollie "Narker" Norris had wound up Spurs players standing in front of free-kicks, gesticulating and jumping around – manager Fred Cox said he did not want a repeat against Duncan Edwards.

Norris' theatricals attracted United's assistant Jimmy Murphy, and the *Express'* Roger Malone, to Dean Court to watch Bournemouth draw 1-1 with Colchester. Norris had been talked to by the referee for a two-footed challenge in the 15th minute. Malone warned him: "Edwards is 13 stone. He has never been pushed around on the field by anyone." Murphy's take, meanwhile, was: "The clash between Norris and big Duncan will be interesting."

On the day before the game, United learned that the final of the European Cup would be held in Madrid on May 15th, but the match would be rearranged to the 29th if United made it to both that final and the FA Cup final. If it went ahead on May 15th, United would be without their England players, as Walter Winterbottom's side were playing Denmark in a World Cup qualifier. Then, the under-23s were touring the Iron Curtain with further Babes likely to be in that team. So the incentive for success was increased – even though, strangely enough, the FA Cup final was scheduled for May 4th, and did not clash with anything else.

Edwards was still having treatment for the ankle injury which had caused him to miss the Charlton game. Tommy Taylor was also injured, however, and he was definitely out of the game at Bournemouth, so the pre-match hope of a direct confrontation between Norris and Edwards was dampened when Duncan was named in the number nine shirt at Dean Court. In the end, United were lucky to even have Edwards – and Colman and Foulkes – as the Army only granted leave very late.

"We shall win by about the same score as we beat Spurs – 3-1," a confident Norris said before kick-off. And for a while it looked as though it might be a repeat. Brian Bedford scored early and then Norris left his mark on Mark Jones, causing the United defender to have to come off.

"Centre-forward Duncan Edwards moved back to centre-half and all the defenders except goalkeeper Wood took it in turns to move up to bolster the four forward survivors," reported Maurice Smith in *The People*. "It paid off – but only just!" Johnny Berry scored twice in a five-minute spell to take United into their second semi-final of the season.

The Army had insisted that Edwards would not be released if the Bournemouth game went to a replay, and they were good on their word. As United played at Everton in the league on the day the replay would have been held, Duncan – and Foulkes, Colman and Charlton – were all in Cosford for a game against an RAF XI. If United hadn't shown their impressive strength to win, Busby may have been aggrieved that Colman didn't even play for the military side. Edwards was the star in a "stylish" performance, scoring in a 5-1 win.

Charlton recalled this display: "On this day he was particularly dominant. Duncan's desire for possession was insatiable. The move that I will never forget started when he shouted for the goalkeeper to give him the ball. Then Duncan passed to the full-back, who promptly delivered it back after receiving the firmest order. I was next in the chain. I received the ball and duly returned it to sender. By now the RAF was in full retreat. The last act involved the centre-forward. He held the ball for a moment, then rolled it into Duncan's path. He shot immediately, straight at the head of the goalkeeper. The goalkeeper made no attempt to save. Instead, he ducked as the ball rocketed into the back of the net."

Forty years later, Charlton bumped into the goalkeeper in Wisbech – who told him it was the proudest day of his life!

Colin Webster had scored the goals at Goodison, deputising for Edwards, who was in turn a deputy for Taylor, in the number nine. Duncan was back in that shirt for the visit of Aston Villa, but was told by Busby to play a deeper role than centre-forward. This brought him in direct confrontation with Villa half-back Stan Crowther, and the pair had a memorable clash.

"Stan Crowther was giving Billy Whelan some tough treatment," Tom Clare recalls. "In the second half, Duncan decided to act. A ball bounced between them both. Duncan set it up for one of his classic tackles. He took the ball, Crowther, and about five yards of turf! Crowther went up in the air like a rag doll. He came down so hard he broke a rib. He took no more part in the game."

Those sort of physical challenges were one of Duncan's favourite parts of the game. "The most spectacular tackle is the slide," he said. "It brings glamour, uncertainty and danger to the game, and it is one to be used only in the moments of direst peril... a fraction out in the timing and a free-kick or worse – a penalty – follows. A bad sliding tackle always looks so dreadful, too... yet the sliding tackle can also be the most devastatingly effective way out of the worst kind of trouble. My own golden rule for the slide is never to tackle the man with the ball from a square position, at the right angles. The margin of error is too large."

Duncan had timed this one right – he usually did – but Crowther still had to leave the pitch. Against 10 men, United couldn't quite turn 1-1 into 2-1. "United had a reserve half-back line, and Duncan Edwards was still at centre-forward," reported Cyril Chapman in the *Birmingham Post*, "but United reserves are a race apart, and no credit should be deducted from Villa on the score that United could not field their usual team."

It was a positive result nonetheless, and another opportunity for Busby to try Edwards in a different role without any negative consequence. The evolution of Busby's side was arguably complete with the 1956 First Division title but even he might have felt their progression was ahead of schedule this season. At the end of that first championship-winning season, Edwards had three full seasons behind him in terms of league games. Pegg (69) and Jones (64) could claim two. Colman and Whelan, 25 and 20 respectively.

If you were to average the appearances of the first team in total, they'd played between two and three seasons – the average was 97 appearances, down to 81 if you took out Taylor, Berry and Wood (the totals being 1067 and 654 respectively). This highlights the remarkable and rapid success of the youth system that in effect, as a group, they took one full season to come to terms with the First Division and in the next they were the best side not only in the country but arguably, considering the size of their margin, the greatest British football had ever seen.

United were now so proficient that there was none of that late 1954 concern about where Duncan's best position was. But there was a notable difference between the ease in which Edwards was moved around in the first team compared to the youth side. At Chelsea in the Youth Cup it had been a case of 'give it to Duncan'. At City in the Youth Cup it had been a case of Duncan taking on that responsibility himself. In the early months of Duncan's first-team career, many observers had noted how he had looked better in some roles than others. He didn't appear to have the instinct of a Tommy Taylor, so missed chances meant he looked like an unnatural finisher. He didn't have the wispy finesse or guile of a Whelan or a Viollet so he was dismissed as clumsy. As though he was trying too hard.

Busby had preached about his pattern and his system. He had talked about the individuals. Let's remind ourselves. "It is a pattern formed by the players and the staff, formed by individuals who are all different." Even the manager was having to understand that within that ideology, Duncan Edwards was not a regular case. Almost every other player had an obvious position where they excelled. Through the fire of Murphy and calm of Busby, those players had come through final processing to become masters of their field. To labour a point made earlier, there is no doubting that Edwards possessed the skill set to become one of the best players, if not the best, in any position. It was obvious that United benefitted most when he was at left-half. It was obvious from his own admission that this is where Duncan saw his natural position.

But the interesting point within all this is how Busby's 'individuals in positions' mandate had slightly evolved. This was a season where Duncan realised that replacing Dennis Viollet didn't necessarily mean trying to *be* Dennis Viollet. It was a moment of liberation. He brought the Duncan Edwards quality to inside-left – yes, that meant dropping deep, as he did against Dortmund to control a game that most definitely needed controlling. Rather than being a player who deputised in a position, he was Duncan Edwards, picked to play in his way no matter where he was on the pitch. It was the maturity in Duncan's play that elevated him from the level of one of the best players in the league to the best without question.

Duncan was back in the number six for the visit to Wolves. It was a creditable 1-1 draw and a good homecoming in more ways than one as Gordon Clayton, the boy who had travelled to Manchester with him on Duncan's very first day, made his own first-team debut for Busby's side. Once more, Clayton would be thankful for Duncan's presence, as the latter cleared off the line to preserve United's point.

All players had one eye on the FA Cup semi-final against Birmingham at Hillsborough. There was no doubting the intent of this Manchester United team with Colman and Edwards at wing-half. "Manchester are essentially an attacking side," Tom Duckworth previewed for the *Sports Argus*. "And when they attack, it is all-out attack with those two brilliant wing-halves, Eddie Colman and Duncan Edwards, giving their forwards every support."

Duncan, though, was set to feature as centre-forward. Tommy Taylor was injured and so too was Dennis Viollet, but his late recovery from a groin injury eased Busby's concern. "Duncan Edwards, chosen as Taylor's deputy in the last game, looked the logical choice," Frank McGhee wrote. "But Busby decided that big

Duncan's partnership with clever Eddie Colman was too valuable to be broken up."

United were good. Very good, in fact. Berry scored in the 12th minute, and Bobby Charlton (in his first ever cup tie!) scored a minute later, with Edwards and Colman never giving up any control. Whenever the Blues felt a renewed sense of urgency, they found Edwards even more competitive. "No one had greater drive than Duncan Edwards," read one report.

"Manchester United are sure to win the FA Cup now," wrote Joe Hulme in *The People*. "They've become the team who can't be stopped. On Hillsborough's Wembley-like turf United proved to me once and for all that they have everything."

Everything and more. After their successful entry into European competition, United had finally been able to afford the floodlights for Old Trafford, and two days after the semi-final, they were switched on for the very first time to welcome Bolton.

"No risks shall be taken about league points in spite of our lead," Busby said. "So if possible I shall field the full semi-final side for our First Division match against Bolton."

It was not possible. Viollet bowed out with a groin injury and with Taylor still absent it meant Edwards had to play in attack. Archie Ledbrooke reported that Duncan and some of his colleagues would be travelling to London the day after the game to play against the Belgian Army at Highbury two days later (it was also announced that he was in the England team to face Scotland on April 6th). "Soldiers Duncan Edwards, Eddie Colman, Billy Foulkes and Bobby Charlton are all available (for Bolton). It was Edwards who dominated the Sheffield semi-final. He is the footballer of the year. He is the footballer of almost any year. He could be given England's captaincy NOW and carry it lightly on those giant shoulders."

When Bolton scored early against a tired United side, Duncan once more exerted himself to his limits trying to recover the result.

"Edwards was labouring heavily," Don Davies wrote, "though straining to pull his weight like a willing dray horse. It cannot be said that he was receiving too much support from the others. Hopkinson in the Wanderers' goal saved brilliantly from Berry and Edwards. One shot in particular from Edwards spurted upwards from the goalkeeper's foot almost to the height of the illumination towers."

In the dying moments, with United 2-0 down, Edwards moved back into defence in Busby's attempt to get some control of the game; Blanchflower moved into attack. It was to no avail, but United still had a three-point lead and a game in hand.

In London, the Belgian Army came away with a 2-1 win. "Not even the inclusion of Busby Babes Duncan Edwards and Bobby Charlton could give the front line the necessary zip," Clifford Webb reported in the *Herald*. "I got the impression that Edwards and Colman could do with a lay-off."

There was no rest just yet – United were at Leeds three days later and Duncan was keen to test himself against the great John Charles. The Welshman was heavily linked with a move to Italy, and signed off from this fixture with an equalising goal, cancelling out Johnny Berry's opener. With two minutes left, United got a corner. Berry swung it in – Edwards rose to meet it, but the ball bounced off his hand. While the Leeds players appealed, the ball dropped to Whelan, whose effort was saved, but Charlton was there to score a dramatic winner. United now had a five-point lead with a game more to play than their closest rivals.

In the build-up to the Scotland game, Duncan complained about soreness so he was rested from training. However, as the *Glasgow Herald* reported: "The enthusiastic Edwards could not refrain from kicking the ball when he went out for a run round the pitch and on one occasion he took a corner kick."

While with his England team-mates he learned that he had come second to the legendary Tom Finney – who turned 35 that week – in the Football Writers' Footballer of the Year award.

Within 90 seconds at Wembley, England were behind, when Tommy Ring smashed in an unexpected goal. It should have been two in the 25th minute. A long free-kick was missed by everyone and was bouncing towards the goal until the big bounding thighs of Duncan Edwards came striding across, and one swing of his right foot cleared it from danger.

The image was captured by the photographer for the *Daily Mirror* and it would later be immortalised by a statue in Dudley town centre. Due to the classic arm-back, leg-raised pose, it looks as though Duncan is striking a shot towards goal. However, perhaps the fact that it is Duncan there at the last, saving his team, is even more poetic. Especially considering what was to come.

England levelled in the 63rd minute, with Derek Kevan – the other debutant – converting a cross from Colin Grainger, who was, ironically enough, playing his seventh and last international, as Winterbottom's regeneration continued.

One man who definitely was the future was Duncan Edwards.

"It is 4.35," Maurice Smith wrote in his dramatic match report for *The People*. "The shadows on the green Wembley turf grow long – long as so many of these England footballers' faces. The score is 1-1... and up moves Duncan Edwards, six-foot half-back wonder boy of those amazing Busby babes, 20 yards out. Out of shooting range? Ah, but you don't know this giant Edwards. Out flashes his left foot. The ball cuts along like a jet-driven lawnmower and that is the end of Scotland. It was one of the greatest goals I have ever seen to make up for one of the poorest of internationals."

Smith was a little too excited – it was a right-footed effort, but no less worthy of flowery prose. Edwards cut across the ball with remarkable technique, sending the ball fizzing into the net. England had won the Home Championship.

"That they won the match and with it the Championship, was due to a remarkable piece of late individualism by a half-back who was having his worst international to date – Duncan Edwards,"

Cyril Chapman wrote in the *Birmingham Post*. "With five minutes to go the left half-back came bursting through on his own, tearing past ineffective English forwards and astonished Scottish defenders alike, to let drive a shot of immense power which went in off a post. The Scotland goalkeeper had no hope of saving."

Duncan's captain, Billy Wright, was in awe. "That is the sort of game he revelled in," he said. "We had not been playing well but Duncan somehow kept us going. I have a photograph at home taken during the match of me on my backside and Duncan picking up the pieces. Duncan was a kind of footballer's footballer because he had absolutely everything. He had class, control, skill and craft. He was as hard as nails and tackled like a demon. He was 13 stones of solid muscle, totally nerveless and very mature... he just loved football."

"It was a terrific shot," said Tom Finney. "It went in like a bullet. For a youngster to come into the side and play at Wembley and be so outstanding, it was something we hadn't seen for some time."

Edwards, the man of the hour, could add two newspaper clippings to his collection that week. First he was featured in Alan Forward's 'personality spot' in the *Mirror*. "He's the biggest Busby Babe of them all – and probably the brightest," Forward wrote. "No wonder Manchester United's manager, Matt Busby, once said: 'I have never seen anything quite like Duncan Edwards.' Today this giant has the soccer world at his feet. In an age of colourless youngsters, he stands out as a positive, cheeky, cheerful personality. Never over-awed, yet never over-confident, Edwards is the complete footballer... Strong in the tackle, a master in the air, a dynamite shot with either foot, he is always quick to spot the right thing to do. The lad who played for England at 18 was only narrowly pipped by Tom Finney last week for the 'Footballer of the Year' trophy. He need not worry. For he is certain to win that title one day."

In the *Daily Herald* there was 'The Duncan Edwards Story':

Without the high-powered publicity which turns young men of his age into film stars, the hullabaloo, the baring of his private life, displays of temperament, and gossip paragraphs in the papers – without all these things, Duncan Edwards has become the hero of a million people. He is more than that. More than a great footballer. To thousands of youngsters he is more than an idol. He is their ideal. They hold up a mirror to themselves and hope to see his reflection staring back. Yet despite all this admiration, this unaffected young man, whose like has never before been seen in football, refuses to talk about the game he loves away from the ground. In fact, apart from a list of Manchester United's fixtures hanging in the kitchen, there is nothing in his parents' home which has a bearing on football. Duncan's badges, international caps, photographs and scrapbooks are locked away.

With six months to go to his 21st birthday, Duncan Edwards is within reach of one of our national sport's greatest honours – a cup-winner's medal. The chance comes to claim it when he plays for Manchester United in the cup final next month. I expected to find there was nothing in the Duncan Edwards legend beyond the obvious facts... that he is a big lad endowed by Nature with a big heart to match his husky frame, and a gift for controlling and kicking a ball extraordinarily well. How wrong I was!

Hard work marked everything he did at school, as Mr Jimmy Patrick Murphy, the Welshman who is Manchester United's assistant manager, found when he made enquiries about the boy before signing him. His teachers still remember how expert Duncan was at folk-dancing. "So light-footed, you know, so nimble." As for football, Mr Booth recalls that he was "a pure fanatic in his treatment of the game." After every match they would return to the school and go over every move together to correct mistakes.

Duncan's path to fame was cut out for him when he was only 12. Reg Priest, Manchester United's Midland representative, sent a report to the club: "Have today seen a schoolboy who merits special watching."

From then on his progress was carefully checked. Reg Priest watched him play 20 times. The shrewd men who were building the finest football team this century investigated his background, because they place as much emphasis on character as ability.

They were satisfied with what they discovered. And when Duncan left school at Easter, 1952, his destination was Manchester. His success since has been meteoric. But it hasn't affected him. A group of his old teachers follow him around to see him play. When Duncan meets one of them after the game he says: "Good afternoon, Sir," as deferentially as any well-mannered schoolboy. Yes, it has been triumph all the way.

There was to be no let-up in proceedings. Just five days after that thrilling goal against Scotland at Wembley, Duncan was playing the biggest club game of his career at the Bernabeu stadium.

Matt Busby had been to see Real Madrid's second leg with Nice. He was so impressed by Alfredo Di Stéfano's two-goal display that he said, "I have never seen a better player."

Busby, though, was less than impressed with other factors waiting for him in Spain. He instructed players to drink bottled mineral water and to even use it to clean their teeth, and also instructed the manager of the Fénix Hotel to tell his cook that only "English-style meals" for his players would do.

United's players were in awe of the vast stands of the stadium as they arrived a few hours before kick-off. The concrete of the steep terraces seemed like marble under the sunlight.

Busby's gameplan was to have Colman watching Di Stéfano. He was not going to make too many tactical concessions, as he wanted to see just how good his own players could be. Just before the pre-match talks from Busby and Murphy, there was a knock on the dressing room door. It was a couple of Real officials, here to supply photographs of the 11 players on the team-sheet to prove it was the team who would be playing – and asking United to provide the same. Busby didn't have them.

"When we get back to the hotel after the game," he said, "you are welcome to examine the players' passports. That is the best I can do for you."

For the first hour, United held their own. But when Héctor Rial scored in the 61st minute, they discovered what 135,000 jubilant Spanish fans sounded like – and then conceded another within two minutes when Di Stéfano evaded the attention of his shadow for a moment. The English side were rattled and it was almost three – Byrne and Wood got in a muddle, but Edwards was on hand to clear off the line. He was not going to give the game up just yet.

Psychology is a funny thing in football. At 2-0 up, players and supporters can relax and lose some of their previous intensity. It can offer a trailing team a way back as long as they are ambitious and confident. United were. They hit the post. They had a penalty appeal turned down. And then Tommy Taylor scored. In the heat of the moment, there is a rush of blood. United, young as they were, felt seven minutes was long enough to try and get an equaliser. Madrid, experienced as they were, counted on that impetuosity, and scored within 60 seconds of the restart to restore the two-goal advantage they would take to Manchester.

After the game, George Follows reported that United's players were upset by the referee because of "many mysterious handling offences attributed to Duncan Edwards." Duncan himself admitted: "We simply did not get going until they went 2-0 in front, and by then it was a little too late."

His performance was the most redeeming aspect of United's evening, according to the English press. One described him as "like a tank", Don Davies commended his "oak-tree strength" while Henry Rose's take was to "Salute Duncan Edwards who performed noble deeds in defence."

Bobby Charlton believed the performance was proof that Busby's handling of Duncan's career had been spot on. "As he proved when he came to face the cream of European football in Real Madrid, he was simply beyond intimidation," he said. "Victory was not a challenge but a right. There was no point in holding him back. The old arguments about carefully nurturing talent didn't apply in his extraordinary case. Those high crowds came to see United's youth footballers because they were fascinated by gauging their progress… but Duncan was plainly already a finished article."

Off the pitch, the strange sportsmanship, or gamesmanship, continued at a post-match banquet where all of the United players were presented with a gold watch.

Just like the Bilbao first leg, United travelled back to Manchester already looking at the return. There were still four league games to play – a spell in which they could win the league – but even club captain Roger Byrne described it as "the least glamorous" of their ambitions now.

Taylor scored twice, and Edwards hit another post-rattling drive, in a 2-0 win at Luton. "Duncan Edwards and Roger Byrne completely blunted Luton's danger right-wing pair," wrote *The People*'s Larry Lorne after Busby's side had put themselves on the brink of retaining the title. "Three minutes from the end, Edwards came within inches of repeating that wonder goal he snatched for England last week. Awarded a free-kick just outside the penalty area, Edwards smashed in a mighty left-foot shot which almost snapped a post off at its base."

It was then time for the second part of the *Herald*'s Duncan Edwards story, written by John Bragg:

I must admit that I expected to find Duncan Edwards suffering from an inflated ego. Here you have a boy who, within five years of leaving school, has the world of football at his feet and the applause of thousands ringing in his ears. Manchester today is football crazy. Every youngster in the city wants to play for the fabulous United. The players are feted, and swamped with invitations to parties. Duncan Edwards enjoys his share of the fuss. He goes to parties… and is always one of the first to slip away. He has made friends with young people whose parents have means vastly superior to those of his own family. It is typical of Edwards that he takes those friends with him when he visits his mother and father in their home on a council estate in Dudley. This is the tribute he earns from Matt Busby, the Manchester United manager: "He is the greatest player of his age I have ever seen. Yet, although he has soared up among the stars, his feet are still on the ground." And assistant manager Jimmy Murphy, says of him: "One in a million." Sportswriters say he cannot be faulted, either as a player or an individual.

I hope I have managed to convey the essential fairness that stamps everything Duncan Edwards does. He shuns publicity. He doesn't seem to know what temperament is. He plays wherever Manchester United want him to play... without a murmur. He was just the same at school. When Duncan first went to Manchester after leaving school, he started work as a joiner. The following September, just before his 16th birthday, he asked to join United's ground staff. He was paid 50s. a week to sweep the terraces and clean players' boots. One pair of boots he used to clean belonged to Henry Cockburn, who played for England. On April 4, 1953, Cockburn was out of the first team and the ground-staff boy was there in his place. A new star had arrived.

United won at Burnley – Billy Whelan getting a hat-trick – on Good Friday, meaning Saturday would be excellent if they could defeat Sunderland at Old Trafford. It was. United were a goal up early on through Whelan and in the last 16 minutes hit one of those 1-2-3 Busby blasts that thrilled not only crowds but also young players, just like Duncan Edwards in 1948. Now he was one of the players scoring in one of these frenzies, as he notched his team's third of four with a 30-yard rocket that was rising all the way into the Stretford End and might have carried on into the Manchester Ship Canal had the net not stopped it. United were champions again – the second league title for the Busby Babes, and the third for the manager.

Chapter 17
Perpetual Motion

Manchester United's future continued to look rosy. While the first team were winning the league, the juniors were still thrilling in the Youth Cup. Jimmy Murphy's latest golden apples overcame Southampton in a goal-filled semi-final, entertaining greatly in the second leg, and Don Davies simply purred at their quality. "Had it not been for a little too much elevation in their sights United's sharp-shooters might have cracked half a dozen thrilling goals home in the first half-hour," he wrote in *The Guardian*. "This was from growing lads, not from seasoned professionals. The writer of these notes is at pains to stress that he is not given to flights of imagination. He merely feels it his simple duty to bear honest testimony to some of the most attractive football he has seen this season. They played with a zest which carried the spectators along with them in the stream of excitement."

The latest side had young forwards like Mark Pearson and Alex Dawson. United's early clinching of the league meant that Busby felt comfortable resting enough players to give Dawson his debut. Six players were missing against Burnley – Byrne, Edwards, Berry, Whelan, Taylor, Pegg – with, according to Frank McGhee of the *Mirror*, "bumps, bruises, strains and plain old-fashioned exhaustion": "With the League championship, the first leg of their fantastic treble, already so gloriously won, all six will probably be resting so as to be ready for the match of the year, the return European Cup semi-final against Real Madrid on Thursday."

The visit of Real Madrid became the first ever European Cup match at Old Trafford, owing to the recent installation of the floodlights.

Ahead of the game, Spanish newspaper *ABC* insisted that the occasional hostilities of the first game needn't be repeated: "The Manchester public has no reason to show an aggressive attitude... we trust that the European Cup, which in its first season was a tournament of perfect sportsmanship, will retain this character."

Matt Busby, though, followed Stan Cullis' lead in watering the Old Trafford pitch. On the morning of the game, Madrid representatives saw pictures of the sprinklers in the newspaper. No translation was necessary. They made their way to Old Trafford, demanding the sprinklers be turned off – or they would go home. United agreed. Not that they were helped at all – within 33 minutes they were 2-0 down to goals from Kopa and Rial. It could have been more. "Nothing could have been more fortunate for United than the fact that the referee brought the ball back from a throw-in on the halfway line just as Edwards floored Gento in the penalty area with a reckless tackle," noted Don Davies.

It was 5-1 on aggregate to the Spanish giants. This time there could be no sage words that would turn things around. Even if Busby had felt the urge to abandon his previous cool approach and urge his players to 'give it to Duncan' in the Murphy fashion, even he would not have been able to turn the tie around in 45 minutes. Madrid's experience of playing in the competition, and experience in years, was far too great. It was all Busby could do to insist that his boys keep going because the crowd deserved a respectable result.

They achieved that. Taylor scored in the 62nd minute. Charlton in the 85th. United's players – dreaming of the impossible – became incensed with what they felt was time-wasting. "Duncan seemed to believe that left enough time to pull off something even more remarkable than the defeat of Bilbao," Charlton recalled. On one occasion, an Edwards cross was blocked by Manuel Torres. Torres stayed down, as if the ball was a bullet, causing an infuriated Edwards and Byrne to try to lift the player over the touchline. This was one game where Duncan's anxiety to win in hopeless circumstances caused the temper to flare. He'd never experienced anything like this and it did not feel good. United ended with a creditable 2-2 draw, but, according to reporters, deserved little credit.

"Manchester football fans helped to knock their own Red Devils out of the European Cup at Old Trafford last night – and threw away their own good name as sportsmen," wrote George Follows. "They were guilty of a squalid show of one-eyed partisanship, a public display of bad manners that made me ashamed to be English. They booed the players of Real Madrid when they did a victory dance at the end, though the Spaniards had well proved themselves the more skilful soccer-men. They cheered when Duncan Edwards fouled Mateos near the end of a game disfigured by 48 free-kicks. They incited Edwards and Roger Byrne to actions they will want to forget. Edwards lost his head. He attempted to drag injured Manuel Torres off the pitch so that the game could be restarted."

The tone was echoed by Desmond Hackett in the *Express*. "Let us candidly admit Manchester United were well and truly beaten by Real Madrid... Manchester United, the pride of English soccer, were given a public football lesson. Let us also feel heartily ashamed that after Real Madrid had so competently won this semi-final, the only thing this 62,000 crowd could do was to boo. I never felt more ashamed of any English soccer crowd."

United's players remained frustrated as they walked off the pitch. Edwards remarked that the game had been "damn rough" to Frank Swift, and Roger Byrne complained about "a lack of sportsmanship" from the holders.

"I'm a little disappointed at the team's failure to overcome such accomplished opposition," Busby sighed. "It was a great game between two great sides."

It had been an unforgettable experience for United's supporters, too, who had felt a slight sense of optimism with the second-half performance in that second leg. "Real Madrid had a great team," admits Tom Clare. "But United were learning. They went all out attack the first time and got caught out. Real started time-wasting with 15 minutes to go. Their right-back went down and was taking his time. Duncan came over with Roger Byrne and literally hoisted him over the touchline to get on with the game. He got some bad press for that."

So the great first voyage into European football ended with bitter anti-climax. The recriminations could last for however long the United players wished to console their bruised egos, but two things were true – Real Madrid were not bothered because they were in the final, and United had been beaten by a side who were both better and more experienced. United's players would have to hope that this experience would stand them in good stead for any future rematch.

Busby had a premonition that this temporary setback may yet come with long-term benefit. "Duncan was the most valuable member of one team I ever saw anywhere," said the manager. "He was worth two of most and two good ones at that. We seldom lost a match, but if we did, most players tried to banish defeat from their minds. Not Duncan. It didn't finish there. He regarded defeat as a personal reflection on himself. 'What am I doing letting that lot beat us?' he would say."

Sensing the line between exhaustion and frustration may be blurry, Busby continued to give most of his players the last couple of league games off. The reserves did well again – winning at Cardiff, and then drawing at home to West Brom. Alex Dawson scored in both games, in the latter netting United's final, and 103rd, league goal of the season – a new club record.

Chapter 18
Calypso

And so to Wembley. In the 1970s, it became popular for clubs who had reached the FA Cup final to release a song. Some were better than others. United did it more often than most clubs, releasing songs in 1976, 1983, 1985, 1994, 1995 and 1996. Some were good. Others, well... But some things can just never beat the first time around. The *Manchester United Calypso*, written by Trinidad-born Edric Connor, had enjoyed its first airing at Old Trafford over the public address system on the day United won the title against Sunderland, with the lyrics printed in the match programme that day: *"If ever they're playing in your town, you must get to that football ground. Take a look and you will see, football taught by Matt Busby. Manchester, Manchester United. A bunch of bouncing Busby Babes, they deserve to be knighted. It's the greatest thrill that you've ever seen, they are known as a soccer machine. They are the best, there is no doubt, so raise a cheer and give a shout, for Manchester, Manchester United..."*

Though a little late in the season to truly replace "U-NI-TED" in the stands, some gave the chorus a go, and it is fair to say that a new song was born. The refrain would, in actuality, be more common after the turn of the 21st century, though that was probably in relation to the jovial tone and its relation to events to follow.

Manchester United arrived for their FA Cup final completely transformed from the side who had been here nine years earlier. The only thing that remained was that Busby style and Frank McGhee of the *Mirror* felt that would be the decisive factor. "Sudden death at Wembley," he wrote. "That is what I expect to see on the famous lush green battleground this afternoon – with Aston Villa as the victims. I expect to see them killed stone cold dead by a couple of quick-stabbing goals in the first half-hour. By 3.30 this afternoon Manchester United should be well on the way to victory... Their achievements already this season in the League, the European Cup and the FA Cup have set them apart. A win will place them alone on a proud pinnacle of glory, above every other team in British Soccer history... Another vital match-winning factor on United's side is the occasion itself. The arrogant young men of Manchester are used to the big matches. The size of the crowd, the desperate importance of it all won't cause any dry mouths, stomach cramps and trembling knees in THEIR camp. They will walk out with the easy familiarity of men who know the dressing rooms, the long walk from the tunnel and the billiard-table turf intimately from international experience."

McGhee had predicted it would be all over by 3.30pm – but the game had effectively gone from United at 3.06pm, when Peter McParland headed a cross towards goal. It was comfortable for Ray Wood, who collected the ball with two hands – but then McParland inexplicably decided to charge for the ball. He would deny any malice but it was clear that the goalkeeper had full control. The only thing to be gained was hurting Wood – and that objective was accomplished, as United's stopper collapsed with a broken cheekbone. "The ball was, in cricket parlance, 'dead', and there was no danger to United," said Matt Busby. "McParland's motive for his extraordinary action remains a mystery, but what a costly business it proved for my club."

A year earlier, Bert Trautmann suffered a broken bone in his neck after colliding with a Birmingham player in the final – on that occasion, City of course won, but it had breathed new life into the conversation about substitutes, especially for goalkeepers, with the potential to ruin a game being so high if one was hurt. Only that season, of course, Wood had suffered an injury in the Charity Shield, with City sympathetic enough on the day to allow United to replace their goalkeeper.

The rules did not allow for that on FA Cup final day, even though Gordon Clayton had travelled just in case. So United were immediately down to 10 men and weakened further still when Jackie Blanchflower was forced to go in goal, and Duncan Edwards had to move to centre-half – but not before he had a few choice words.

"Only once did I see him lose his temper, in the FA Cup final," recalls Wilf McGuinness. "He lost it with McParland – but, luckily for the Villa player, he had regained his composure by the time he reached him!"

Edwards went on record to state how much he detested this sort of action. "If there is one subject I do feel vehement about it is the charging of goalkeepers," he said. "By all means harry the goalkeeper, worry him, chase him, but please don't bounce him on his back every time he gets the ball in his hands... an unfair charge has only to be slightly awry in its timing and it has put out of action the most vital man on the other side. There is little fun playing against a side mortally handicapped, and, as gallant as these 10-man fights may be, football has enough to offer without relying on them for thrills. The ironic thing is that when I play for England on the Continent I am told to take it easy with the goalkeeper."

United made it to half-time level with 10 men. Busby was keen to see how Wood was doing. "Ted Dalton, the United physiotherapist, tested Wood by throwing and kicking the ball to him, but poor Ray saw no more than a couple out of every six balls," Busby recalled. "It was a depressing session, staged on that deserted grass strip outside the packed stadium, but a young cockney kid did relieve tension somewhat when he told Ray, 'Look, mister. My mates and me have got a game on just round the corner. You can come and play with us if you like.' Imagine the situation. A hundred yards away 100,000 feverish spectators, who had paid £50,000 for the privilege, were waiting to see Ray Wood return to the cup final arena... but, instead, Ray had been offered a kick-about with a dozen cockney youngsters on a deserted patch of grass. The offer was turned down, but not too abruptly!"

Wood was brought back on to play on the left wing but was a passenger. United were spirited but Villa's patience finally won out as McParland – of course – scored a double in quick succession to move the game firmly in their favour. McParland then went through to score a hat-trick, but Edwards was in no mood to allow more insult to be added to injury, and threw himself into a goal-denying tackle.

With seven minutes left United won their 10th corner of the half. Duncan, so desperate to turn the result around, had now abandoned all reason and had become that boy on the playground, taking the corners instead of being the lighthouse to be targeted. However, where there is a will, there is a way, and Edwards' corner was knocked into the net by Taylor. Game on. Busby asked if Wood could stand the last few minutes in goal. Try as they might, the Babes could not get an equaliser, and cup heartache was theirs again in the cruellest fashion.

"I felt very tired midway through the second half," admitted Duncan after the match. "It had thrown a big responsibility on our 10-man team... I still felt we might get the equaliser."

After the match, what had happened to Wood was, of course, the major talking point. Should there be substitutes? Interestingly, there was also a split about whether or not Busby himself was to blame. Was he irresponsible to put Wood back on the pitch? Alternatively, surely if he was fit to go back on, he should have been back in goal much earlier?

"Substitutes? I say the soccer bosses are crazy and even cruel to deny replacements for injured players," Desmond Hackett wrote.

"Did manager Matt Busby boob by not putting Wood back into goal earlier than the last seven minutes? Manchester United fans turned on Busby and accused him of losing the game because he did not make the Wood switch sooner. Manager Busby was quite correct and certainly humane."

Why was Wood allowed back in goal at all? Club captain Roger Byrne: "Because in the last few minutes it didn't matter how many Villa scored. We could have stood up to extra-time in spite of being a man short for so long. At half-time I looked ahead to that possibility and told the lads not to chase too much, but to play to one another so that we wouldn't be exhausted."

Busby told journalist Frank McGhee that Wood "did not know where he was, why he was there – or what was happening around him". Meanwhile, McGhee insisted: "If it had never happened, I am convinced that United would have fully justified my pre-match forecast of an easy victory. Duncan Edwards, instead of being at centre-half, would have been up supporting every United attack... that forecast of mine so upset the Villa players that – according to goalkeeper Nigel Sims – they planned to throw me in their bath if they saw me afterwards. Sorry to disappoint you Villa fans, but I walked out of Wembley bone dry – and unrepentant."

Duncan would be unrepentant too. He remained emphatically against the charging of goalkeepers, but calmed down sufficiently to offer the ultimate sporting gesture. "I would also like to thank that great sportsman, Duncan Edwards, for the way he came over to me to congratulate me as we left the field," McParland said. "There were no hard feelings." Edwards had heard that McParland had been distraught in the dressing room at half-time and it had convinced him that he had not intended to hurt Wood.

So how did Duncan do in his first cup final? In the *Express*, Henry Rose harshly wrote that Edwards "was not the giant he was when pressed to play at centre-half at Bournemouth in the FA Cup. He tackled strongly and fairly, broke up repeated Villa attacks, but did not make the impact on the game I thought he would in United's heartbreaking uphill struggle."

It would surely be fairer to say that Duncan's one-man show was inspirational; that he was simultaneously the reason why Villa's scoreline remained relatively low and why United remained competitive, despite him having to command the play as a wing-half from centre-back.

"In the cup final when he had to drop back to centre-half... the ground he had to cover that day," Tom Clare sighs. "Phenomenal. He glided past players and would leave them for dead. He was desperate to rescue that game."

He almost did it.

Duncan would later make two statements which revealed much. The first was directly about the final. "The most heartbreaking defeat I ever figured in was when we were beaten by Aston Villa in the cup final," he said. "There it was, the great anti-climax. You would be justified in thinking that our dressing-room as we trooped off the field after receiving our medals was like a mortuary. You would be wrong... the boys made their usual cracks as they packed their gear. There was no sign of depression. Rather was there an attitude of 'we'll be back.' Everyone was quite confident that this was only a temporary setback that had merely delayed the arrival of the cup at Old Trafford. When we returned to Manchester to a civic welcome, the feeling was even more marked. I can remember thinking as we stood listening to the thousands of our supporters as they cheered us, 'They can be like this when we have been beaten. By golly, they deserve the cup and we'll get it for them.'"

He also said, perhaps even more tellingly: "Defeats will come, and when they do accept them as quietly and philosophically as I hope you do your victories."

It's an old adage but unavoidably true; you learn more in defeat than you do in victory. Defeat can be literal, in the case of a football match. It can be overcoming a setback, such as receiving personal criticism. It can even be in taking on advice. There was evidence that even someone with the reputation Duncan had from a very early age could absorb advice. He realised Eric Booth was right when it came to his position in the team. He'd learned through United's growing up period of 1954 and 1955. He'd taken the defeats. He'd experienced players almost twice his age singling him out for an aggressive welcome to senior football. Every time, the response had been emphatic. With normal footballers these things are gradual. Duncan knew as soon as the final whistle went. He knew what would need to be right next time. If he could play the 90 minutes again straight after a defeat he would. When he predicted that United would bring a cup for their supporters, this was no flippant point. He meant it.

He was itching for the new season to get started, but before that, he had England duty to attend to. The United players had been accused of looking leggy in their last few matches, and it was suggested this was a reason for their failure to win the FA or European Cup. England won 5-1 against Ireland – with Tommy Taylor scoring a hat-trick – but the narrative remained, with Hackett commenting: "The big boy from Dudley looked slow and stale after his heavy season and a rest would probably do him good."

But Duncan was not only required for the senior England team, he was also called into the under-23 side which was touring straight after the older players had finished for the season. And there were two more World Cup qualifiers to go before that was done. The first was in Denmark, a game which marked Stanley Matthews' last-ever international. Matthews was a paragon of sportsmanship, and of course the Danes had previously expressed their idolatry of Edwards, too, but on this evening, they were inclined to boo the Manchester United man for a foul in the first half and then for what they deemed to be some tackles that went beyond the letter of the law. "He can have no complaints about his treatment from the crowd," Hackett said. "England will go down in the record books as the winners against Denmark in the World Cup qualifying series tonight. They will also go down as one of the poorest teams ever to put on the white shirts of England. I just don't know what got into them."

It was a similar story in Ireland, as England grabbed a last-minute equaliser to qualify for the 1958 World Cup, but earned little praise, especially Edwards, who put in an early crunching tackle on his club-mate Whelan. In the *Express*, Hackett wrote: "Duncan Edwards performed with the air of a man who is tired of it all. And once again the big boy Edwards was endlessly booed for fouling." The afternoon was also notable for the long-awaited international debut of David Pegg, who had become the bene-ficiary of Matthews' retirement.

Chapter 19
Lucky?

No sooner had he been promoted to the senior England side, than David Pegg was returning to the under-23s. Their 1957 tour of eastern Europe was already underway, with a game in Bulgaria played on the same day as England qualified for the World Cup. Pegg was accompanied by Duncan, Ronnie Clayton and England manager Walter Winterbottom on the trip to Romania via Belgium. What followed was extraordinary.

"Whenever we played for England we roomed together," Clayton recalled. "On pre-match nights, Dunc and I would wander off for a quiet meal – and to talk about football. Only one thing in this world gave Dunc a feeling of fear – the knowledge that he was having to fly. He could never quite quell those butterflies in his stomach as he walked up the aircraft steps."

Fear of flying is not uncommon. Duncan had not had pleasant experiences of flying, or even international travel in general. Mostly, though, the fear is in our heads, and not related to actual physical danger to our lives; and even in the 1950s, when commercial air travel was a fairly new thing, the completion of a journey without incident was common enough to take for granted. That was the case for the first part of the journey to Belgium. After refuelling, the plane was back in the air.

"On the second leg of the flight from Brussels to Bucharest, the pilot apparently got a little off course," Clayton said. "We didn't know this at the time, but we did get a shock when one of the players exclaimed: 'Look – out of the window!' And – only a couple of yards away, it seemed – we saw another aircraft, bearing on its fuselage a red star. Even as we sat, wondering what was going to happen, we got the answer – in the shape of tracer bullets which began to zip across the nose of our aircraft. Suddenly the MiG (Mikoyan-Gurevich, a Soviet fighter aircraft) shot beneath our plane – and we zoomed upwards. We must have missed a midair collision by inches.

"Dunc and I, as usual, were sitting next to each other, towards the rear of the plane. Dunc turned to me and, in a voice which sounded strangely unlike his own, said: 'You don't look so good.' In a faint voice I managed to answer: 'Neither do you.' I felt like being sick. And from the look of him Dunc's stomach was tied in knots, too. We felt even worse when seconds later the MiG appeared again, zooming above and below us. It seemed uncomfortably close, and someone suggested that the pilot was trying to force us to land. But our own pilot wasn't having any. Calmly, he spoke to us over the intercom: 'There's no need to worry.' And he kept an even keel and stayed steadfastly on course. For 15 minutes that MiG tried everything to shake us out of our steady flight; and as we sweated through the whole ghastly performance it seemed like 15 hours. Suddenly the ordeal was over. The 'enemy' plane had vanished. And we breathed again."

Upon landing, Duncan confided in *Express* writer Bob Pennington. Pennington asked if it would be okay to report the story – but Edwards asked him not to. It was already informally known that Duncan hated flying. Even going to Ringway Airport with Molly to watch the flights take off sometimes made him apprehensive. Whether or not this particular story would be one of embarrassment more than it might stir some political unrest was not quite certain – Duncan was due to be demobbed, and may well have had that on his mind too.

This would have been a traumatic event for anyone, and yet, it was not Duncan's last brush with death on this day. On the evening in Bucharest, some of the players went out to the circus, where Ronnie remembered how Duncan had, "for the second time within a matter of hours… escaped death by inches". "Duncan was finicky in a number of ways," Ronnie called. "Finicky about his food, for example. And finicky about animals, too. They were all right, so long as they stayed their distance. Circus animals at any rate. And at that circus he was sitting too close to them for comfort. His seat was pretty near the spot where the animals made their entrance into the arena. I was sitting next to him, and felt somewhat relieved, too, when he suggested that we should move a few yards farther from the entrance. It was a good job he decided to make that move. For if he had stayed in his original seat he would have been crushed to death. As it was, he made the switch only seconds before the accident happened. For a giant spotlight toppled from its mast high above the area and crashed – smack into the seat where Dunc had been sitting. That seat was splintered into hundreds of pieces – and if Dunc had stayed there's no doubt he would have been crushed to a pulp."

Lucky Duncan Edwards. The players had training the next day, and 24 hours later they were in action against Romania. England had Edwards in six at left-half but looked toothless up front. Bob Pennington pondered: "Considering our limited resources here, there was one obvious choice at number nine – Duncan Edwards. I was told officially today that Edwards does not like playing in the attack. He must be England's regular left-half for the next 10 years. But he should have been switched in Bucharest."

In *The People*, Maurice Smith complained about the presence of Edwards on this trip – not for his performance, but for his own benefit. "Duncan Edwards, Johnny Haynes, Alan Hodgkinson, Derek Tapscott – the bright young men of British football – are being flogged to death," he blasted. "I ACCUSE the FAs of England and Wales of dereliction of duty; of cheapening national prestige. I accuse the English FA of suicidal short-sightedness;

of crass stupidity in taking part in meaningless International 'B' team tours... with players who would be better off now lazing on a seaside beach... Duncan Edwards, in cup-ties, European Cup-ties and league games for Manchester United and oddly-assorted international matches for England, has played his heart out in nearly 70 burning, blistering, nerve-racking top-class games in 10 months. On top of that, Edwards has been playing twice a week, on average, with his Army unit."

Despite that, and despite Romania illegally making a substitution at half-time, England won 1-0 with a goal from Johnny Haynes two minutes from time. "Edwards, at walking pace after collapsing with cramp, whispered to Haynes to be ready for their free-kick routine," Pennington wrote. "The Romanians lined up and braced themselves to be blasted by the famed Edwards power drive. Instead, Edwards gave a mere flick of the ball to the right. The waiting Haynes cracked the ball high into the corner of the net with his right foot. A handful of Union Jacks waved like fury. I have never heard 20 people make so much noise."

Frank McGhee described the goal as "the best I have seen this season". Despite this, McGhee described Edwards as the only player "below form", adding: "The strain of his tremendously busy season is written plainly on him. In the 75th minute, Edwards collapsed with cramp. In the second half he never managed to raise enough steam for one of his dramatic dashes upfield."

In the first half, Edwards had still been driving his team forward. Walter Winterbottom recalled: "There was a moment where he dribbled up to the edge of the area, could have scored himself, but he wanted to bring David Pegg, his team-mate from United, in, and he passed to him to involve him in the game. That's how generous he was in spirit. We had to try and correct him. We told him, 'When you go on a dribble like that Duncan, for heaven's sake, go all the way... shoot!' This became a feature of the England players. When they saw him go on a dribble they'd shout, 'All the way Duncan'… and sure enough we went to Czechoslovakia soon after and he scored two goals like this."

On the day before the game in Bratislava, Duncan and Ronnie went for a walk and found themselves at a boating lake. They decided to have a go on the water. "Trevor Smith and Dick Neal, of Birmingham, were with Duncan and myself on that boating expedition," Clayton remembered. "The fresh air and exercise seemed just what the doctor ordered. But, of course, we had to start fooling around. And the boat was rocking so much that Dunc feared we would capsize. In no uncertain manner he told us that he would take over and row the boat back to shore. And, with determination showing in his every stroke, he began to send the oars cleaving through the water. We began to skim along, and there's no doubt we would have made the shore in record time, only Dunc underestimated his own strength.

"Suddenly, there was a double crack and the oars had snapped like matchsticks. The boat rocked even more fearsomely than when we had been in command… somehow we paddled our way slowly back to the bank. And there the boatman was waiting for us with a torrent of abuse. It cost the distinguished and disgusted Duncan Edwards something like the equivalent of £4 in English money to soothe the outraged boatman's feelings and pay towards the cost of replacing those oars!"

If he was tired of either playing or the rowing, the Czechoslovakia game seemed to be an outlier; perhaps it was the exhilaration of it being the last game of a long season, so everything would be left on the pitch. "Boom-Boom Edwards beats Czech tricks" read the headline.

"Two cannonball goals from 25 and 35 yards by left-half Duncan Edwards shattered the Czechs to give Young England a power and prestige win," one report stated. "There was plenty to cheer. Edwards was inspired by his 25-yard right-foot smash-hit after eight minutes. He roused himself of the lethargy that had settled on him at the close of an exacting season. No wonder the Czechs called Edwards "Pan (Mr) Boom Boom" after blasting a 35-yard second goal in the 51st minute with his left-foot."

Jimmy Armfield recalled it fondly. "He was the difference between the two sides," he said. "He scored both goals with terrific shots from outside the box, and every time he had the ball the Czechs went into immediate panic. It seemed to me that they were physically afraid. Every time he strode forward not one defender would risk the challenge. And that's how he got both goals. Duncan was perpetual motion. That came from his strength but also from his dedication. He trained hard and his superb fitness made a perfect partner for his tremendous confidence. It was an almost unchallengeable combination."

Peter Lorenzo of the *Herald* described Edwards as "so much the strong man behind this heart-warming England display", continuing: "Deadly Duncan so demoralised this sad-faced, dispirited red-shirted outfit that after the second of his cannonball specials had nearly shot its way out of the Iron Curtain, the Czechs put on a substitute keeper, Hason, to replace a very ruffled man in black, Rufus."

From the touchline, Edwards had heralded the cry of 'All the way, Dunc'; he was hoping that the following season, he would be going 'all the way' with Manchester United.

Chapter 20
A Standard Of Excellence

The manner in which the Busby Babes had illuminated European football encouraged eyes from foreign clubs to observe their talent. Italy was the headline destination for John Charles, and it seemed as though other clubs were keen to follow Juventus' lead in the acquisition of the legendary Welsh star.

In late May 1957, Inter Milan made an offer of £65,000 for Tommy Taylor. "The offer is so tempting that I cannot resist it," Taylor told the *Manchester Guardian*. Matt Busby responded with some emphasis, "We will never agree to the transfer." Busby pre-empted any further transfer speculation with a stern warning. "Duncan Edwards is not for sale."

Busby was looking forward to finally having Duncan back around the club full-time. "In peacetime, two years' national service is not a good thing for a professional footballer," Busby said, "yet some young players have returned home much better chaps than they were when they were recruited."

The United boss dismissed any concerns about Edwards being tired. "Work-rate would never even have had to be mentioned to Duncan," he said. "He couldn't have enough matches. And he couldn't find enough work in any of them. He was utterly indefatigable... he was full of life, full of football. He used to come and ask me could he play in the youth team. I know players can have too much football, but when I hear some of the complaints I always think of Duncan Edwards. He played more than 90 games in one extended season for United and England teams. And no player did more per match than Duncan. He was never in an ounce of trouble. He lived for the game."

On May 31st, Duncan flew back to England, and travelled to Nesscliffe for one last time. At 2pm on June 6th, 1957, he was officially demobbed from the army. An article in the *Express* carried the headline: "A Soldier Ends Double Life: From Now On It's Soccer", continuing: "At 2 o'clock yesterday, he stopped being a 9/- (45p) a day 'Lance Jack' and became once again the full-time soccer star said to be worth £50,000 in the European Common Market – Soccer Branch."

Edwards himself said: "Naturally I am glad that my National Service is over, but I have been treated marvellously and I have no complaints."

Duncan made the most of his summer relaxing before what was sure to be an incredible season. He went to Jersey for a brief holiday and a charity football match, where he bumped into Peter McParland, and showed there were no ill-feelings. "The big Dudley lad was a good friend of mine," McParland said. "I had some grand times with him in Jersey. I can remember him now. His burly frame, clad in singlet and brief shorts, came bursting into the hotel room I was sharing with Ray Hogg, all set to take us round to the local football ground."

In the real business, United had the defence of their league to look forward to, which was almost taken for granted these days. But Edwards, like his team-mates, was desperate to win the FA Cup and even more keen to come face-to-face with Real Madrid, who had gone on to retain the European Cup after knocking out the Babes. For United's stars, their dented pride meant that winning against the Spanish side would probably mean as much to them as winning the trophy. The two would probably have to come hand-in-hand anyway. Then, after all that, there was the World Cup in Sweden, and England's run of good results boded well.

In July, Duncan and Molly became godparents to Julie, the daughter of Molly's best friend Josephine. At the christening Duncan made efforts to not be the centre of attention. "Molly was my closest friend and they came as a couple," Josephine said. "He was smashing, a very kind young man and very genuine. He sat in the kitchen drinking milk because he was teetotal. He knew that he was a big star, but didn't want the day to be all about him." Josephine revealed the pair had got engaged – altogether it was never made official with an announcement.

Ronnie Clayton got married, and Duncan was there to wish his pal well, buying Ronnie and his new bride a full tea-service. "Judging by the quality of the china, it must have cost him more than a few pounds, too," Clayton said.

The Manchester United first-team dressing room was perfectly composed as far as Matt Busby was concerned. The average age of 24 meant there was still at least three or four years until their peak should be expected to begin. They were already the best in England, arguably the best of all time from the British Isles, and may well follow that up with becoming the best in Europe. And that was now. How good could they be in three years?

The journey to realising that potential meant ironing out any kinks. Roger Byrne had been cited as a possible weak link but he was an England regular and club captain. He and Johnny Berry were the remaining players from the 1952 title-winning side, and perhaps most importantly he was a Manchester lad who had not been brought up on the indoctrination from Murphy and Whalley about Busby being God-like. Byrne would answer back. Busby appreciated that. He considered it healthy to have a voice that would not be too deferential. On the other side of the pitch, Bill Foulkes was already being earmarked for a place in the centre of defence. Still, he'd have to wait for an opening in the middle – it was a competitive area, as Mark Jones found out to his cost, with Jackie Blanchflower waiting in the wings.

Up front, United could not boast richer talent. Berry and Pegg were as good outside players as anyone in the country. John Doherty and Albert Scanlon could step in and deputise superbly. In the inside-forward and centre-forward positions Busby was almost embarrassingly blessed. Taylor was clearly number one in the middle but Colin Webster and Alex Dawson had already demonstrated a taste for the occasion too. One week Taylor might find Viollet and Whelan alongside him. Another he might find Whelan and Charlton.

Perhaps the biggest concern Busby had was the increasing injury issues of Ray Wood. Was there someone more durable, more intimidating? Could there possibly be a way of a goalkeeper adding something to the outfield? Regardless, Wood had recovered from his fractured cheekbone and was not about to be dropped just yet.

Busby's half-back line was even healthier than the forward selection. Wilf McGuinness and Freddie Goodwin were ready for First Division football but in Eddie Colman and Duncan Edwards, United boasted, respectively, one of the, and *the*, outstanding half-back in the country. This was Colman's third season and all he had tasted was success. He was to go on a learning curve, but as far as Duncan Edwards was concerned, he was now at a peak and getting better with experience. Of all of the talent in this remarkable team, he was the one. He was the driving force in comfortable games to ensure standards were maintained. He was the one encouraging his sides to win in style like Busby wanted, or simply heavily, like Murphy demanded. If standards dropped it would be Edwards showing his colleagues what was expected.

He had grown up with these lads. This was his team. He was immensely proud that they were recognised as the best in the country. It was Duncan believing his team could overcome a three-goal deficit against the European champions with 10 minutes to go. It was Duncan who believed his team, even without a goalkeeper, could recover a two-goal deficit with seven minutes to go in a cup final.

Busby and Murphy could well have created something extraordinary if Duncan Edwards did not exist. They would have created a team of style and resilience. But what Duncan Edwards provided the Busby Babes with was more than style and resilience. It was the personality which said – *why should we be defined by what is expected? What does it matter if we are three goals down and they are the best team? We are here to win.* Bobby Charlton remembered it as extraordinary even amongst this level of talent. And that was the standard being set by the best player in the team. A new standard of excellence was expected. If Duncan Edwards was putting in this commitment, no other player on the team could afford *not* to. He was redefining on the pitch what it meant to represent Manchester United.

He was the greatest player in the greatest club side, arguably, of all time. The United players knew that. They could feel the aura. "I don't think we'll ever see someone like Duncan again," said Bill Foulkes. "It was really incredible for someone of his age and his maturity both physically and mentally. Although he was unassuming he was very confident. He was a man who knew what he wanted. Everyone respected him, as a person and a player. He was the perfect player. He could do everything."

Any summary of Edwards from his team-mates came with similar descriptions. "I once asked Jimmy Murphy who was the greatest footballer he had ever seen," said Albert Scanlon. "He said, 'I've seen them all and Duncan Edwards must be the greatest of them all.' Give him a ball and it was as though a whole new horizon opened up before him, because what he did with it was magic. I once saw him in a European Cup match run all the way down the field from the halfway line, with players coming at him from all sides and there he was bouncing the ball on his head as though he was just at a practice match! That man was magic."

Portsmouth had won back-to-back league titles in 1949 and 1950. Arsenal won three titles consecutively in the Thirties, inspired by the prolific goalscoring of Cliff Bastin. Duncan

Edwards, with two league titles, was only 20. He was re-writing history. The football writers knew what they were living through.

"It takes most footballers a lifetime to achieve the success of Duncan Edwards," read a feature in *Charles Buchan's Football Monthly*. "The Duncan Edwards record is astonishing for so young a boy. It has come about because this tough product of the Black Country not only has above-average skill, but is the most powerful footballer in Britain... probably in the world. He could justly be described as the Iron Man of the England and Manchester United teams. Good and not-so-good footballers come and go as frequently as buses. Only great footballers stand the test of time. Duncan Edwards has only just fallen out of the soccer cradle, yet already he qualifies for a top game. Matt Busby is firm in his opinion of the secret of Edwards' success: 'Power, ability, enthusiasm and character,' snaps Matt. 'He is the most complete footballer I have ever seen.' Matching Edwards with a shoulder-charge is like trying to check an advancing tank with a pea-shooter. Average opponents just bounce off him. You cannot help being thrilled by Edwards' play. Better still, you'd like him as a young man, a very human young man at that... Duncan Edwards cannot avoid publicity. He is respectful, but not over-friendly with football writers. Just as he doesn't resent a rough tackle, he doesn't wince under criticism."

The magazine also gave this description of his style: "Ideally built for the position, he also has the temperament of the great player, and the great virtue of consistency. Edwards has the happy knack of being able to vary his play to suit the occasion. He can be forceful when necessary, and artistic if desired. For his size, Duncan is amazingly quick on his feet. He has the foot-work of the professional boxer and the ball control of a first-class inside-forward. In fact, he is never more dangerous than when dashing through opposing defenders with the ball at his feet. But his biggest asset is his ability to part with the ball to advantage. Edwards has split-second timing in sending the ball through to his forwards. One of his specialities is the long, cross-field pass to the outside-right, made quickly and accurately."

United's pre-season consisted of a tour to Germany, where they played in Berlin and Hanover. In the first game against Berliner Stadtelf, United won 3-0, and all 60,000 in attendance were hoping that one of the many long range shots from 'Boom Boom' would go into the net – not that they were left disappointed when none did, as they had seen the great Duncan Edwards play for the famous Manchester United. As usual, Duncan had been embarrassed by the attention – when they had arrived at Tempelhof Airport, there were fans and journalists chanting "Boom Boom, Boom Boom!" Edwards asked journalist Frank Taylor if he would go out and distract them, but Taylor laughed, saying there was no way the crowd would fall for it. As Edwards reluctantly greeted the crowd, he made sure that all of his colleagues were in the photographs.

The champions started their title defence in menacing style against Leicester City thanks to a Whelan hat-trick. "The way United played the ball from man to man was uncanny," wrote Joe Hulme in *The People*. "They always had a man spare. The defence under pressure was an essence of coolness and those crosses from Duncan Edwards to outside-left Pegg were a delight."

Everton, once a team with a hex on United, were also beaten by three goals. Manchester City, once another bogey side, suffered the same fate.

"I remember talking to Jack Dyson, who played inside-left for City," remembers Tom Clare. "He said, 'Duncan was phenomenal. We at City used to lay traps for him. He had a habit of carrying the ball, so we'd let him have it until the 18-yard line and then we'd close him down. After a while it didn't work. He got wise to it. He would physically go through us.'"

The proof was here – after 15 minutes, anticipating that the City defence would sit back, Duncan played a one-two with

Whelan, beating the offside trap and scoring with a sensational shot from long range. United, with their star man in imperious form, won 4-1.

They were strolling 2-0 at Everton when Blanchflower had to come off injured. The hosts fought back to earn a 3-3 draw. However, Blanchflower was fit to play against Leeds three days later, and United were on song, treating the 50,842 fans to one of those breathless goal sequences – Viollet 60, Taylor 62, Berry 65 and Taylor again in the 69th minute sealing a 5-0 win.

A 4-1 win in the sunshine at Blackpool, in which Duncan struck the post ("almost breaking the upright in two" according to one writer), earned the left-half this write-up in the *Herald*: "Manchester United's mighty man of muscle, Duncan Edwards, put the padlock on his old England pal Stan Matthews last night – and the Red Devils whipped Blackpool."

Archie Ledbrooke went one better. "Duncan Edwards was at his majestic best and therefore nearly the best player in the world," he said. "One minute he was clearing off his own goal line, the next he was running through half the Blackpool side in a solo dash that owed as much to artistry as it did to sheer strength."

Just when it appeared all of United's jinxes were done with, along came Bolton Wanderers to remind Busby of their existence.

"Just in case you believe I would have you regard him as a superman, let me hasten to add that Dunc was human," recalled Ronnie Clayton. "He feared no football foe – but there were two matches he was always glad to get over every season... Bolton seemed to put a hoodoo on Manchester United whenever the two teams met. And this was gall to a player like Duncan, who played to win every time out."

Old pals Dennis Stevens and Ray Parry scored to help Bolton win 4-0 at Burnden Park. Stevens, however, had cause to grumble with his relative, as he was the latest to try and win a physical duel and was left to hobble through most of the second half.

Blackpool got some revenge while the champions' heads were dropped. They scored in the first and 31st minutes to get a lead they would not relinquish. As ever, United's hopes rested on Duncan's inspiration, the midfielder having a number of efforts before finally scoring in the 86th minute.

Against Arsenal three days later, Busby made a tactical switch to deal with the attacking threat of Vic Groves and David Herd. United moved to a four-man defence, with Edwards shifting alongside Blanchflower, and Whelan and Berry asked to drop in to help Colman with his midfield work. It worked, with United getting back on the winning trail with a 4-2 score.

It had been a week where Busby's opinion had been sought more often than usual, considering the release of his new book, *My Story*. Don Davies reviewed it in *The Guardian*, and felt readers would enjoy the stories and would "appreciate, too, Busby's realism. Proud as he is of his 'Babes' achievements in the European Cup, he makes no false claims as to their standing in relation to the great players abroad. Old Trafford has yet to produce its Puskás, its Koscis, its Boszik, or its Di Stéfano."

If the comment makes your eyes widen considering all the accolades given to Duncan Edwards, consider two things: first, the fact that as good as he had been, there was probably at least one thing missing. That was the evidence of either a European Cup winners' medal, a World Cup winners' medal, or a European Player of the Year award. The second thing to think about was his style of play. Frank Blunstone has an interesting take, even if it sounds somewhat critical of Edwards. "When you looked at players like Georgie Best or Stanley Matthews, those were players who had more ball skill than Duncan," he says. "But what Duncan had was strength and size. He could play anywhere. He could win the ball and move it on, but he wasn't what anyone would class as a dribbler. He could hit any type of pass you wanted. Ten yard, 20 yards, 50 yards. It was exceptional."

Yet Blunstone is also quick to point out that Duncan was the best in his team. "United were a great team," he says. "Even in company like Colman, Charlton and Pegg, Duncan stood out as the best player in the team. I don't think people realised how good he was. That has to be because of his style, because he wasn't a dribbler. He was a winner of the ball, a player of immense positional intelligence and a player who never wasted anything. He was wonderful. He knew what his strengths were and he played to them. No, he wasn't a natural dribbler, but there were a few times I saw him go through people, he was so strong!"

Duncan's greatness was not questioned by potential suitors. Maurice Smith went to Rome to get the inside scoop on the big money being spent by Italian clubs. "Hush, this is secretissimo but I have just been shown a list of English names guaranteed to rock English soccer to its foundations," he wrote in *The People* on September 29th. "Those names are of foreign players whom the Italians want in their game as soon as possible. That list is Tommy Taylor, of Manchester United, followed by Johnny Haynes, of Fulham, Duncan Edwards, another Manchester gem, and Peter McParland, Aston Villa." Smith reported the £45,000 bid for Taylor had already been rejected but his source at Inter Milan had admitted they had underbid. "Now we must pay for Taylor our biggest ever price," the source told Smith, "bigger even than the £120,000 Juventus paid for South American star Sivori."

The wages on offer were astronomical by British standards. If Duncan had been tempted to make the move he would be expecting to quadruple his salary to £60 a week and then get the same amount for every home win and £120 for an away win. The Italians were not successful with their chase of Busby's Babes. Nor were they successful with a £20,000-a-year offer for Busby himself. Smith suggested the transfer fees could have been as high as £350,000.

Edwards was not going to rock the boat. His reverence of Busby was always obvious. "I feel he must be the ideal model for all managers," he said. "He has established himself as 'the Boss' by his knowledge and personality. He is unfailingly courteous and quiet-spoken to all his players, yet firm. In a dispute with a player he will always listen patiently while the man tells his story, and then give his decision... The players at Old Trafford would do anything for him."

It's fair to say that much was true of Duncan himself. He was idolised by his fellow players and also by the staff at the club. Jimmy Murphy's tributes were never less than glowing. "On or off the field Duncan was an amazing fellow, he never smoked nor drank, and even as a boy he was so professional in his approach to the game he was a shining example to all youngsters," he said. "Even when he was an England international I only had to say, 'I've got some youngsters at the ground, Duncan, will you come along and give me a hand?' He never refused and came to play with boys little younger than himself who idolised him. At big banquets and receptions he would sidle up to Matt or myself and say, 'I know I have to be here, but after the speeches can I slip away? I have some new LP records I want to hear.'"

He believed he could achieve everything in football with his beloved club and friends under the stewardship of the great Busby. The case was emphatically stated at Dalymount Park as United kicked off their second European Cup campaign with a 6-0 win over Shamrock Rovers. 3-0 up in the 79th minute, Busby's side struck three times in seven minutes to demoralise their Irish opponents and render the second leg a formality.

Life was not all rosy for the young champions. Busby was beginning to notice one or two issues. The first came when United's left-hand side – usually impenetrable – was run ragged at Wolves. "As Duncan Edwards joined Wilf McGuinness, unhappy as a left-back, in the joyless trailing of Deeley," Ross Hall of the *Mirror* wrote, "Peter Broadbent and Eddie Clamp made hay down Wolves' right flank." McGuinness was in for the injured Byrne;

Edwards' partner at half-back was Freddie Goodwin, with Eddie Colman in and out of the team as Busby tried to deal with the Salford lad's growing ego. "Eddie started to get a little too big for his boots," says Tom Clare. "He'd be late for training and he liked a pint. Roger Byrne told him he had to fix his ways or he'd be out. Busby eventually dropped him."

An enforced absence was to emphasise the issue. Duncan had told press that his 21st birthday would "be a quiet celebration." He said that none of his family would be going to Manchester, but he did receive a gift from his parents which he cherished, a watch to add to his collection.

How much Duncan actually celebrated was doubtful. It was reported in the *Herald* on October 2nd that he was suffering from the Asian Flu, one of millions estimated to have caught it as it swept through the UK in the second half of 1957.

Duncan had been named in the England under-23 side, but with Stan Crowther named as reserve 'just in case', the United player was not well enough by the October 16th game date with Romania, so the emergency selection was required.

Desmond Hackett's report in the *Express* on October 2nd would have been enough to have sent Busby's own pulse racing: "Duncan Edwards, the most highly regarded ration of beefcake on Britain's soccer parade, is now 21 years old. Before he reaches the ripe old age of 22 he could be one of the wealthiest young inhabitants of this crazy mixed-up game. Yes, those lira-label Italians are here again… John Charles has been a sensation in Italy. In fact, to Juventus, who lavished upon him £10,000, a car, a villa, and rich bonuses, Charley is their darling. But the Italian importers of our finer football crafts rate Duncan Edwards even greater than Charles. They want him, and when these Italians want a player they open the safe with a flourish and implore: But amico, help yourself! The Italians are endlessly patient, but equally persistent. They are here for big business, and young Mr Duncan Edwards, now come of splendid soccer age, is extremely big business. I know that Manchester United will fiercely denounce this as so much nonsense… oh, dear me. With all this sordid talk about money I almost forgot. Sorry it wasn't such a happy birthday, Duncan Edwards. I mean you in bed with flu and a temperature as high as, well, an offer from an Italian soccer club?"

That evening, Italian representatives had to watch McGuinness in the number six shirt in the second leg against Shamrock Rovers. "It must have been as great a relief to the Irish players as it was a disappointment to the home crowd that two such artists as Edwards and Whelan had to stand down from the Manchester team," noted Don Davies in *The Guardian*. Colman was back in but the complacency was on show again – United were 2-0 up by the 22nd minute but then became sloppy and had to be jolted back into life by a goal from the visitors in the 55th minute. Viollet immediately struck another goal to make it 3-1, but the Irish side got another of their own and came away with a respectable 3-2 defeat. A similar story occurred against Aston Villa, with United eventually winning 4-1 to make any talk of a concentration lapse seem ridiculous.

Thankfully for Duncan, his recovery from illness wasn't as problematic as his previous experience with the flu. He had been well enough to attend the game against Villa and provide his column for that day's *Evening Chronicle* where he responded to the rumours of a move. The article carried the plain headline "Italians haven't made me an offer" and the following statement: "In common with Tommy Taylor and most of the other star footballers in this country, my name has been linked with Italian football. There has been no official approach to me, and, if there were, I should refer it immediately to United manager Matt Busby. I would regard such a situation as club business, and, after they had made up their minds, I might be in a position to consider it."

There was never any question that Duncan – clearly viewed as a bargain at double the world record fee – would even contemplate asking to move away from Old Trafford. "To Duncan's way of thinking, there never was a club like Manchester United; and never a manager like Matt Busby," said Ronnie Clayton. "I don't think he ever considered seriously the possibility of leaving Manchester United."

Duncan had not allowed fame to change him and it was indeed his affable nature that added to the aura around him. He was approachable to the kids on the streets. That feeling extended to the young boys at United, the next generation breaking through. "There's a lovely story Nobby Stiles told when he took an autograph book into the first-team dressing room," Tom Clare remembers. "Duncan looked at him and asked if he was the young lad who'd recently played for England – he took the book and got the lads to sign it. They were all mates, there were no cliques."

Clare tells a story of how he was watching United play at Preston, and ran on the pitch at half-time to get close to David Pegg. Pegg laughed and put the young fan on the bench for the second half. A little while later, at Blackpool, Tom tried to get a word with Duncan: "After a game at Bloomfield Road I ran on to the pitch and approached him. 'Oh no, not you,' he groaned with his beautiful Dudley twang, 'not now son. See me at home!' He wasn't pissed off. It was good-natured."

It was this sort of spirit which made Duncan love being at United. "Probably the most important factor in any club is an intangible thing that has nothing to do with the technicalities of the game," he said. "It is called club spirit. It is a cross between confidence and faith that makes a man say, 'My club, right or wrong.' It is the unseen asset that sends a player on the field having complete confidence in himself and in all his team-mates. He starts the game with the unshakeable belief that he is the member of a great side and that his colleagues are no more likely to let him down than he is them. Driven by this belief he and the other 10 will constantly search for the ball, ask for it, fight for it, do anything to gain possession of it, not to perform any tricks of individual brilliance, but solely to keep their side on top... club spirit is the most powerful single element in football today. Develop it and there is no prize too great to reach for."

The Babes were at their best for Duncan's return to the team at Nottingham Forest. United scored early on, and after Forest had responded just after the break, Busby's side seized the initiative again – Viollet's 59th-minute goal the eventual winner. Edwards looked fresh, as though he had spent 10 days on the Amalfi Coast entertaining offers from every Italian club, rather than just recovering from the flu, and was once more the major influence in a magnificent game of football.

"There was only one moment of disappointment in the entire 90 minutes – the moment when the referee's whistle signalled this magical match was over," raved Bill Holden in the *Mirror*. "Both Forest and United were brilliant, but Manchester had the extra edge which meant victory. And that extra edge was the tremendous performance of Duncan Edwards, the young giant left-half whose magnificent performance pulled United out of a succession of scrapes."

Don Davies described it as his favourite post-war league match: "In Nottingham circles, perhaps, the furious exchanges of that exciting second half may seem in retrospect almost like a continuous bombardment of the United goal, with only the broad frame of the peripatetic Edwards, and occasionally the safe hands of Wood, intervening to save their side from disaster."

The *Express* referred to Duncan as "the most effective one-man performer in British football", and the *Times* had Duncan as the "one man (who) stood out above all others" with a "massive performance". Another report said: "He kept popping up like a hero of a film serial to save his side from disaster."

Forest manager Billy Walker admitted: "I don't mind defeat when it comes like this. I was proud of my boys for the quality of their football and for the way they fought. I was so excited about it all that I did not sleep a wink. I lay awake and relived every kick of it all over again."

Chapter 21
Chunky

Duncan's importance to the heart and personality of the team could be seen by his absence again when United capitulated 3-0 to Portsmouth at Old Trafford in October 1957 – Duncan, Roger Byrne and Tommy Taylor were in the England side that day, playing in Cardiff against Wales in the Home Championship. Perhaps another reason for United's defeat was the absence of Jimmy Murphy, who could now add manager of the Wales national team to his CV due to his immense reputation as Busby's assistant.

"I had gone through the tactics to play England," Murphy said. "I dealt with all aspects, until Reg Davies piped up: 'You mentioned everyone Jimmy, but what about Duncan Edwards?' 'Just keep out of his way son,' I said, 'I don't want you to get hurt.'"

Once the laughter had died down, Murphy tried to give some calming advice. "Edwards; I know all about this lad," Jimmy told his players. "You have nothing to fear from him. He has got two arms, two legs, a head and two eyes just like the rest of you fellows. He just thinks he's a good player, he just thinks he's tough and strong, but he's just a big softie."

Goalkeeper Jack Kelsey was not convinced. "This was typical Murphy kiddology," he said. "Most of us who were aware of Duncan were not taken in by it… a big softie he certainly was not."

England scored after two minutes and were in complete control when Johnny Haynes notched just before the break. Finney and Haynes would complete a 4-0 drubbing in the second half. Four goals in front, England won a throw-in close to the Wales bench. Duncan took it and noted Murphy's presence close to him. "Are there no early trains back to Manchester, Jimmy?" Duncan joked. "You're wasting your time here!" Murphy scowled and said he would tell Duncan where he was going wrong when they got back to the Cliff.

The Times described Duncan as "a young oak", adding: "Edwards nonchalantly picked off Davies and all others as if they were flies. And he did it all at walking pace."

Desmond Hackett repeated his line from the Forest game in the *Express*: "Duncan Edwards was just the same – the most effective player in British football. He wiped out the Welsh right-wing as completely as a damp duster cleans a blackboard."

George Follows' write-up was entertaining in itself. "The roaring red dragons of Wales were squeaky white mice. Admittedly this was a walkie-talkie international. Duncan Edwards was only prevented from playing the second half with his hands in his pockets by the fact that there were no pockets in England's trim new nylon shorts. But he was able to carry on a snappy conversation with his pal and Welsh team manager, Jimmy Murphy, without missing a trick on the field."

Duncan was happy with some revenge against Aston Villa in the Charity Shield, as United won at a canter with four goals in the second half at Old Trafford. This was, incidentally, the first time ever United wore black shirts and socks with their home kit.

There was, perhaps, one piece of news that rivalled even the latest medal for Duncan's collection – when he was told he'd passed his driving test. On Friday October 25th he wrote a letter to a friend, Eric Dorman, who lived in Canada, quoted verbatim below, where the United midfielder revealed his new nickname:

Hi there Eric

I'm sorry for not writing a littler sooner, but this last fortnight I have done nothing but chase about. First Eric let me tell, yesterday I went for my test

*and beleave it or not I passed. Mark Jones was there the same time I was &
he also has passed.*

*We Babes are not playing to well at the moment Eric, or should I say
we're not scoring goals like we used to. On Tuesday night we played Villa, we
won 4-0 Eric, but I wish you could see there side… mind you, on Tuesday
the forwards had a bit more punch about them and they managed four goals.
Tomorrow, Sat 26th, we're off to my home town, we play West Bromwich,
up to now D Viollet won't be able to turn out for us as on Tuesday night he
twisted his knee. I think they will play Bob Charlton, as he was at the ground
this morning. I have only just rushed from the ground as I have to see Gordon
in town for dinner at one o'clock, we're off to the new C.A men's shop opened
up in town, see what we can buy. I close now Eric for a few hours and return
about 4.30.*

*I'm back, the time 4.15, not bad. This afternoon Gordon & I were at
C.A. I brought a pair of flannels, cost me only £2.9.o, there smart to.*

*From there we ended up at Jesse Marolls. We both measured for a suit,
not a bad afternoon's work old boy.*

*By the way here's something for you. I told you we play West Brom tomor-
row. Guess what, Eddie Colman has been dropped for that match, Freddie
Goodwin takes his place. I'll have to mind how I go.*

*Listen to this, Mr Kershaw has just brought a new Jaguar, it can go at a
speed of 140 not bad. As for myself my car should be here anytime now, roll on.*

*All of the gang are quiet well, Molly had a little flu, otherwise everything
is just the same. Well that's the low down for now Eric, Keep well, also keep
out of trouble. Yours, Duncan, if you like, Chunky.*

Chunky was well enough to buy himself a belated birthday present,
a Morris Minor, paid for by the work he'd done promoting
Dextrosol. The car was acquired from Paragon Motor Company
in Oldham on November 21st. It was a time of increased responsibility in almost every aspect of Duncan's life. Two days before
buying the car he'd renewed his life insurance, covered for the
sum of £500. He accepted the presidency of the newly-formed

Dudley Youth Football League and agreed to write the soccer edition of publisher Stanley Paul's *Tackle (enter sport name here) This Way*, a professional's guide to their chosen sport. He would write it himself, on his own portable typewriter, as he did when writing any article on football.

Duncan was incredibly prudent and saved money where he could, always ensuring he sent some home for his parents. He also had a tidy amount in savings, so it was only when he had this small windfall that he allowed himself the indulgence of a car. A car, by the way, he couldn't even use until he received his licence.

"Even though he couldn't drive it, it was his pride and joy," remembers Tom Clare. "He'd clean it and we'd just hang around the other side of the road, watching our hero from a distance."

Duncan had received driving lessons from Molly's father. That was not the only act of benevolence from his future father-in-law – he had told Molly and Duncan that their wedding present would be the deposit for a house. The engaged couple had fallen in love with a house for sale in Timperley, so the father of the bride-to-be decided to give them their present early. It was arranged that they would move in after getting married.

Manchester was where the heart was for Duncan. But there is no doubting that he had captured the imagination of the football world. He received correspondence from fans and admirers from afar, including one Portuguese reporter from *A Bola* who wrote requesting a feature interview to be conducted over letter. It included questions like *what is your name, what is your preferred position, have you always played there* – softball starters with an increasingly suspicious angle that was beginning to look like a scouting mission rather than a tribute.

From the exotic Libson to familiar hometown opponents. *Sans Viollet* and with Colman getting some tough love in the reserves, United went down 4-3 at West Brom, thanks in large part to two goals from Bobby Robson.

"Duncan Edwards was a colossus," future England manager Robson said. "Magnificent in stature and build with enormous strength and power to go with it. However, that was just a part of him. He had extraordinary ability and technique, and in defence and attack he was superb. He was the finest two-footed player I ever saw. Recovering the ball, then running it through midfield to finish with an explosive and devastating shot was a sight and a joy to behold and Duncan could do this continually. Duncan Edwards was one of England's and the world's finest players."

His efforts received greater reward in the next match. "United beat Burnley because of Duncan Edwards," read one match report, and although strictly speaking the win was earned by a Tommy Taylor goal, the point was emphasised: "He reached peak form and was the complete footballer – the pillar which held up United – well worth £60,000, whether Italian lira or pounds sterling. Powerful in defence with his amazing facility of turning defence into attack. He spoon-fed his colleagues and inspired them."

Duncan was back in the England team which faced Northern Ireland on November 6th. Winterbottom's team were unbeaten in 16 and, according to Tom Duckworth in the *Sports Argus*, their hopes of winning the World Cup were never brighter: "Billy Wright, Ronnie Clayton and Duncan Edwards make up the finest half-back line England have had for years. Clayton and Edwards are the complete wing-halves, equally good in defence or attack."

However, they faced some hard reality when they were a goal down at half-time.

The England manager told a familiar tale: "Duncan came into the dressing room as the other players were feeling a bit down. 'Walter,' he says. 'Don't worry. I'll get you a goal in the second half.' This business of him being able to score goals was a real feature of him. The Busby Babe confidence was in the England team and we felt sure we'd win the World Cup. It stemmed from Duncan."

As usual, Duncan was as good as his word. But his 82nd-minute strike was a consolation as Northern Ireland went on to win 3-2 – capitalising on nervous defending from new England internationals Eddie Hopkinson in goal and Don Howe at right-back, as well as a generous not-offside decision in their favour and the miraculous goalkeeping of Harry Gregg. Even Edwards and Wright had been culpable for the second Ireland goal, running into each other and giving the Wembley visitors a tap-in. Edwards and Wright were seen "slanging each other after they had collided" according to Desmond Hackett, who was feeling pessimistic after the result: "Tommy Taylor still cannot convince me that he is the best centre-forward England possess. Let it also be said that the men we rely upon, Billy Wright, Duncan Edwards and Johnny Haynes, looked extremely ordinary soccer mortals."

If Edwards had shown any flaw in his game it had been the eagerness he still showed in defence, more apparent if he was trying to compensate for weaknesses elsewhere in the team. There were no nerves, even though now he was not so offended by the mere suggestion of pre-match tension. "If you suffer from butterflies in the stomach, don't despair – so do I and every other player I have met," he said, betraying that youthful bullishness he'd once expressed to a schoolteacher. "Go round the England dressing room before an international and you will find every man suffering from nerves of some description... My own butterflies last until the bell goes to tell us we are due on the field, and from then on I am just another player in another football match. The roar as we come onto the field acts as a boost to my morale, like a quaff of champagne. In this I am lucky, for I have played before so many large crowds since I was a schoolboy that I accept them as a normal part of my football. Indeed, the only times I feel below par in a game are when the crowd atmosphere is lacking."

Another factor from the early days of Duncan's career returned at Preston, when a penalty was awarded against him in the first minute for handball. He was furious – and felt justice had been done when Wood saved from Finney. Finney did score, eventually, in the 71st minute, and it needed a late equaliser from Whelan to get a point. Sheffield Wednesday were beaten in a routine game before United welcomed Czechoslovakian champions Dukla Prague to Manchester.

"Duncan Edwards was in brilliant form, giving outside-left David Pegg a stream of passes," read the *Mirror*'s report, while the *Times* described Duncan as "the real hero once again".

Henry Rose in the *Express* suggested that Dukla would have had a first-half lead "but for the magnificent, brilliant, superb Edwards. What a player! Once again he stood out as the best of his side."

The Czech side were resilient, but in the end, goals in the 53rd, 65th and 79th minute gave Busby a 3-0 lead for the second leg.

Duncan lived up to that hero tag at Newcastle; United were 1-0 down and flagging, causing Busby to take the extraordinary step of switching him with inside-forward Billy Whelan. The gamble worked. Edwards was influential, and the home side panicked. The equaliser duly arrived in the 85th minute, "thumped" in, according to *The People*. Three minutes later, Taylor scored a sensational winner.

Taylor and Edwards were once again in the England team, to face France in a friendly at Wembley on November 27th. "All defenders tackled grimly with a spirit which suggested that each realised at long last that no place in the national team is his by right," Cyril Chapman wrote in the *Birmingham Post*. "Duncan Edwards played as though Manchester United's European Cup hung in the balance."

One might think that is a summary of a tight game. Not so. England won 4-0, and were 3-0 up at half-time – Taylor scoring twice, and debutant Bobby Robson getting goals either side of the break.

Taylor was not in the United team for the visit of Spurs a few days later. In fact, Busby had achieved something remarkable even for him – the entire team were 'homegrown', with David Gaskell in for Ray Wood. Gaskell had been responsible for a training-ground injury to Mark Jones, so he too wouldn't feature. Duncan was vocal in helping his housemate out.

"I got to play against Tottenham in November 1957, just after my 17th birthday," Gaskell recalls. "Our entire team was developed by the club. And that was even without Mark Jones, who missed the game because I'd given him a whack in training. They had a big centre-half who kept standing close to me and even standing on my feet. Duncan saw what was going on. 'Smack him,' he said. 'Give him a smack!' The ball was coming in from the corner and I could still hear Duncan telling me to 'sort him out'. He was about a foot taller than me!"

It was another difficult day defensively for United. Gaskell, on his first league start for the club, faced five shots in the first half – and all of them were effectively clear-cut openings. Spurs scored four times. James Samuel of *The People* wrote: "Gaskell can blame his first-half nightmare almost entirely on atrocious lack of covering by centre-half Jackie Blanchflower." However, he praised United's spirited response. "I have rarely seen a fight-back to match the intensity and courage of United after the interval. It was ruthless raiding, spearheaded by the dapper Eddie Colman and two goals were chipped back by the 68th minute. Picture the scene as Spurs reeled back... picture Danny Blanchflower going full-length to punch the ball away from the boots of the on-rushing Duncan Edwards one foot outside the penalty area... picture Edwards punching the air in furious disappointment as he blazed yards over."

United lost 4-3. George Follows had spent the morning watching Peacock Street beat Beaver Road in a school cup tie on a cinder pitch. He likened Duncan's attempts at a heroic recovery to the sort of disorganised chaos you would see in a local game, and gave an interesting perspective as to how that suited United's style.

"I have hailed Duncan Edwards as Britain's best footballer... but I don't see his death-or-glory dashes as soccer according to the

Busby blueprint," Follows claimed. "Edwards is every schoolboy's hero for several reasons. One reason is that he can still play with a schoolboy's enthusiasm despite all those well-deserved international caps. And this was one of Duncan's most enthusiastic games. He was the most thrilling player in one of the most thrilling league games I have seen. But I hope the kids liked little Eddie Colman better and I hope they liked Danny Blanchflower better still.

"Edwards is a wonderful fellow to have in any team. He is also a wonderful team man. Every time his side is losing he thunders into his party piece, a dramatic version of 'The Charge of the Light Brigade'. But I don't see it as soccer according to the Busby blueprint. In fact, death or glory Duncan is doing it so often that I categorise it as 'X' certificate soccer – not to be shown to children even though accompanied by an adult. This show of strength though fairly executed is a bad example to the would-be internationals of Peacock Street and Beaver Road. I also think it is not good for Duncan Edwards. It concertinas the play until you can't see the goal for footballers. It infringes the first rule of football that the ball must do the work. The work is done by Duncan Edwards instead. And it was certainly not a good thing for Manchester United against Spurs. They were three down... something most certainly had to be done. But they had the men to do it. Edwards has been hailed by some critics as the best player in the world. He can only be that if he adds some of Danny Blanchflower's skill to his own strength. I think he can do it. But for the time being Danny Blanchflower is the man to pin on the wall at Peacock Street and Beaver Road."

Follows' observations are fascinating because of how they elevate Duncan in comparison to his club peers. *I don't see it as soccer according to the Busby blueprint.* That these comments were made in November 1957 are even more compelling. What was Duncan Edwards if not the embodiment of the Busby blueprint? And if he was, then what is the truth? How does one of the most important players in the club's history fit into its identity?

Frankly, there is a lot of truth to Follows' point, because Duncan was so different. And it is the difference which gave him his place in United's history. By the outstanding nature of his gift, Duncan's contribution to Manchester United history – quite aside from being a fantastic player – was to create the significance of any great side the club would possess carrying a player like this. Not quite like Duncan, but someone possessing an individual talent that was so unique and yet so complementary for the group of players around it. Jimmy Murphy referred to Duncan as one of the two players he coached but could not teach. The other was George Best. So Follows could well have been right. Maybe it was not according to the Busby blueprint – but maybe it was that little bit of difference which was the spark, the energy which fused potential into greatness. Without Duncan Edwards, there would be no platform for Best to follow. There would be no history of a spotlight where a beloved team could still find special treatment for one, and so no indulgence for an Eric Cantona or a Cristiano Ronaldo; four players all different from each other in style, and all four sharing the common trait of being so different to their contemporaries that what separated them made them, in the most delicious of twists, more bonded.

The other element to the assessment by George Follows is the implication that Duncan himself needed to get better. Aside from the hiccup of the handball against Preston there was no significant suggestion that his form had dipped. Most of the time he was his team's best player. It was a remarkable level of consistency that Manchester United didn't see until Bryan Robson, and haven't seen since Roy Keane. Keane was in his late 20s when he reached that level of personal discipline. Duncan was 21. And yet the other side of this is the conventional wisdom which tells us that *because* he was 21, maturity and experience was only going to help.

"He could have improved," says Johnny Giles. "Great players always strive for that. Duncan had that desire. He was improving all the time. People say football is a simple game. That's not true. It's complicated. The great players, the great managers, make it look simple. The day you think you know everything is the day you move backwards. If you told Jimmy Murphy you thought you knew everything, he'd take your head off."

So what were the faults which could be improved upon? It seemed a complicated case of shared responsibility. Duncan needed to relieve some of that incessant desire to be everywhere and do everything. It was present in the defeat against Spurs and also in 1-0 losses to Dukla Prague and Chelsea. In the mix of this run was a draw at Birmingham.

United's preparation for that Brum game had not been ideal. The travelling party was stranded in Prague because fog in England kept aeroplanes grounded. United had to travel to Amsterdam and then complete the journey to Manchester via ferry and coach. They arrived on Friday, 24 hours before kick-off on Saturday at Birmingham.

In Prague the *Herald* reported how Duncan had gone in too eagerly for one headed challenge and then Dick Millford, in *The People*, wrote how Duncan had become too preoccupied by the personal nature of the Chelsea match. "United looked as if they could collect the points any time they wanted. But their rhythm and confidence seemed to go when Colman was left limping by Les Stubbs' 37th-minute tackle. United, and especially Duncan Edwards, made the mistake of trying to fight it out with the Chelsea battlers. If United had continued their attempts to win by the text-book, they might eventually have won comfortably."

Some of these problems could be resolved by maturity. They would come with time. Duncan would pick his battles more wisely. He would become less obliged to get involved in confrontations where opponents were following colleagues, because he would learn that opponents were doing it to get under his skin. The other United players would recognise this too. It was a collective experience and it applied just as much domestically, where they were the best team, as it did on the continent, where they were trying to be. Colman appeared to have learned his lesson. He had been outstanding in Prague. According to Roger MacDonald in his book *Manchester United in Europe*, Colman "gave a brilliant display in Czechoslovakia, dictating the game with nitric footwork... Colman slowed and even stopped the play whenever Dukla threatened to get on top."

The 3-3 draw at Birmingham a week before the Chelsea defeat had convinced Busby to finally take external action to address the complacency. Ray Wood was picking up too many knocks. The kids were too green. Busby needed a goalkeeper with as much presence and endurance as quality. That man was Doncaster Rovers goalkeeper Harry Gregg – and a world record fee for a goalkeeper, of £23,500, was paid to get him.

"Busby was getting a little frustrated with the players," Tom Clare says. "He wanted the European Cup but he also badly wanted three successive league titles. United were throwing silly points away, giving stupid goals away. There was youth, complacency. It really was a case of you score one, we'll score two. It was almost careless, but it was part of a learning curve. He signed Harry Gregg because he wanted, as he put it, a European goalkeeper. When Harry made his debut everyone expected that Busby would change the defenders – but he dropped Johnny Berry, Billy Whelan and David Pegg, three forwards! And from then on, they never lost a game."

Gregg would later admit to the size of the stage daunting him, but at the time, he appeared to revel in his new arena. "I was signed as the world's costliest goalkeeper but that doesn't tell the real truth," Gregg told this author in 2013. "I was playing 'follow the leader' in many respects. I just kept my trap shut and got on with it. That's not to say I didn't enjoy it. I loved it. I joined what I thought was the 'Hollywood' of football. There were four teams at Old Trafford, the first, the reserves, the A and the B. 42 or 43 players. And out of those 43 players, only four had been signed from the outside. Ray Wood. Johnny Berry. The great Tommy Taylor, and then myself. The strength of the club was in what it had developed itself. It was incredible."

In addition to what Busby knew he was getting with Gregg, there was also a bonus he hadn't really accounted for. "I wanted to play football," Gregg said. "And I mean, as a goalkeeper, I wanted to play football. I'm not saying this to be clever... when I was starting out in the reserves at Doncaster Rovers, most goalkeepers stayed on their line. I couldn't understand why, if the ball was 70 yards from me, I should handicap myself by 18 yards by staying on the goal-line. It was basic common sense to me. I never did anything for show. Everything I did in a game, I did because I had to. In the 1958 World Cup, when we played against Germany, I came out of the box on three occasions to beat players to headers. But it wasn't for show. It was effective. I couldn't understand why others didn't do it. Good players, great players, always move in relation to where the ball is. It is instinct, subconscious. I knew that I did things differently to other goalkeepers."

What Gregg brought to the role was a command of the entire penalty area which often meant United could condense the play further up the pitch. It was a masterstroke of a signing.

"I knew Duncan and I would be friends," Gregg said. "He was one of the nicest, and most honest, people that I've ever met. Potentially Duncan would have been the best ever. They said Duncan was a giant... well, he was about 5ft 11in and built like a brick shithouse... thighs, shoulders, the lot. I liken him to Roy Keane, I said Roy was the closest thing I'd seen to Duncan. I got a lot of stick for saying that. People seemed to think Duncan would glide past you like a beautiful bird. Listen, if Duncan couldn't go past you he would go through you. Keane was the same. He had to win every game, every five-a-side, every race in training. Duncan was obsessed with football and with winning. He was potentially one of the greatest all-round players. And yet he was such a shy young man."

Harry Gregg, on the other hand, was not. Ahead of facing Leicester on his league debut, he had already imposed himself in training. He was a battering ram when he came to collect crosses. He asked his team-mates if they minded this style. Gregg told the *Mirror* that the response had been: "If you come out for the ball and I am in the way – hit me."

It was put to the test in the first half. Leicester won a corner. "I came out for a high ball inside the penalty area," Gregg said. "I clattered Duncan Edwards. I just about took his head off. And Roger Byrne just said to me, 'Hey big man. Keep coming.'"

"Left-half Duncan Edwards and centre-half Mark Jones should have bruises to prove that Harry took them at their word," read the *Mirror*'s match report, after United had scored four times without reply to provide instant vindication for the manager. It was two clean sheets in a row when United won against Luton on Christmas Day (a game in which Duncan scored the first goal, a penalty, having taken over that responsibility following missed kicks from Byrne and Berry), but in the return game 24 hours later, it was Duncan who had the unfortunate displeasure of deflecting the ball past Gregg for his first concession in United colours, in a 2-2 draw. Further draws at Maine Road and Elland Road sandwiched a routine win over Workington Reds in the FA Cup. Going into 1958, fourth-placed United trailed league leaders Wolves by eight points. They had a fight on their hands if they wanted to win the league title they'd started to take for granted.

Chapter 22
To Belgrade

On New Year's Day in 1958, Duncan Edwards joined Manchester City players Ken Barnes and Bert Trautmann at an event at Oxford Street Cinema. Some 800 schoolchildren were there to watch David Niven star as Phileas Fogg in *Around The World In 80 Days*, and shortly after they were seated, the footballers walked in to see them. After the event the children wrote on cards that would be attached to balloons and released from Belle Vue Stadium, with prizes awarded for those whose balloons went farthest.

If Duncan had written his own card, one imagines that he might have been wishing for his prize to arrive in 147 days, 433 miles away from Manchester in Brussels – the city that would host the European Cup final that year.

Instead, he was writing for news agency Hayters, submitting typed columns every week. On January 7th, Duncan wrote about the scarcity of top strikers in the game. "If you want your boy to make good as a footballer, Mrs Worthington, put him in a number nine shirt," he wrote, presumably in response to a query of a curious mother. "Seldom in the history of the game can there have been such chance for centre-forwards as there are in these days of famine. A list of the best centre-forwards I have played with or seen in this country would go Nat Lofthouse, Don Revie, Tommy Taylor, Ronnie Allen – and then end. Of that quartette all except Taylor have put a fair number of years at football behind them. For a country that plays as much football as England the list is pitifully small. The plain truth is that centre-forwards with the stamp of class on their play are just not about."

A week later, Duncan's column concentrated on transfers. "There seems to be a feeling abroad at the moment that there is something criminal about spending money in the transfer market," he wrote. "Arsenal, suffering from the sort of hangover that hits all great clubs, demand to know where they can buy top class players at a pre-inflation era price. Our manager, Matt Busby, spends £20,000 on a goalkeeper and a number of gentlemen make smart cracks about 'Busby Babes'. This line of thought is one I cannot follow. At Manchester we have achieved no little success with a crop of players spotted, cultivated and then introduced into league football at an age when the players of most other clubs are fighting for a place in the reserve side. These teams have been built up by the diligence of the management, scouting and coaching staff and have probably saved United a reasonable amount of money. Yet United have never made youth a fetish. If Mr Busby has considered that we needed a player he has bought him – and hang the price."

If Arsenal had their way, they might well have tried to succeed where the Italians had tentatively tried but failed. On January 13th, there was a report from Bob Pennington of the *Express* regarding the transitional period at Highbury. They had attempted to sign Johnny Haynes of Fulham. "It has also been demanded that Arsenal buy Duncan Edwards from Manchester United, Jimmy McIlroy from Burnley, and Johnny Brooks from Spurs," Pennington wrote. "Is there no hope of new stars for Highbury? Every club I contacted in my nationwide probe yesterday gave me the same emphatic 'No sale' verdict."

Pennington went on to suggest that Arsenal could do worse than plump for a 17-year-old rookie by the name of Denis Law, who he rated even higher than Haynes.

Manchester United's quest to get to the European Cup final would resume with a tie against Red Star Belgrade of Yugoslavia.

Red Star were an exceptional team, as proven by their own semi-final appearance in 1957. In addition to the many great players they had, they also had their own 'Duncan Edwards' by the name of Dragoslav Sekularac. In the *Manchester Evening News* on the day of the first leg, Tom Jackson predicted "the whole pattern of the match may well rest on the outcome of the class between 19-year-old Sekularac and England's powerful left-half Duncan Edwards", and hailed Sekularac as a "wonder boy" who was "regarded as a stonewall certainty for the Yugoslav international team in next summer's World Cup finals. But Edwards, too, is a hot candidate for the World Cup and I'm sure he will make this duel with Sekularac the key to the match."

Edwards had been described in the Yugoslav press as "a wonder of a child, the unsurpassed left-half with six on his back". Red Star were already well aware of his reputation. United, for their part, were also aware of how good their visitors were – and stood almost in awe as they scored through Lazar Tasic in the 35th minute.

It needed an impatient Old Trafford crowd and a spirited Duncan Edwards performance to rouse the United players in the second half. Perhaps the one thing Red Star had not been prepared for is just how inspirational Duncan could be in adversity. If his team-mates could rise to the occasion too, then who knew what they might accomplish?

This was a night when magic seemed to happen for the first time. United took almost 20 minutes to get going – but when they did, according to Miroslav Radojičić, one of the greatest Yugoslav journalists, "… everything started from Edwards. The ball for Scanlon, who inserted to Bobby Charlton, and it was 1-1."

Edwards had charged past three challenges before playing the ball – a sign of the urgency which was now required. "The persistence of Edwards won the first goal," Frank Taylor wrote in the *Chronicle*. "He roared past two men to put Scanlon in the clear."

In the 81st minute, Colman had a coming-of-age moment, scoring a dramatic winner – finally, a moment where he could realise what hard work was needed for such a glorious achievement. United had spurned chance after chance before their most local of lads gave them a crucial advantage. But it was Edwards coming out on top in the game's pivotal duel which was key to the 2-1 victory.

"Edwards had completely dominated Red Star's most menacing forward," wrote Roger MacDonald in his book *Manchester United in Europe*. "Sekularac, who pinched the ball off him early in the match, dawdled arrogantly in midfield and was caught by Edwards, whose tackle, while meticulously fair, was quite devastating. Sekularac hit the ground like a sack of potatoes; his contribution to the remainder of the match was negligible."

Frank Taylor recalled the incident. "Like a wild buffalo robbed of his prey, Edwards turned in a flash, sprinted like fury after Sekularac, and with a thundering tackle whipped the ball away; his powerful thrust coming quite fairly into contact with the little Yugoslav. When Sekularac finished his cartwheeling on the turf, he was in no fit state to challenge Edwards' possession of the ball; nor in fact did he do much more in the match. This was proof indeed, that at that time the master footballers of Europe were only master footballers until they faced strong, powerful and fair tackling. They were not so used as our men to this style of play."

United's lead was narrow but theirs nonetheless. It earned them much praise from the country's top sportswriters. George Follows in the *Daily Herald* described Charlton, Edwards and Colman thus: "these three boys were the terrible triumvirate who eclipsed Red Star."

In the *Express*, Henry Rose was beaming. "Wonderful, wonderful Manchester United, Duncan Edwards, and Bobby Charlton. They did British soccer proud at Old Trafford last night. The test of real champions is the grit and ability to fight back after being knocked down. And that's what United did against the ball-jugglers from Belgrade... Edwards, surely the greatest player in soccer, inspired that second-half fightback. He was backed up by the 20-year-old Charlton. Mercifully, the mist luted so the crowd could see and thrill to every second of it. Edwards ploughed through a defence reinforced by every Red Star forward. Charlton zigzagged and fired three shots I swear would have beaten every goalkeeper in the world except Beara. Each time, this immaculate former ballet dancer saved. But United's wholehearted efforts had to succeed – and they did when Edwards bulldozed through. He passed to Albert Scanlon, whose centre was hooked into the net by Charlton for a 64th minute equaliser."

Tom Jackson had an interesting take in the *Evening News*. "Manchester United may not be the brilliant, all-powerful team that captured the hearts of the soccer world last season – BUT, by golly, how these do-or-die Busby Babes can fight back when the odds seem stacked against them!" he wrote. "For it was undoubtedly sheer fighting spirit, determination, and seemingly unlimited stamina that swept Red Star off their feet… The players who deserve extra-large medals are Duncan Edwards (how he rose to the challenge!), little Eddie Colman and Bobby Charlton. Edwards revelled in the heat of this tremendous battle and the result was that Red Star's 'wonder boy' inside-right, Sekularac, was limited to only brief flashes of his undoubted uncanny ball skill."

In his column for the local paper, captain Roger Byrne reserved special praise for the man who really provided the inspiration when it was needed. "I must pay tribute to Duncan Edwards," he said, "who carried out his job of marking Red Star's much vaunted 'wonder boy'… to such brilliant effect that I'm sure much of the danger was drained from their attack. No doubt Sekularac can be very good when he is given the room to indulge in his tricks, but Duncan afforded him so few chances that Red Star's attack gradually disappeared from the game." Byrne should have taken some of the credit. Colman had initially been tasked with marking Sekularac; after an initial struggle, the United captain showed his experience by instructing Edwards to switch sides.

United then came up against Bolton, a team who had their number many times in the past. On January 18th, however, it was a different matter. It was time to end the latest 'hoodoo'. The Babes were rampant, scoring after three minutes – and though Stevens levelled in the 20th minute, United responded with three rapid goals to go into half-time with a lead of 4-1. Bobby Charlton completed his hat-trick and Viollet got his second goal either side of a Lofthouse consolation.

With three minutes to go, United were awarded a penalty. Up stepped Duncan Edwards, the man who, as a boy, had apparently struck one so hard it cannoned off the crossbar, rebounded down the pitch and went out for a corner for the opposing team. If he could generate that much power as a teen, what might he be able to do as a 21-year old? The Bolton goalkeeper was not in the mood to find out.

"I spoke to Eddie Hopkinson, the Bolton goalkeeper, who used to live near me," Tom Clare recalled. "He said, 'If the truth must be known, Tom, I got out of the way of it!' Don Davies in *The Guardian* described it as probably the hardest shot he'd ever seen." The scored spot-kick helped United record a handsome result of 7-2.

Duncan explained why he liked to wallop the ball. "The push-penalty has only to be placed a foot too far inside the post and it is easily saved," he said. "That is the reason I favour the hit-'em-hard method. I slam the ball at the iron stanchion support-ing the net – and congratulations to the goalkeeper who saves it."

United faced Ipswich at Old Trafford in the FA Cup. Charlton scored twice in front of 53,550 fans; a subdued occasion where one player from the visiting team actually received plenty of praise. Bill Fryer of the *Express* said John Elsworthy looked "every bit as good as Duncan Edwards". In the *Coventry Evening Telegraph*, however, Brian Glanville insisted that Edwards was still "widely accepted as Europe's finest left-half" in a column discussing the virtue of placing faith in a young team.

Duncan wrote a timely article where he referenced the tendency to build up singular players in a team game, and although he never discussed himself, his comments on the matter are intriguing. "Blackpool, I am frequently told, are a one-man team," he said. "The one-man being the incomparable Stanley Matthews. Preston, I am reliably informed, are in the same boat, with Tom Finney as their ace of trumps. I hear similar reports about Fulham and Johnny Haynes, Bristol City and John Atyeo, Leyton Orient and Tom Johnston. And I don't believe any of them, because I have never yet seen the team where one man was greater than the whole. In short, the whole thing is a myth, but a dangerous myth because once it has grown sufficiently it can affect a team's performances. Take the example of Finney North End, as Preston were once called. With or without the genius of Tom, they are a first class side, yet I believe one of the major worries of manager Cliff Britton is making his players believe it when Finney is not playing. For so long have the other players listened to the story that they are nothing without Finney that a special effort is needed to key them up when Tom is away."

With all the changes in recent weeks, there could be no suggestion United were less than a team. They had clawed back two of the eight-point deficit before a trip to Arsenal on the first day of February. Before they ran out, Duncan gave that familiar battle cry. *Well, lads, we haven't come here for nuffin'*. "His confidence was supreme and infectious," Busby said. "As we were going away he would say [it] to all around him, the great and the greater (our players at that time were all great)… and he saw to it that we seldom came away with nuffin'."

Duncan was no stranger to being accosted by youngsters who would now not only wait for him after games, they would run on to the pitch – one young Arsenal fan by the name of Derek Bushby took it upon himself to approach Duncan before kick-off, to ask for his autograph. The United man obliged, and the moment was captured in an iconic image – the young boy in a long overcoat, and Duncan signing his scrap of paper, resplendent in a gleaming all-white strip that was doomed to be coloured in the mud of the Highbury pitch.

Derek wasn't the only young boy there to see the famous Busby Babes. In attendance at Highbury was a young Harry Redknapp. "I was 10," he recalls. "I saw Duncan Edwards, Eddie Colman, Roger Byrne, Tommy Taylor. All those incredible players. It was a great team, and I was only a kid, but I'd always say they were the greatest... I wasn't a United supporter but I had a real affinity for them. There was no tribalism or nastiness at football. Me and my dad would stand at Arsenal, there was no segregation, we'd stand next to people from Manchester or Sheffield. Dad would have his flask and offer cups of tea. We all stood together."

And even though the Babes were beloved as a complete team, one player stood out as a spectacle on his own. "Duncan was a colossus," Redknapp says. "He was incredible. When you think Bobby Charlton – a player who was poetry in motion – said Duncan made him feel as if he couldn't play, you get a sense of how amazing he was. That a player like Bobby would be looking for a player like Duncan to get the team out of a bind and he'd deliver two goals to do just that. He had an aura like a Diego Maradona or Zinedine Zidane. He had the power as well. You could see him power past people, and hit a 40-yard pass or 30-yard shot. He was a one-off."

The Gunners felt the full force of his power early on. "As the game unfolded, Arsenal simply couldn't cope with the level of our confidence or our touch," Bobby Charlton recalled. "Duncan scored after 10 minutes, from 25 yards. He bounded across the muddy surface before giving the fine Welsh international goalkeeper Jack Kelsey no chance. As was so often the reaction of opponents when Edwards exerted himself so powerfully in the early going, you could see Arsenal heads drop."

Charlton added a second. Taylor got the third. It was 3-0 at half-time. "When Duncan was in your team, the game was never won or lost until the final whistle was blown," Harry Gregg remembered. "We were winning by three goals and Duncan spent the entire half-time break telling us the game wasn't over."

What unfolded after the break transformed this from a procession into one of the greatest league games in football history. Arsenal's comeback was spectacular, as they scored in the 58th, 60th and 61st minute to draw level. Everyone at Highbury was still catching their breath when Viollet showed predatory instinct to give United the lead again.

Edwards, who had been so dominating in United's control of the first half, had become less so in the frenzy of the second period. The press were critical of his performance, particularly his role in Arsenal's next goal, with Jack Peart, the *Sunday Pictorial*'s correspondent writing that he did not "think his display in this thrilling game would impress England team manager Walter Winterbottom. He was clearly at fault for Arsenal's fourth goal when, instead of clearing, he dallied on the ball." Thankfully, by that time United had already struck a fifth, and saw out the game with their lead intact.

However, Duncan's role in United's win was not underestimated by his colleagues. "Duncan, as always, took Arsenal's recovery as a personal affront," recalled Charlton, while on the journey back, they joked that Edwards had earned the right to become captain of the England team. "We were all taking the Michael out of him," Gregg said. "Billy Wright was in this run of games for England but there was speculation Duncan was going to succeed him as captain. We were ribbing him about that and he was embarrassed. You know what he said? He said that Mark Jones was a better centre-half than him, and he should replace Wright if anyone should."

The conversation bore a passing resemblance to the one Duncan had shared with Jimmy Murphy on a trip *to* London a couple of years earlier, where he insisted David Pegg should remain captain of the youth team, and was another reminder of how much he loved the club and the players he played alongside.

The praise also came from United's opponents on the day. "They just kept coming at us," remembered the bombarded goalkeeper Jack Kelsey, "and the score could easily have been 10-7. It was the kind of game, even one which was played in ankle-deep mud, which would pack grounds all over the country at any time. It was the finest match that I ever played in, and in Duncan Edwards, Manchester United had a player with all the promise in the world. Even in the conditions that day, his strength stood out. He was a colossus."

It was not the first time United had been casual, but by far the greatest takeaway from the afternoon was the wonderful game of football. "The thermometer was doing a war dance," Geoffrey Green wrote in his book *There's Only One United*. "Spectators and players alike were breathless as the teams left the field arm in arm."

A repeat of such complacency could cost them dear in their next two games – the knife-edge second leg against Red Star in Belgrade, and the visit of Wolves in the league. But Edwards knew how good his opponents in Yugoslavia were, and was not going to take it for granted. "Let's get this Red Star side out of the European Cup first," he said, "and then we'll deal with Wolves. If the boys play like they did against Arsenal, Stan Cullis's boys will need to go some to beat us."

Before travelling to Belgrade, Duncan had two administrative jobs to complete. The first was his newspaper column, where he discussed his theory that northern clubs were more likely to 'giant kill' in the FA Cup than southern ones, due to a glut of great players from the past featuring in their ranks.

Then, before he packed his suitcase, he made certain that the final pages of his forthcoming book were sent to his publisher, ready for sign-off. United's travelling party left for Belgrade on Monday February 3rd, stopping in Munich to refuel. The decision had been taken to hire a charter plane, considering the problems they'd had returning from Prague. They had been waved off – once the late Mark Jones turned up – by Jimmy Murphy on the Old Trafford forecourt. Murphy was due to take charge of Wales in their World Cup play-off against Israel and so remained in the UK. "I usually sat next to Matt on the plane whenever the team went away," Jimmy said. "I had suggested that I went to Belgrade, with it being such an important European Cup game. He had said, 'No, Jimmy, you have a job to do,' so Bert Whalley went to Belgrade in my place."

The weather in Belgrade was terrible, with low clouds and snow making for poor visibility. The conditions were deemed the minimum permitted for British European Airways to allow their pilots to land in. Airport engineers only realised the plane had landed when it was taxiing on to the apron.

More pleasant a greeting was theirs at the gate. "A crowd of autograph hunters stormed the Customs Hall," read a report in the *Daily Mirror*. "Officials tried to keep the fans back but they swept past them and through the barriers."

United trained in the afternoon the day before the game, while the reporters soaked in the atmosphere of Manchester United's latest grand occasion. "Sekularac is almost a legendary figure here," Don Davies wrote on February 4th. "His play is said to rival that of Sivori or Boniperti yet in Manchester we saw very little of it, thanks to the unremitting attentions of the mighty Edwards."

The respect was healthy from Red Star just as it was from United and the travelling press. "We played against an extremely big team that had high quality players in its ranks," Vladimir Popovic, the midfielder, said in 2007. "They were mostly extremely young. The matches were very important for both teams and were played in front of a large number of spectators."

The best and most frustrating of Busby's side were on show in the big game. After just two minutes Viollet made it 1-0. Charlton scored in the 30th and 31st minutes to make it 3-0, and 5-1 on aggregate. George Follows congratulated Charlton's magnificent influence. "He interrupted a foot-juggling act by Jostic, ran the ball three yards forward and hit a sensational 25-yard left-footer that even the bounding Beara could not touch," Follows wrote. "Three minutes more and Charlton scored again. A crisp right foot from 10 yards – after Duncan Edwards had bulldozed through from a free-kick… with three goals in the bag at half-time there seemed no need to worry about the goals that had got away."

Edwards had been majestic. "Duncan retained the dominant mood he had displayed at Highbury, and for most of the half we seemed to be quicker to the ball and to have plenty of time to play it," remembered Charlton, who had taken his goalscoring tally to 12 goals in 11 games.

"Duncan ran the show against Belgrade," said Bill Foulkes. "It was unbelievable. The pitch was muddy but it made no difference to the way he was able to pass. He had this way of just skimming the ball over the top of the mud with power and accuracy that it made no difference. Us lesser mortals were struggling in the mud."

"The bigger the occasion," Matt Busby said, "the better he liked it."

United, however, then conspired to do exactly as they did at Arsenal – and within 13 minutes of the restart, Red Star had levelled the score in the game and were one goal away from forcing a replay. "Jones, Foulkes, Byrne, Edwards and Colman, who had played magnificently throughout, as had the rest, saw to it that that goal never materialised," wrote Don Davies.

With a much more competitive edge to proceedings, tempers flared in the closing stages. United were just about professional enough to see the game out at 3-3 – and qualify for the semi-final.

"Manchester United added another shining page to their glittering history today," Henry Rose wrote in the *Express*. "They reached the semi-final of the European Cup for a second season despite inflamed Yugoslavs, one-sided refereeing and injuries… I found it easy in this white-hot battle to forgive Duncan Edwards for protesting over a free-kick. The referee took Duncan's number."

Edwards hobbled through to the end of the game. In the early editions of February 6th's *Manchester Evening News*, the fans at home were relieved to read that he should make the important game at the weekend. "Edwards is *hors de combat* with an ankle injury," wrote Eric Thornton, "but he is expected to be fit for United's top-of-the-table tussle with the rampaging Wolves."

United were through. Perhaps their greatest educational experience to take from this trip was not the on-pitch concentration, but the grace in which Red Star took their defeat, considering the Babes' own frustrated response to elimination against Madrid ten months earlier.

Sekularac, the top player of the Red Star team, developed a particular affection for the United players. "I knew all of Manchester's players very well, we played two top games," he told *Danas* in 2014, and in Jonathan Wilson's *The Anatomy of Manchester United*, he told the author: "Their friendship, their kindness, how they received us in the first leg in Manchester and how they behaved here, and how we greeted each other, even today I take my hat off to them."

Of the second leg, Sekularac described Duncan as "maybe the best player in the world", and added: "The game was amazing, Manchester led 3-0, and then we managed to equalise, and we had the opportunity for a complete turnaround. The best chance was mine, 100 percent! But I missed. If I had scored to make it 4-3, the replay would have been played, most likely three days later in Italy. We made an incredible friendship with them! They were all nice and polite, real English gentlemen. After the game, I went to the Metropol hotel with Bobby Charlton and Tommy Taylor."

Sekularac recalled how Taylor had invited him to go on a cruise after the World Cup in the summer – the Yugoslav accepted, and said he would visit England afterwards.

Popovic's memories are equally warm. "The match was played in an extraordinary atmosphere where the fans cheered us on for all 90 minutes," he said. "We only needed one more goal. We were not lucky enough to give it, but it is indisputable that that game, like Manchester, remained in my fond memory. Already in those young days, Bobby Charlton showed that he would be one of the best English players in history. I had countless duels with him and I could immediately feel the quality. Duncan Edwards was one of the top players, who was a real leader on the field, a player who carried that team. After that game, we all went out together and celebrated. The first thing was dinner at Majestic... we had an extremely nice evening, because they were top athletes and top people. I still remember those moments, even though it was back in 1958."

There was no lack of humour. Jovan Cokic recalled of Roger Byrne: "He approached me and asked me through the interpreter to apologise for one rude foul. I laughed and hugged him, and he continued to justify himself in disbelief that I would forgive him."

United's players had attended a banquet at the British Embassy. There, Roger Byrne asked Busby if it would be okay to accept the Red Star players' invitations to go out. Busby not only accepted, but said he would go along. After leaving the Metropol, the next stop on the night crawl was the Skadarija Bar. Red Star officials talked to Walter Crickmer about their plans to build a new stadium. They said they would love it if United would return to open it. Crickmer agreed. Miroslav Radojičić spent time in the company of Matt Busby and Don Davies, who complained, "Why didn't your boys score just once more, so we could have met again?" before Busby and Davies departed for bed and left Radojičić in the company of Taylor and Edwards to talk about football in a pub whose name, when translated into English, was 'Way of Life'.

When the United players eventually left to get some sleep ahead of their flight the next day, the journalist made an impulsive decision – he was going to go with the United team back to Manchester, and write an article or a book about the human experience of what they had created. The following morning, Radojičić went through with his plan, but when he arrived in Belgrade, he realised he had left his passport at home – by the time he had returned, the plane carrying the Manchester United party was on its way to Munich for its changeover.

The plane landed with a hard bump in snowy conditions at Munich-Riem Airport. Pilot Captain James Thain and his co-pilot had been with the United party on both legs of the trip. Thain had flown to Belgrade, with Kenneth Rayment taking control of the return. After stopping to refuel, the plane was ready for its final journey to England. On its initial attempt to take off, Thain noticed a strange sound from the engine while accelerating, and some fluctuation in the boost pressure gauge. The attempt was aborted. Three minutes later, a second attempt was made, but within 40 seconds the pilots halted again after noticing over-acceleration. As this was a common issue with this type of plane – an 'Elizabethan' – Thain and Rayment were not unduly concerned, but they did ask the passengers to leave the plane and to wait in the lounge in the terminal until the technical issues were resolved.

Snow was now falling heavily. It seemed unlikely that another attempt to fly would be made, so Duncan sent a telegram to landlady Mrs Dorman, which read: "All flights cancelled, flying tomorrow. Duncan."

Chapter 23
Dreamer

Fifteen minutes after departing the plane on its second aborted take off from Munich on Thursday, February 6th, 1958, the Manchester United party was called back to the aircraft amid the snow. After conversations with engineers where the option of remaining in Germany overnight was discussed, pilot James Thain felt that the length of the runway would be sufficient to generate the requisite velocity to take off, and, keen to remain on schedule, took the decision to try again. David Pegg, who had been compelled to move seats after feeling uncertain on the hazardous flight to Bucharest the previous summer, did so again, sitting with Duncan Edwards, Mark Jones, Eddie Colman and Tommy Taylor at the rear of the plane.

The plane started moving again at 2.56pm, and reached the holding point at the runway at 2.59pm. As the aircraft gathered pace, a couple of the players joked to try and lighten the mood. Bobby Charlton told Dennis Viollet, "I'm not taking my coat off this time." Tommy Taylor asked Viollet if the wheels had left the ground yet. Roger Byrne joked that it was "all or nothing". Johnny Berry, however, felt uncertain. "It's no laugh; we are all going to be killed."

Bill Foulkes recalled the "strongest possible feeling of fore-boding" hitting him. "Somehow I knew we were not going to make it," he said. The sound of the throttle of the plane was replaced by the screech of brakes and the searing cry of metal grinding.

One last voice. Bill Whelan, above the din. "If this is death, I am ready for it."

The plane could not be stopped from skidding off the end of the runway. It smashed through the perimeter fence and the port wing was torn off in flames after striking one of the residential houses nearby. The conclusion of the harrowing incident, told by Roger MacDonald: "The rest of the aircraft continued its wild path of destruction. The right side of the rear fuselage hit a wooden hut with concrete foundations about 100 yards behind and was torn away with explosive suddenness like the wrath of a giant. The remainder, still attached to the starboard wing, scraped and slithered on, reducing trees to stumps, until one big impact made it spin crazily, like some enormous Catherine wheel. Then it stopped, a wreck of jagged metal facing the runway, with carnage and debris marking its path."

In the cockpit, Thain acted swiftly. The air stewardesses had miraculously survived. They escaped through an emergency window. Rayment was trapped in his seat by fuselage, but implored Thain to go on – Thain said he would be back as soon as the fires were dealt with.

Harry Gregg, for a moment, thought he was the only survivor. The first body he saw was Bert Whalley. "He was motionless, his eyes were open and there wasn't a mark on him," Gregg said. "Somehow, I knew he was dead."

As Gregg crawled out of the aircraft, Thain raced past him with a fire extinguisher, screaming at him to "run, you stupid bastard, it's going to explode!" Then, Gregg heard the cry of a baby, just as other people began to emerge from the wreckage. "Come back, you bastards, there are people alive in there," Gregg blasted. He went back into the plane to rescue the baby and its mother. He saw Ray Wood, Albert Scanlon, Bobby Charlton and Dennis Viollet, and presumed they were all dead. He had not been able to pull Wood and Scanlon free, but did so with Charlton and

Viollet. He found Matt Busby and Jackie Blanchflower, and was then horrified to find Roger Byrne, who had died. Eventually Gregg waited with Blanchflower – "The lower part of his arm almost completely severed," recalled the goalkeeper – as assistance arrived on the scene.

Bill Foulkes and Bobby Charlton had also stumbled clear of the flames. They watched as explosions blasted even more devastation onto the landscape. A truck arrived to take survivors to the local hospital. Reluctantly, Gregg joined Foulkes and Charlton, all three unaware of the fate of many of their team-mates.

Seven players were killed in the impact. Roger Byrne, Geoff Bent, Eddie Colman, Mark Jones, David Pegg, Tommy Taylor and Billy Whelan. Three members of the club staff had perished – Walter Crickmer, one of the men responsible for creating the culture for which Manchester United were so celebrated, and coaches Tom Curry and Bert Whalley. Journalists Don Davies and Frank Swift – dead. Willie Satinoff, a fervent supporter of the club and a close friend of Matt Busby, the only fan who could claim to have been to all of United's European fixtures. Dead.

As the bodies were rushed to the Rechts der Isar Hospital in the Haidhausen region of Munich, the survivors were desperate for news of their friends whose fate remained unknown.

In Manchester, Jimmy Murphy arrived back in town after successfully getting Wales to the World Cup. He was in high spirits with United's success in the European Cup, and he was excited to welcome back Matt Busby at Old Trafford that evening with a glass of whisky to toast the victories of the week. He was picked up at Manchester London Road and taken to Old Trafford, where he received the devastating news from club secretary Alma George. Murphy recalled the events of the afternoon in his autobiography:

"Mr Murphy, please stop," she said. "Haven't you heard the news? The United plane has crashed at Munich." My feet stopped. So did my heart.

The fingers of the clock on the wall pointed to four o'clock... but now time meant nothing. The numbing horror of that moment will live with me till I die. I dashed into my office, picked up the phone and put calls through to the Police, newspapers, the BBC, asking for news. Then it started to come in. Roger Byrne, Eddie Colman, Mark Jones, Tommy Taylor, Billy Whelan and David Pegg were dead. Killed in a snow storm at Munich Airport. So was Bert Whalley, one of my closest friends and one of the greatest coaches I ever met. Tom Curry, dear, patient Tom the club trainer, and the club secretary Walter Crickmer, they too had been killed and Matt Busby was fighting for his life. To the generation which has grown up since then, they may be just names, but to me they were Matt's boys. My boys! I had seen them come to Old Trafford as part of Matt's master plan to build the greatest side in Europe... and they were gone. Seven of the greatest players ever assembled at one club were wiped out, and the greatest of them all, Duncan Edwards, fighting for his life. I was like a man living through a nightmare. I locked the office door, put my head on my desk and wept like a child. Only last Monday I waved cheerio to them: "See you on Thursday lads... see you do a good job." They did, they won through to the semi-final of the European Cup. Now they were gone, at the very time they had the world of soccer at their feet. And now, 10 years later, I search my memory and still cannot chart the course of the next 12 hours. The fingers pointed to four o'clock when I heard of the tragedy and they were still pointing to four when I left for home the following morning, don't ask me what I did. I was living a nightmare. All I know is there was a bottle of Scotch in my cupboard and the following morning it was empty – and that was extraordinary as I am a beer drinker but I must have drank a whole bottle of whisky without knowing.

The evening newspapers covered the events. The first edition of the *Evening Chronicle* mentioned the plane had been delayed. News rushed through, and the 6pm edition carried coverage of the crash. On the BBC, news of the crash scrolled across the screen while *Watch With Mother* was being broadcast on television. Radio programmes were interrupted to share the news.

Wilf McGuinness recalled seeing a newspaper and being instantly relieved it mentioned the crash had occurred on the runway, as he felt it could not have caused significant damage. But he and a friend went to the offices of the *Evening Chronicle*, where the horrendous truth began to sink in.

In Munich, Bill Foulkes was able to get an update he took positively, once he knew most of the bodies had been found. "I asked the doctor how Duncan was," Foulkes said. "He gave a gesture... I said, 'so, 50/50?' and thought, well, if Duncan's 50/50, he'll be okay." Foulkes had been protected from the hard reality – Duncan had been listed by the doctors as "mortally injured" on his admission to hospital.

The Red Star Belgrade players began to hear of the news late on Thursday. Sekularac had missed a late chance in the game and had previously bemoaned it because it meant Red Star were eliminated. He saw newspapers carrying the headlines after leaving the cinema and immediately began to regret his miss for different reasons. "If we had played a replay in Italy, they would surely not have returned home from Belgrade," he said. "Who knows how many times I said to myself, 'Well, Sheki, if you were a better goalscorer, all those guys would have stayed alive if you had shaken the net?'"

Popovic remembered a surreal feeling. "It happened the next day, that information came very early to Belgrade and I can't explain to you how we all felt at that moment. All those who participated in the game and our football in general felt very bad because they were young players, who had a very great perspective," he said. "That day and that moment remained in my bitter, super-bitter memory."

Back in England, Molly was still in work in her office at Cook and Company, the textile machine makers, when she was informed of the crash. She immediately cycled to her friend's house in Sale. There, she – like Sarah and Gladstone in Dudley – waited nervously by their radio and television for updates. The names of the survivors were read over the radio. Duncan's was listed.

Arrangements were immediately made for members of the victims' families to travel to Germany if they wished. Many decided to brave the conditions. On the first plane which left Manchester for Munich, Jimmy Murphy was accompanied by Matt Busby's wife and children, Jean, Sandy and Sheena, Sheena's husband Don Gibson (the former United player), as well as Molly; the plane was diverted to Frankfurt due to heavy snow.

The *Manchester Evening News* carried a haunting headline on Friday – "MATT 50-50 : EDWARDS 'GRAVE' : BERRY COMA" – with the first updates of what condition Duncan was in. "I don't think Edwards will be able to play football any more," said one doctor, and his injuries were listed as "shock, broken ribs, fractured right leg". Molly had pleaded with reporters not to ask her any questions.

The *Birmingham Evening Post* reported "Dudley Relief At Edwards's Survival", beginning: "There was relief at Dudley last night when it was learned that Duncan Edwards had survived the crash. In Elm Road, Priory Estate, Dudley, Mr and Mrs Gladstone Edwards anxiously awaited further news of their son. Edwards's career has been watched with pride by his townsmen. Late last night Mr and Mrs Edwards received a telegram from British European Airways offering to fly them free to their son's bedside. Mr Edwards said that he will accept the offer. Duncan is their only child."

In the days before around-the-clock television news, most of the public had to rely on radio bulletins, the irregular news programmes on television or the morning and evening editions of daily newspapers. Things were changing rapidly with the condition of different individuals. Duncan was reported to have "showed a slight improvement" by the *Halifax Evening Courier* on Friday 7th.

That evening, Gladstone went to London Airport with the father of Kenny Morgans to catch a direct flight to Munich. He left Dudley Port Station in good time – telling reporters "I am confident that Duncan will pull through" – but bad weather again meant this flight was delayed until the following morning.

Molly was devastated to find Duncan in critical condition and delirious from the impact of the crash, as well as the medication he had been pumped with. He didn't recognise her. As he came around, he realised Molly had been there, and asked for a message to be passed to her. "I'll be all right."

There were conflicting reports on Saturday 8th. "It is most unlikely that John Berry, Duncan Edwards and Bert Scanlon will be able to play football again, Dr Maurer, head surgeon at the hospital, told me," said Douglas Slight in the *Manchester Evening News*.

Perhaps the answer was dependent on the way the question was asked. Peter Lorenzo of the *Daily Herald* described Edwards as "the mighty man of British football. His right leg is broken and he has severe shock and concussion. I asked Professor Maurer: 'Will he ever play football again?' He shrugged his shoulders and said: 'He is a strong boy. It is possible, but first let us get him well.'"

It was against this backdrop of hysteria that Jimmy Murphy, Matt Busby's assistant, was trying to make sense of everything. Back in Manchester, the remaining staff at the club were wondering what to do. Chairman Harold Hardman – who had decided against taking the flight after what had happened on the Bilbao trip – told the *Liverpool Echo* that as soon as possible United would resume their full League, Cup and European Cup programmes. They had a duty to football and a duty to the public, he said. "We shall carry on, even if it means we are heavily defeated."

That had been the message passed on from a gravely ill Matt Busby to his number two. Murphy told the *Liverpool Echo*: "He said to me. 'I'm feeling a little better now. Take care of things for me, Jim.'"

In another account, Murphy mentioned that he had spent around three minutes with Busby, who had also said "Keep the flag flying."

Jimmy left Matt and was walking down the corridor when one of the sisters on the ward approached him. Duncan had been asking for his watch – the one that had been presented to him by Real Madrid. The boy who had – in his early days – grown so accustomed to winning things that he would just toss his schoolbag on the chair and leave his mother to sort it out, had this one sporting memento he kept with him at all times.

Unbeknown to Jimmy, Harry Gregg had heard the nurse telling other people earlier that Duncan had been complaining. Harry was moved to perform his next act of heroism. He left the hospital and returned to the airfield to search for the watch that Duncan believed in his confusion had been stolen from his wrist. Harry saw the gold of the watch glistening against the snow. It was mangled. Almost destroyed. But there were few men with as much integrity as Harry Gregg, and he was insistent that it should be reunited with its owner. He picked it up and took it to the hospital. This important fact was never made public, as Harry never shared the story publicly with anyone but his family, and even then, he did not like to talk about it as it would bring him to tears.

Upon hearing the nurse share the distress with Jimmy, Harry got his attention and the pair went in to see Duncan. The other element of this story that Harry, in his modesty, never made public was that it was he who carefully placed the watch back on Duncan's wrist – and because he never said anything, it was always presumed that Jimmy had done it.

It was this act which prompted the following event.

"I sat with him a while, and then he turned his head," Jimmy said, "it was the saddest thing I've ever seen or been a part of. He turned and said, 'Oh it's you Jimmy,' I said yes. I had to put my head to his mouth. He said, 'What time's kick-off tomorrow?'"

Jimmy smiled and said 3pm. Duncan's reply: "Get stuck in."

Murphy – a devout Catholic – left Duncan's bedside and walked to one of the hospital stairwells where he broke down in uncontrollable tears. He left Munich a changed man, determined to follow through on his promise to Busby. There was another telling incident before he left.

"I woke up again later in Munich to hear a voice saying, 'Albert Scanlon will never play football again,'" recalled Scanlon. "Jimmy Murphy came in and I was crying and I told him what I had heard. He said, 'That's not true, Albert, you are all right.' Given that it came from Jimmy, it was enough for me."

Murphy faced reporters. "I have seen the boys," he said. "Limbs and hearts may be broken, but the spirit remains. Their message is that the club is not dead. Manchester United lives on. My boss and my greatest friend, Matt Busby, would want me to tell you that the Red Devils will survive this. We have a motto at Old Trafford which means 'work and wisdom'. The work of the country's finest players, and the wisdom of the country's finest manager have made the club what we were. It is going to be a long, long struggle, but together we hope to be back 'there again'. And we know that they will be back. They have to be, because they are the greatest."

Murphy knew how serious the situation was with Duncan. "We all knew how desperately ill Duncan was," he said. "And even if he lived, his right thigh was smashed and it was doubtful he would ever play again... (but) nothing could quench the great spirit and courageous heart of this boy."

But as the United assistant manager prepared to return to Manchester, he did so with that resolve to do good on his word to Busby. His logical conviction to do so was galvanised by the fact that Duncan had survived at all and the emotional push was inspired by the illogical. It was not logical to think Duncan could play football again – but Duncan as a player and Manchester United as a club had made a mockery of convention. It was not practical to create a competitive team from the best homegrown players. It was certainly not practical to expect that team to be the best in the country. And to go toe-to-toe with the best sides in the world? Busby, aided by Murphy, had pulled off a sporting miracle. A work of art. And Duncan was its masterpiece. The fact that one doctor had said it would not be completely futile to rule out a return to playing was the ignition to the spark of the conversation Murphy had with Busby. Manchester United would be born again.

Murphy hadn't even left the country by the time the next update was provided.

"Edwards and Frank Taylor had a slight relapse," a hospital official said on the afternoon of February 8th. "But everything is being done, and it is felt in the hospital that the worst is now over."

Doctors treating the patients gave the following report to press: "Duncan Edwards – Still in danger. No change this morning."

The *Sports Argus*, printed that evening, reported: "Duncan Edwards: Very seriously ill. The Dudley man's condition was said to have deteriorated somewhat today when his temperature was 104 degrees. Later it fell four degrees."

Some newspapers were trying to take a blunt line in order to properly align the public's expectations. The *Green 'Un* in the *Sheffield Star* reported: "Jackie Blanchflower and Duncan Edwards are thought unlikely to play first class football again. We do not like writing this report. But our public charge is to record the truth. These are the facts."

On Sunday, that was the line being carried in *The People*. "Duncan Edwards, the brilliant footballer who was being groomed to be England's next captain, will never play again," wrote Peter Forbes. "Edwards has highly complicated features that have weakened his condition."

"He lost a lot of blood in the crash," Professor Georg Maurer, who had been given the responsibility of looking after Duncan, said. "He has had several transfusions. Now we can only wait and see." Maurer was a man of great dignity – he had been awarded the Iron Cross for his work saving the lives of British and German soldiers in the battle of Dunkirk, and his tireless contribution to help these representatives of England's most famous club would go a further step towards strengthening Anglo-German relations.

Maurer, or one of his colleagues, would provide regular updates. On Sunday, it was the turn of Dr Lang, one of the senior doctors of the hospital, who said the condition of Captain Rayment, Berry and Duncan Edwards was "changing hour by hour – slightly up and slightly down."

However, on Sunday morning, Duncan fell into what was described in the press as a coma – only to be 'taken off the danger list' that evening.

"Duncan Edwards has come out of a coma and recognised and spoken to people," reported Peter Lorenzo on the events of the previous evening on Monday February 10th. "He has also taken some soup." That day, the bodies of the deceased were flown back to Manchester, with the exception of David Pegg and Billy Whelan, who were taken to Yorkshire and Ireland respectively.

Back in England, all around the country grown men and women and young children waited for news. "The whole country said prayers," recalls Harry Redknapp. "We did every day at school. You were waiting for the newspaper every day. One day the paper had a picture of Duncan sitting in bed, looking like he was recovering. I cut it out and put it in a scrapbook."

Duncan's condition progressively declined. While the *Mirror* reported that Duncan had shown a "glimmer of improvement", the *Birmingham Daily Post* said he was "still unconscious and in acute danger", and the *Newcastle Evening Chronicle* shared a worrying update: "Earlier this morning, doctors at the Isar Hospital reported his condition as unchanged, but at the last examination this morning doctors were alarmed at the unusually high percentage of nitrogen in the player's blood. Besides the high percentage of nitrogen in his blood, Edwards has a series of broken ribs on his right side and a complicated fracture of his right thigh. Three specialists are attending him in the hospital's emergency ward."

In the *Liverpool Echo*, it was reported that Edwards was "receiving food intravenously".

It was the most concerning day yet since the crash, and saw Duncan's parents urgently summoned back to Germany. Gladstone had returned to see Sarah, but events in Munich meant a rush back for both of them to see their son.

"In a desperate attempt to save the life of Duncan Edwards, an artificial kidney was rushed from Freiburg University clinic to the Isar Hospital here today," disclosed Douglas Slight. "His condition was growing steadily worse. And then came new drama. Three attempts failed to detour his blood through the machine. A tube was put in his throat to aid breathing. Then, after several adjustments, the machine began working at 2pm. A team of leading surgeons was battling non-stop to save him. Surgeons said the kidney was their last chance to save Edwards… his injuries include severely damaged kidneys, broken ribs, pneumothorax (collapsed lung), broken pelvis, and complex fracture of the right thigh. He is also suffering from severe shock. Edwards was said to be near death after the nitrogen content of his blood rose to '500 promille' during the night. A '45 promille' content is normal. Doctors reduced the nitrogen in his blood by yesterday evening, but when it climbed during the night doctors put an emergency call through to Freiburg for the artificial kidney. Edwards was also being given a four-and-a-half pint transfusion. The brilliant 38-year-old specialist travelling with it, Dr Sartorius, arrived later after losing his way in Munich. He was conducting the operation. He was immediately taken up to the fourth floor, where Edwards was already in the operating theatre. The ambulance, accompanied by Dr Sartorius in a fast police car, had been driven through the night… during the night, alarm buzzers with flashing coloured lights had sounded several times and two doctors were called in at 3am, one of them in a police car."

While waiting for the kidney to arrive, Dr Lang told reporters Edwards was "still young and therefore has more chances".

The *Aberdeen Evening Express* reported: "Duncan Edwards' parents, Mr and Mrs Edwards, and his brother-in-law, Mr I P Wooley, are making a dramatic dash to the bedside of Duncan, lying gravely ill in Munich. Early this afternoon they left Dudley on a three-hour race against time by road for London Airport in the hope of catching the 5.15 flight to Munich. BEA officials were preparing to secure the waiving of customs formalities to get the three relatives on to the Lufthansa Convair."

They arrived just before midnight on Tuesday, and the dramatic events of the day were relayed in the press the following morning.

Of the many heartbreaking elements of this tragic conclusion, perhaps the most devastating are the events of Wednesday, February 12th, which contain a story rarely told.

Professor Maurer explained that Duncan woke up after the emergency procedures, and murmured, "Where am I?"

"Doctors are much more hopeful of saving his life," the *Manchester Evening News* reported. "This afternoon a bulletin said he was maintaining his improvement, and doctors had been able to set his leg in a cast. The bone is broken in seven places. Edwards, whose kidneys are working normally again, has pleased doctors with his remarkable powers of recovery. Professor Georg Maurer, chief surgeon, said, 'His condition is very gratifying.' Today his parents, who arrived here last night, visited him. For six hours yesterday an artificial kidney, rushed from Freiburg to Munich, was connected to Edwards's blood circulation to take the strain off his injured kidneys."

Prior to that, however, there was a moment of grave concern followed by the most beautiful tragedy. "Before the connection, the nitrogen and potash content of the blood were so high that his heart was about to stop beating," Maurer told the press. He went on to explain that when Duncan was in his state of semi-consciousness, he "seemed to imagine he was still playing football and once shouted: 'Goal, goal!'"

It is no less distressing to consider, more than 60 years after the event, the image of this young man, slipping out of lucidity; the heartbreaking poetry of Duncan being so obsessed with football that he was dreaming of it at the time where he could have lost his life at any moment. *In* the moment, as the events were unfolding, one could only marvel at the miraculous work done by the doctors.

"His kidneys appear to be functioning again. The machine has done its job excellently," said the professor. "This morning we gave him a little milk and he said a few words."

Duncan still seemed in possession of his faculties. His mother recalled a private conversation: "When he was in the hospital he said, 'Get me out of here, Mum. I've got other things to do besides lie here.' I said, 'I'll get you out of here just as soon as I can.' I told him he had to get out because he needed to see to his car. 'Keep it on the road, Mum,' he said to me. 'I'll get better.'"

Later that day, however, another doctor warned: "It is still too early to be optimistic. He is still gravely ill."

The *Mirror* reported on Thursday 13th that Molly was still in Munich. "Arrangements had been made to rush her to the hospital yesterday if she was needed suddenly." Elsewhere, other newspapers carried the report of a South African woman, born with two pairs of kidneys, who was trying to alert international press that she would be willing to donate a pair to Duncan.

The following day, updates were provided to the press by Dr J Graham Taylor of British European Airways. Dr Taylor said Edwards knew what had happened to him but did not know of the deaths in the crash, and added that while he was conscious he spoke to Molly. "Edwards's condition is unchanged," Taylor said. "He is still rather restless. As this morning his kidneys had not yet started functioning properly, it was decided that the artificial kidney would be used again."

The *Western Mail* reported that he had begun to ask questions: "First coherent sentence spoken by Duncan Edwards since last Thursday's air crash came through half-closed lips in a Munich hospital yesterday as his mother and father sat at his bedside. Edwards said simply, 'How are the others?' His parents told him: 'They are all right.' For neither Edwards nor Matt Busby, now on the recovery list, knows the terrible death-toll."

Busby had been read the last rites but pulled through – doctors did not want to shock either of them and potentially set their recovery back. Bobby Charlton had been kept in for observation but stayed long enough to see his friend awake again. "Where have you been?" a weak Duncan scolded him. When Bobby departed for Manchester after being discharged, he remained uncertain of the fate of his former housemate.

On Saturday 15th, Dr Taylor told *Reuters* that Duncan had suffered a "little internal bleeding during the night" but that it was "not a major crisis".

In *The People* the next day, the question was asked: "How long can a man hover between life and death – without the scales tilting one way or the other? That is what doctors attending Duncan Edwards were wondering last night. For nine days and nights the 21-year-old 'Busby Babe' had been on the brink of death. And he was reported to be still dangerously ill. During Friday night, Edwards had a haemorrhage and immediate blood transfusions were ordered. Dr Graham Taylor, British European Airways medical chief, said, 'Only his tremendous physical strength and powerful fighting spirit are keeping him going. He is an amazing man. No ordinary person would have survived so long.'"

The *Weekly Dispatch* reported there had been no recurrence of the "severe haemorrhages", but that the RAF was on standby at Halton to fly out another artificial kidney if it was required. On

Monday 17th, the *Manchester Evening News* appeared to take the line that no real news was good news: "Surgeons say there are signs his badly bruised kidney may be starting to work again. But doctors warned that the improvement is only slight and it would be wrong to be too optimistic."

In a sign of how rapidly things were changing, the *Belfast Telegraph* reported that afternoon that there would be further treatment with the artificial kidney machine. That treatment had to be "interrupted for technical reasons but it was later resumed" according to the *Birmingham Daily Post* on Tuesday 18th. The *Manchester Evening News* described events of the last 24 hours as a "double crisis in the fight for his life", continuing: "First crisis was in the early hours when the artificial kidney broke down after three hours' working. Technicians on the spot repaired it. Doctors reported no adverse effects on Edwards. But crisis number two soon followed. Doctors said, 'Because the level of poisonous nitrogen in the blood is rising, the kidney will have to be used again.'"

It had been a dramatic fortnight but there was a growing sense that there was to be no positive outcome. Treatment was keeping Duncan alive but aside from one or two moments of consciousness, there was no indication that he was recovering, and the continuous use of the artificial kidney was beginning to do more harm than good. On Wednesday 19th, it was reported that he had been given another blood transfusion. The morning bulletin had described his condition as "rather weak'.

"Doctors today gave grim news about the condition of Duncan Edwards," wrote Douglas Slight. "He has taken a turn for the worse and is 'showing signs of distress.' The bulletin said he was weaker following further treatment with the artificial kidney. He has been given direct person-to-person blood transfusions. Use of the artificial kidney has developed into a vicious circle which is gradually sapping his strength. A BEA doctor said Edwards' condition was 'about the worst' since the kidney treatment was started last week."

However, that doctor, Dr Taylor, also later said that Edwards had "rallied somewhat" and was now out of his oxygen tent. He added to the *Belfast Telegraph* that Edwards was still dangerously ill and "is still not quite back to where he was yesterday".

Duncan remained unaware of events in the world. He was not aware that Busby had been read the last rites again – only to pull through for a second time. He did not know that back in Manchester, United were taking to the field that evening. Jimmy Murphy had fought through the emotion to put a team together to face Sheffield Wednesday in the FA Cup. The Football League had permitted the postponement of the game against Wolves, so this was the first time United had played since the disaster. Gregg and Foulkes were somehow deemed able and willing to play – and Murphy fielded Greaves, Goodwin, Cope, Webster, Dawson, Pearson and Brennan, all rookies with the possible exception of Cope and Webster. That was nine players. Murphy had been inundated with offers from clubs willing to help but he was still keen to do things as close to the Busby way as possible. So only two players were signed. Ernie Taylor, the inside-forward who Murphy had described as the heartbeat of the Blackpool team of Matthews and Mortensen. And, in the number six shirt – registered just before kick-off – was Stan Crowther, the former Aston Villa player whose last experience of this ground was being booted off it by the previous owner of the jersey, and who was given special dispensation to play having already featured for Villa in the cup. United, riding a wave of emotion from the Old Trafford crowd, somehow overcame the odds to triumph against Sheffield Wednesday.

Meanwhile, the bulletins updating the public of Duncan's personal cause seemed calm. Doctors said that they might repeat treatment. A medical officer for BEA said on Thursday that Edwards had "now overcome yesterday's setback and has regained his general condition of two days ago." On Thursday evening, Molly, Sarah and Gladstone were at their hotel, attempting to get some sleep. The morning edition of the *Birmingham Daily Post* on Friday February 21st reported Duncan's condition as "unchanged" and that artificial treatment was "almost certain".

Tragically, even that was hoping for too much. Duncan had passed away just after midnight.

The most comprehensive account of the following hours came in the *Newcastle Evening Chronicle*:

For the second time within a week the flags over the Old Trafford stands, Manchester, hung limply at half-mast in the rain today. They were in memory of Duncan Edwards, the brilliant 21-year-old England and Manchester United left-half who died in Munich Hospital at 1.16 today, the eighth member of the team to die and the 22nd victim of the air crash at Munich on February 6. Groups of schoolboys and workmen stood silent in the rain outside the United ground as the flags were lowered. Shortly after the United players had assembled in the dressing room this morning they stood in silence for one minute. Edwards' team-mates, Ray Wood, Ken Morgans, Dennis Viollet, and Bert Scanlon, who are convalescing, were also informed of his death. They wept as they heard the news from Professor Maurer. The more seriously injured Manchester United men, including the team manager, Matt Busby, John Berry and Jackie Blanchflower, were not told that Edwards had failed to recover. Edwards died suddenly. His parents and his fiancee, Miss Molly Leach, were not at his bedside. They were in their Munich hotel.

The British European Airways medical officer issued this statement: "At about midnight local time Thursday, February 20, the doctors attending Duncan Edwards noted his circulation showed some signs of failing. Restorative injections were given and they produced some improvement. However, the improvement was not maintained and his circulation failed completely, causing death at 0216 local time on Friday, February 21."

Later Mr and Mrs Edwards, Miss Leach and three friends of the Edwards family, left by air for London. A special BEA aircraft is flying to Munich tomorrow to take Edwards's body to London. The body will then be taken by road or rail to Dudley, Worcestershire. It is understood that the funeral will take place next Wednesday.

The *Coventry Evening Telegraph* reported he "died peacefully" without pain. A BEA spokesman said that it was caused by failure of his blood circulation due to an increased urinic condition. "His death was not unexpected, but not immediately anticipated," the statement read.

Fifteen days after the catastrophic disaster at Munich-Riem Airport had rocked Manchester United to its foundations, the club was plunged into a whole new period of heartbreak as it mourned the passing of its greatest ever player.

Chapter 24
Shock And Loss

Tributes flowed as relentlessly as tears as the news broke of Duncan Edwards' death. In Munich, his parents and fiancée had been the first to find out.

"The lion-hearted Edwards died peacefully in sleep, with no pain, at 2.15am today after a desperate last-minute battle to save him," reported the *Manchester Evening News*. "About midnight doctors noticed that his circulation was failing. Injections caused a temporary improvement, but his strength ebbed away. Nurses at his bedside broke down and wept as the flame for life for which they fought so hard flickered out. First to be told were Edwards' parents and his fiancée, Miss Molly Leach. After visiting the hospital, they were given sedatives and told to try and rest."

The sedatives were to calm Sarah and Molly; Gladstone succumbed to a state of shock from which he never truly emerged.

Doctors knew that they had to handle the news delicately, so decided that only certain players could be told, and the news was still withheld from Jackie Blanchflower and Matt Busby. Jimmy Murphy confessed that the wounds felt fresh all over again. "I broke down and cried," he admitted. "The club and England had lost a great footballer. I had lost a very dear friend."

The players were told at the club. "It was like a new knife had been plunged into us. I thought he'd make it," McGuinness recalled. "He was so strong. The iron man. It was such a blow to everybody. A tremendous blow."

The first public statement from the club was issued by club chairman Harold Hardman. "He was a most model servant and a highly skilled, efficient footballer," Hardman said. "He had great qualities, character and footballing ability. He was a man that the game itself can ill afford to lose. The club was mostly greatly indebted to the hospital at Munich. He could not possibly have had better attention."

Jimmy Murphy talked to the press later that day. "Duncan came as a boy to this club. He was a diligent pupil, always willing to learn; yet in spite of all the success which he earned, Duncan always kept his feet on the ground. He was a grand lad, and one of the greatest players in the world. In every match one could see big bustling Duncan battling away; he gave everything he had, no matter how the game was going."

Walter Winterbottom was just one of many to provide accolades to what was, instead of what was to become. "Duncan was a great footballer and he had the promise of becoming the greatest of his day. He played with tremendous joy and his spirit stimulated the whole England team. It was in his character and spirit that I saw the true revival of British football."

It was not the time for a grief-stricken United squad to add their own tributes. One ex-player did, however. "This is a great blow to soccer everywhere," said former club captain Johnny Carey. "He was the greatest wing-half of his time. I recognised his possibilities when he was only 16, and he has fulfilled all I forecast for him."

So too did fellow professionals. "He was a magnificent young player and had he been spared, might have gone close to beating Billy Wright's record of England caps," said Don Revie. "His death is a grievous loss to world football."

Stan Cullis, the manager who sat outside the Edwards home when the boy was 15, said: "Duncan Edwards was a player dedicated to soccer. He had just one aim – to get to the top and stay there, and the fact that he had already accomplished so much is testimony enough to his ability."

One of Duncan's personal heroes, Stanley Matthews, paid a fine compliment to the lad who actually became his team-mate. "His death is a loss not only to Manchester United but to English football," Matthews lamented. "Once he had reached his peak he would have been among the greatest half-backs the game has ever produced."

It was a public and personal loss. Mrs Jessie Dorman told the *Manchester Evening News* that it was like "losing my own son":

Surrounded by cups and gifts brought from abroad by Duncan, Mrs Dorman, mother of three, said: "He has left hundreds of friends and thousands of happy memories. He was a quiet and reserved boy any mother would be proud of." Mrs Dorman, a keen United fan, said Duncan, who did not smoke or drink, lived for football. "But he never liked flying," she said. "He always seemed to go quiet a couple of days before flying. He always insisted that the safest place in a plane was at the back."

Among her happy memories are Duncan's love for outdoor life, tennis and golf; pride at being a Busby Babe; meeting his girlfriend Molly Leach; his new car bought soon after his 21st birthday in October. Mrs Dorman said: "He used to spend hours cleaning his car. He was a clean, tidy lad who preferred watching TV to publicity seeking." Duncan will be missed by children at Gorse Park Junior School. Duncan was in his element when he and Tommy Taylor had a snowball fight with the boys, said Mrs Dorman.

It was particularly tough on the remaining boy in digs at Gorse Avenue, David Gaskell. He was one of the players forced to endure a traumatic experience on February 10th. "Mark Pearson, Alex Dawson and myself were at Old Trafford and a wagon came to the ground," he says. "We were asked to unload the coffins and put them in the gym. I couldn't bear it."

The tragedy was only compounded by Duncan's passing. It all became too much for Gaskell. "I had to give the clothes and possessions of Duncan and Bill to their families," he recalls. "It was very brief but very sad. It was a moment that stayed with me. I spent some time with Duncan's mother at a memorial service and it was such an emotional experience. It was distressing. I had to move to Wigan. I couldn't bear being close to the club."

Because the news broke on Friday morning, it meant that Saturday's newspapers were the ones carrying tributes from the sportswriters, on the day Duncan's body was flown to London on a special BEA aircraft.

"Into four years as a professional footballer with Manchester United, Duncan Edwards had crammed a lifetime of achievements," John Trickett explained in the *Manchester Evening News*. "At 21 he had won every honour the game could give – except an FA Cup winner's medal and a European Cup winner's medal. He was striding out boldly towards those milestones when death stopped him in his tracks… He left the limelight and the glamour to those who enjoyed it. He was a modest, unassuming young man… who would go to parties and be the first to leave… who would push aside eager pressmen and photographers and say: 'You want the rest of the lads – I'm just one of the team.' As 23145376 Lance Corporal Edwards D, a national serviceman, he was described by his depot commandant as 'a first rate soldier'. As a 16-year-old 50-bob-a-week Old Trafford ground staff boy he was called 'desperately keen and conscientious.' As a world-wide football figure… let the records speak for themselves… Cold, colourless statistics… they tell nothing of the man. Nothing of the powerhouse, brilliant football that flowed from the feet of this 13-stone genius. When his forwards were toiling in vain for that vital goal, up would come 'Big Dunc' with a piledriver of a shot. He had the ability to steady a faltering team – and did it by his example rather than by words. He let his feet do the talking."

The local Midlands press had their say, too. "The death of Duncan Edwards is a grievous loss," Cyril Chapman wrote in the *Birmingham Daily Post*. "Football crowds love a fighter, they are quick to appreciate a man who really enjoys his game and they are thrilled by the crack marksman. Little wonder, then, that there was such a warm spot for Edwards in the hearts of football followers everywhere. He played football with the zest of a man who loved every minute of it. In a team of stars his was of the greatest magnitude, for brilliant as were his colleagues of Manchester United, his was the name coupled most readily with that club… search where we will, we shall not find another Duncan Edwards."

Duncan Edwards was gone, but his influence remained prominent.

United's game against Nottingham Forest on the Saturday after his passing was a tremendously poignant occasion. "The loyalty of Manchester trekking through the snow to support the new United was shown in a remarkable post-war record attendance of 66,123," Bob Ferrier wrote in the *Weekly Dispatch*. "So this great city expressed again the unique bond which exists between it, the club, and its players. The gates were closed some 10 minutes before the start, during an inter-denominational service conducted by the Dean of Manchester for all the victims, but in particular for Duncan Edwards. This short, simple service compressed the emotions so much that the match and the appearance of the players eased the feelings of the big crowd, and as soon as the game began the United were quick to prove that if they are now only a shadow of the wonder team, it is a shadow of much substance in the code of courage and will power."

United were 1-0 down in a game they had little right to win, before Alex Dawson popped up with a late equaliser. Once more, the spirit Duncan personified had been the quality which kept his old team competing.

On Wednesday February 26th, 1958, the whole of Dudley came to a standstill for the funeral of their favourite son. Crowds were lining the streets for hours beforehand. It was, as many locals have described since, "a state funeral".

The cortège travelled past Wolverhampton Street school, where the hearse paused for a moment as current students stood outside to pay respect, before making its way to St Francis' Church for the service.

Former team-mates and opponents, who to a man loved Duncan, were due to serve as pallbearers: Gordon Clayton, of United, Bobby English, another United youngster, Ronnie Clayton, Billy Wright, Ray Barlow and Derek Kevan. The official reason was given as weather, but it could well have been the weight of emotion that meant Clayton and English did not make it to the funeral, and they were replaced by Peter McParland and Peter Sayward.

"The mark of sacrifice and genius is deeply imprinted on this young Priory community," Reverend A Dawson Catterall told the mourners. "We are proud that the great Duncan Edwards was one of our sons. His history gives us an honoured place in the world. His football record needs no praise within these walls for it was known throughout the world and this great game was something England has given to the world... talent and even genius we shall see again but there will only be one Duncan Edwards. So far as his character is concerned it is sufficient to speak of his pride in his home; his modesty, his presidency of Dudley's young footballers, the friends of his boyhood still his friends, as he sheds lustre upon Old Trafford, Wembley and Belgrade. This greatest team of our post-war era was created by the conscious design and genius of Matt Busby. Having appreciated that, can you really suppose that the superb physique and incomparable skill of the men who formed it are just a whim of chance with no purpose beyond this time? This superb and modest athlete lived and loved his life among us to the full and would have undone no part of it. And it is now fulfilled. Go forward Duncan Edwards from this place – rich in achievement, honoured and loved by us all, forward into the dawn."

Duncan's body was taken to the Borough cemetery to be laid to rest with his sister Carol Anne, where wreathes "made a carpet of colour 30 yards around the grave" according to the *Birmingham Post & Gazette*. Around 3,000 people gathered in the cemetery to pay their respects, and the town hall flag flew at half mast in respect of their beloved son Duncan Edwards.

Chapter 25
Eternal

Duncan Edwards had fought for life, died and been buried, and his manager Matt Busby was none the wiser that anyone other than he had been significantly hurt in the crash. On the day of Duncan's funeral, Busby was reported by the *Manchester Evening News* to be "in cheerful spirit and making good progress. He finished reading a book about golfer Walter Hagen."

It was a couple of days later when the Manchester United manager found out the terrible reality. He said: "I heard a clergyman in the hospital say: 'Duncan is dead.' The clergyman was given a telling off for saying such a thing anywhere near me, but that was when I first began to be really aware that something awful had happened. I was afraid to ask but I asked."

His wife, Jean, visited later. Matt asked Jean to tell him the truth – she refused, but as Busby said the names of his players and colleagues, his wife either nodded or shook her head.

The impact on Manchester and United was significant. First as a community. The boys who had hung around the digs of their heroes continued to do so. They would never see them again.

"Tommy Taylor would not marry Norma Curtis," Paddy Barclay wrote in his book *Sir Matt Busby: The Man Who Made A Football Club*. "Nor continue his rise to international stardom alongside Edwards and Roger Byrne at the World Cup. Over were the career and carefree life of David Pegg. The third of the Yorkshire pals, Mark Jones, would never again see his beloved

June or toddler Gary. Never see or hold the daughter June would name Lynn. Never again set off across the fields with his faithful dog, who would be adopted by his brother Rick but die within a year. Nor tend his birds; June advertised for new homes for them, causing a queue of children outside her house in Kings Road."

One distraught 10-year-old, Roy Cavanagh, took a box of newspaper clippings he had collected of his hero Eddie Colman to Colman's parents on Archie Street because he thought they should have it. No longer could Eddie be followed home by adoring supporters. No longer would Duncan come out to wash his car. Duncan's Morris Minor stood outside Gorse Avenue. It made only one journey – to Elm Road in Dudley, where it sat on the driveway in front of Sarah and Gladstone's house. Apart from a few subtle pictures of Duncan, there had been little which suggested he had lived there. After his death, the front room became a shrine, with Sarah putting caps and medals in cases. Family would visit, and going into the living room was an experience.

"Go on then, do you want to see?" Sarah would say to relatives after a cup of tea, and they would walk through into the room to be shown the memorabilia.

Dudley remained in a state of shock – Manchester was dragging itself forward, inspired by the unlikely efforts of the United team. As Matt Busby finally began to show improvement, Jimmy Murphy continued to look after the team. Joe Armstrong had pitched in more, helping to do the football administrative work Crickmer did. Jack Crompton, the former United goalkeeper, was asked to return to coach the reserve team. That spell continued officially until the end of the 1957/58 season and unofficially for a little while longer as Busby came to terms with the psychological transition that Murphy, much like the players he had rushed into action, had to suppress in order to continue.

The suppression came with less a wave, more a "tide of emotion" according to Bobby Charlton, who – after being so distraught at Duncan's death he had considered walking away for good – had to be convinced by Jimmy to continue playing; and, when he did, he became almost a singular beacon of hope, the representation of the boys who had died so tragically. This was not a disservice to Gregg or Foulkes, but they were a little older than Charlton, and perhaps more pertinently, Charlton was a forward player – the one likely to get the headlines, in place of the likes of Edwards, Whelan, Pegg and Taylor, who now could not. Every time Bobby Charlton scored – and he scored so many times – it was a simultaneous reminder of what he had come through, what Manchester had come through, and what they had lost. It was a reminder that they kept going.

Charlton was impossibly inspirational, as were the rest of the players who stepped in. Alex Dawson, who was thrust into the first team permanently, skipping three years of education, and yet carried the burden of goalscoring in the FA Cup run. He scored against Sheffield Wednesday. Against West Brom in the next round. A hat-trick against Fulham in the semi-final – the last United player to do so. Ronnie Cope, who had been baby-stepped through his first games by Duncan Edwards, stepped into the breach now to replace Jones and Blanchflower. Goodwin and McGuinness, who were tasked with being the new Colman and Edwards when Crowther couldn't play.

United shared a full-page obituary of Duncan in their programme for the replay against West Brom in the sixth round on March 5th.

Still the pages of tragedy turn for us and the death of Duncan Edwards on February 21st made the sadness we have shared the more pointed... we who thrilled to his awe-inspiring demonstrations of seeming invincibility, coupled with a joy of living that infected his comrades whenever and wherever the going was tough, will always remember Duncan. Let the words of Robert Browning be his epitaph.

One who never turned his back but marched breast forward,
  Never doubted clouds would break,
  Never dreamed, though right were worsted, wrong would triumph,
  Held we fall to rise, are baffled to fight better,
  Sleep to wake.

Manchester United, against all the odds, qualified for the 1958 FA Cup final. Mr Eric Booth received his invitation. So did the families of those who had lost their lives. Molly declined to go. "It was absolutely dreadful when Molly found out," her best friend Josephine later said of the accident. "Molly came back from Germany dressed all in black – I'd never seen such a change in a person. At the time Molly was only 22 and I never thought she'd get over it – they had all their lives to look forward to and the plane crash took all of that away. Eventually she moved to Somerset."

Sarah said she would accept the invitation to the final out of politeness. "I'll go to Wembley because I think it would be ungrateful to United not to make the trip," she told press. "But I am not interested any more, although I used to travel miles to watch Duncan. I saw him at Wembley last year. This time I don't think I even want to watch the game. I really don't think I could stand seeing the boys playing."

There was to be no fairytale ending here. First of all, the romance and risk of a cup run could not be replicated in the everyday business of the league. The atmosphere, the jeopardy of a knockout match caught opponents off guard. First Division teams had their own ambitions and, as Burnley chairman Bob Lord would point out in a fairly unkind manner, they didn't all revolve around laying down and letting Manchester United win out of sympathy.

Neither Jimmy Murphy nor Manchester United wanted that. They wanted the reality. They wanted the competition. If it meant the cruelty of Bob Lord was exposed, even better – Murphy could use that, on top of the grief, to motivate players. It didn't always work. Burnley, on that particular occasion, won 3-0. Mark Pearson was upset with being described as "a Teddy boy" by Lord and showed the lack of maturity that came with this sort of rushed development. Pearson had arguably been the man of the match against Sheffield Wednesday, but what was almost certain to be a long and fantastic career in United's front line ended up lasting just 80 appearances. Dawson, like Pearson, was never the same after the reality of their situation hit home.

United, the back-to-back champions of 1956 and 1957, finished ninth in the league. Wolves won the championship. The reality is they probably would have done anyway. Cullis' team only dropped six points for the remainder of the campaign. The Babes would have had to have been perfect for the remainder of the season and hit a few goals past Wolves. More likely than not, it would have had to be a tough lesson for the young United boys about the danger of complacency.

The prize for winning against Red Star was a European Cup semi-final with AC Milan. United won the first leg 2-1, but went down 0-4 in the second. It was a first encounter with an Italian side, the country which had seemed so desperate to lure the Babes to those shores. If they had gone on to the final, Real Madrid were waiting there. An alternative destiny. Would it have been a moment of joy or one more learning experience? Were the Babes ready to take on Madrid? You could predict that Duncan was – but his team-mates may have needed a little more time. It remains, however, the great unknown.

On FA Cup final day in 1958 the cast may have changed but the story was a familiar one. In November 1957, there had been a debate about the charging of goalkeepers. Stanley Matthews said it could be an offence like it was in European football. Johnny Haynes said if you do away with charging goalkeepers you might as well do away with it against all players. Duncan had already gone on record with his views on the matter.

Bolton took an early lead in the final. United tried valiantly. Wanderers treated this scratch side with the professional dignity of the Babes before them. The half-back line where once Colman, Jones and Edwards stood as an impenetrable trio was decimated. In Edwards' place was Stan Crowther, man of the match in the previous final, now with shoes that were just too big to fill.

The guile of Billy Whelan and predatory instinct of Tommy Taylor, gone, with Alex Dawson and Ernie Taylor asked to do so much. Colin Webster, normally a centre-forward, asked to replace the production line of David Pegg, and Ian Greaves tasked with doing Roger Byrne's job. It made for a difficult afternoon, as the inexperience at this level showed. And yet they still dreamed. Charlton – using all of the power usually found in an Edwards shot – let fly with a primal effort which hit the post. Just as it seemed they might be inspired, Bolton broke – Stevens shot from the left. Gregg saved, and appeared to catch the ball with both hands. As he did, Lofthouse charged in, bundling Gregg and the ball into the net. Referee Jack Sherlock deemed it a fair challenge. The 50th-minute goal had ended the game as a genuine contest, but it did not stop United's keen green kids from trying. Although Bolton won, they were never made to stop working. As they commiserated after the final whistle, although some hoped there would be a next time, there could be no bold proclamation of it in the way that Duncan and Eddie had predicted in 1957. Nothing was certain.

Matt Busby had impressed upon his players his desire for them to express themselves to entertain the public. When Murphy was in sole charge, the grit and dark reality of what faced United could scarcely be avoided. The players knew they had to give everything just to compete. It became, over time, a self-fulfilling prophecy, and was the greatest possible tribute to Duncan; although, of course, it is just as fair to state that it was the greatest possible gift Duncan could have bequeathed to Manchester United. He had become immortalised, his philosophy of football now embedded within the red fabric of the shirt he used to wear. Where once his unique presence had seemed distinctive enough from the Busby way to be seen as a separate quality, it was now woven into the tapestry as a key element of it.

Now, just as important as it was to have that expression, it became a fundamental requirement of a Manchester United player to fight for those lost causes. Turning the lost causes into victories made them all the sweeter. Let it be said that Duncan was just one of the Babes and everything those players stood for resonated just as strongly in its own way. Those Babes had perished chasing the unknown and doing it in their own individual style. That too became the benchmark for Manchester United teams of the future. When winning in style could not be achieved, winning in the ugliest, scrappiest way possible was celebrated just as keenly. Sometimes, even more fondly. The greatest triumphs had an element of it all. The big trophies, an element of skill, and spades of desire. In fact, never anything less than desire – the most crucial factor of all. And defeat, if it must be tasted, should be savoured fully, bittersweet flavour and all, so that further setbacks might be avoided, and further successes celebrated with the acceptance of all which had gone before.

Duncan Edwards had died. A new Manchester United had been born.

From his biggest stage to his humble beginnings, Edwards' absence was felt and his achievements honoured. The Worcester Schools' FA created a competition in his name: the Duncan Edwards Memorial Trophy.

In October 1958, on what would have been his 22nd birthday, the design of a new headstone for Duncan's grave was released to the press. The headstone was unveiled on the morning of Saturday

October 4th, by Matt Busby in front of 2,000 people. The fixture list had been generous to United – they were due to face Wolves at Molineux that afternoon. "Duncan was with me as a boy footballer from 15 and he was always a credit to his school, to his town and to his club for whom he played so magnificently," Busby said. "It is indeed a great privilege to unveil this memorial to such a wonderful boy."

United lost 4-0 to the champions Wolves that day, as the size of the rebuild on Busby's hands became evident. It was the first of six defeats in eight games. The new-look United team rallied, however. They won an incredible 15 out of the next 18 games to finish second. It was a false position in some respects – it was going to take a while for United to challenge seriously for honours.

Busby, feeling an immense guilt relating to the tragedy, had to be convinced to return to his job. Once he did, he made it his ambition to win the European Cup, partly inspired by the memory of his boys tragically lost.

United had been invited into the competition the following season after Munich. They were forbidden by the Football League, despite already having been drawn against Young Boys of Switzerland. The Swiss side, having received a bye due to United's pull-out, offered to play two friendlies.

Other acts of generosity had been seen on the continent, starting in Belgrade. Local newspaper *Politika* reported that Red Star sent a telegram to the European Cup organisation committee in the hours after the crash, proposing that United should be proclaimed honorary champions. They suggested the remaining clubs should withdraw and play the rest of the tournament as friendly matches so the cup would go to the "football masters" who were prevented from winning it by only bad luck: "Thus in a solemn way due tribute would be paid to a great football team and in the history of football an imperishable trace would remain of a tragedy which had shocked the peoples of all continents."

The Yugoslav FA suggested the European Cup be renamed the Manchester United Cup, and Real Madrid president Santiago Bernabeu said they would support the move. None of these emotional suggestions were granted, nor were they requested by United.

England, meanwhile, were dumped out of the 1958 World Cup by the Soviet Union in a play-off. In 1962, they were eliminated in the quarter-final by Brazil. Walter Winterbottom was replaced by Alf Ramsey – and, with a new generation of talent coming through, England finally tasted World Cup glory in 1966. The presence of Bobby Charlton in particular in the England team just made the idea of the likes of Edwards, Taylor and Byrne starring in a successful national side all the more plausible, and that's without even mentioning Foulkes or Pegg, or the players like Eddie Colman, who would surely have got their own chance.

United were starting from scratch. Real Madrid offered practical help – they would participate in friendly games and waive their appearance fee in order to help boost United's finances. The games were good tests for United to see how they were getting on in their redevelopment – the first, played on Duncan's birthday in 1959, was a 6-1 win for the Spaniards. Over time, the scorelines drew closer. United started to win.

Once Busby had started to show the old ambition, Murphy promised to deliver him a Youth Cup-winning team again. Out went Murphy on the search for talent. Out went Armstrong. Eyes were everywhere. Players were brought in. At the last of these friendly games with Madrid, one of those players – a youngster by the name of George Best – watched as Alfredo Di Stéfano, the best player on the pitch, worked relentlessly throughout the 90 minutes. Five-and-a-half years later, George was inspirational in the first competitive meeting between Manchester United and Real Madrid since 1957. This European Cup semi-final was won by Matt Busby's team, a team that still included Bill Foulkes and

Bobby Charlton. Foulkes would make his 665th appearance for the club in the final, and for Charlton it would be appearance 509.

In addition to Best, Murphy's orchard had provided Shay Brennan – who had played in the first game after Munich – Nobby Stiles, Brian Kidd, David Sadler and John Aston Jnr. True to their original philosophy, thanks largely to Murphy's resilience to keep it so in the most testing times, United lined up for the final with only three bought players – Alex Stepney in goal, Tony Dunne at left-back, and Pat Crerand in midfield (Denis Law, the main striker, was injured).

Ten years after Munich, Manchester United came up against Benfica at Wembley. Charlton scored twice, Kidd scored on his 19th birthday, and the winning goal was hit in style by Best in the first moments of extra-time. That strike had initiated one of those famous Busby flurries – 92nd, 94th and 99th minute goals finally delivering the trophy United had coveted for so long.

It had been apt that George Best had won it. In many ways he and Duncan were nothing alike – George was three inches shorter, probably more than three stone lighter, and more likely to use sleight of hand than awe-inspiring power, but there were similarities nonetheless. The hunger. The insatiable need for a football. The consuming desire to win. The appetite to be everywhere on the pitch. More importantly than individual attributes, what the pair shared was the spotlight in a team of stars.

The players said Munich was never spoken of and yet always there. On the full-time whistle at Wembley in May 1968, it was clear how much it meant when Busby sought out Charlton and Foulkes first for special embraces. Jimmy Murphy recalled the after-match dinner, where families of those lost in Munich had been invited (as well as to the game). "There were so many memories," Murphy said. "Like Mr and Mrs Gladstone Edwards, the parents of Duncan, coming over to my table: 'Big Dunc would have liked this night. He always said United would win the European Cup, and we are so proud he was proved right.'"

Gladstone Edwards retired from his job as a metal polisher to tend to the grave of his children. He did this for the rest of his days, until he died, 20 years after Duncan in 1978. Sarah passed away in 2003, when she was 93. Just before she died, she showed some of that famous Edwards bravery to chase a burglar out of her house. There was no questioning who Duncan had inherited his boisterousness from.

Sarah remained broken-hearted, and immensely proud. Proud when a statue sculpted by James Butler was unveiled in Dudley town centre in 1999, depicting Duncan in that classic 'belt the ball away' pose captured against Scotland in 1957.

A Duncan-powered kick of a ball from the statue from where it now stands – it was moved in 2015 to a prominent position at the top of Market Street – would have found the museum and foundation set up in his name by Rose Cook-Monk up until late 2021. The museum featured all of the key moments of Duncan's life, remarkably rare artefacts, and heartfelt tributes to the rest of the Busby Babes and some of those more-forgotten victims such as journalists and other passengers.

Duncan's life was prolonged due to his strength, but so was his suffering. As he succumbed to his fate, as his body fought to prevent the inevitable, he dreamed of playing football. Death has never been as poignant.

Duncan could never be forgotten in Dudley. The local youngsters learn about him as soon as they learn about football. They will hear about Cristiano Ronaldo or whoever the most popular player of the day is, but the name of Duncan Edwards will always shortly follow. It is a reminder of two things. Firstly, that Duncan's legacy lives on. Secondly, it remains possible for the greatest of a generation to come from the same streets. The latter point transcends football. It becomes a matter of working hard and dreaming.

It's much the same in Manchester. Manchester United in the 21st century are scarcely recognisable to the club Duncan represented. The players don't live close enough to walk to Old Trafford and they cannot be idolised on their journey to and from training by the local children. Money and fame has changed the sport of football forever. The reign of Sir Alex Ferguson redefined the conventional rules of domestic domination even though there was so much familiar with his success that fans of a certain vintage could draw comparisons with the Busby Babes. In 2011, United became the most successful team in English league history. They have won three European Cups. Four players have won the European Player of the Year award while at Old Trafford. Three of them are immortalised in a statue on the forecourt of Old Trafford – one of those is Bobby Charlton, Duncan's friend and team-mate.

There is no statue of Duncan in Manchester but in 2011 a blue plaque was placed on the front of his old digs in Gorse Avenue. This was the consequence of an application by Stretford High teacher Chris Hirst, who, as part of teaching his Year 7 team about the Busby Babes, realised just how close Duncan and Tommy Taylor, who lived on Great Stone Road, lived to the school. There was a romantic symmetry as Hirst contacted United fan Tom Clare for further information – when the plaques were approved, Tom was proud to have been a part of the process that marked a tremendously vivid chapter of his own life. For Clare, it was important that his hero was remembered for the man he was as well as the player.

"He was prudent, he looked after his parents," he says. "He was a normal everyday boy next door. He was no mug. He left almost £10,000 when he died – an enormous amount of money back then. He advertised Dextrosol, Raleigh bikes. He had a weekly newspaper article."

When one considers that Duncan wouldn't have made more than £4,000 from his wages over the entirety of his professional club career, it demonstrates just how wise his financial management was. But he was not a money-man. He was a footballer. The hero of Tom Clare and thousands of others. "People said Duncan didn't reach a peak," Clare says. "We hadn't seen the best of him. He was 21, he'd won the First Division, he was the best player in a United team looking to win the European Cup. 18 England caps. If he'd have been any better, he'd have been Superman."

There is a paradoxical narrative which comes when looking at the life of Duncan Edwards and it revolves around the mythical nature of his achievements, speculation of what he could have been, and how good he truly was. The temptation to embellish is natural because it's the easiest way to reduce the numbers to meaningless statistics. There is the hyperbole – *Superman* – and it is balanced against a key element. How ordinary he was. How normal. In a sense, to elevate who he was and what he did to a status that is so mythical as to be seen as unrealistic is to do a fundamental disservice to everything he stood for.

So let's go through it. Duncan Edwards wasn't a perfect player. He was getting there, but hadn't quite arrived. There were the clumsy handballs. The positional indiscipline that occasionally led to mistakes. The righteousness with referees. The wisdom that came with playing more top-class international games. Most of those issues had been ironed out. Maybe there was only the last box to tick. The journey could not be completed until Manchester United had won the European Cup. He was almost perfect, of course, and it is easy for those who knew him such as Busby, Murphy and Charlton to describe him as so; it was effectively a formality that United would go on to realise their potential. But it was potential – not actual.

"You have to prove that you're the best," says Johnny Giles. "Real Madrid were dominating the European Cup so they deserved their reputation. United still had a bit to do. They were younger – the Real team had experienced legends like Di Stéfano and Puskas, but United had all this youth... If you were going to name three outstanding players in the world at that moment, then you would have Di Stéfano, Puskas and Duncan Edwards in the conversation."

In 1957, Duncan was named joint-third in the European Player of the Year award. Di Stéfano was the winner, Billy Wright in fact was second, and Duncan shared third place with Raymond Kopa of Real Madrid. (Puskas was ineligible, as he was serving a ban from UEFA for refusing to return to Budapest). A World Cup or European Cup – certainly both – would have surely pushed Duncan to the top.

Because it did not happen, and because Duncan died so young, there is an alternative argument that often rules him out of contention when people discuss the greatest of all time. It is born from reluctance to include someone who died at the age of 21.

"Sometimes I fear there is a danger that people will think that we who knew him boost him because he is dead," said Bobby Charlton. "Sentiment can throw a man's judgement out of perspective. Yet it is not the case with him. Whatever praise one likes to heap on Duncan, it is no more than he deserved… a few are great, and they deserve respect. But Duncan Edwards was the greatest."

Charlton was not a man prone to making over-the-top statements. Nor was Bobby Robson. "Duncan Edwards was a colossus, and if he had lived would I think have broken the record number of England caps," said Robson. "He was physically strong, had great power, a good football brain, ability both on the ground and in the air, he was fast – in fact he was a complete player… Had Duncan Edwards survived in February 1958 and continued his footballing career he would have gone down in history as one of the true legends of the game. For me, he does that anyway."

Then there is Jimmy Murphy. Murphy *was* one to embellish. He loved a story. "All those lads made up the most wonderful team I have seen," he said. "In my time I think we had three really great teams here but they were the best. They could have won anything they put their minds to. The boat race, the Grand National and the Derby, anything."

But when he spoke of Duncan, there was a decidedly serious tone. "He never tired of the game. He was the most complete player I had ever seen," he said. "Men like Matthews and Finney could really only play only in their own position; Duncan could play anywhere. It was desperate that we lost him but it was a credit to his strength that even lying so ill in hospital he could joke about playing again in a few days...

"I described Duncan the first time I saw him as 'The greatest thing on two feet'. When he died I still thought that. There seemed no end to the savagery of Munich. Like everyone in football I mourned the loss of Duncan Edwards, even now I still think it was perhaps the biggest loss to English football. I am quite sure that England with Roger Byrne, Tommy Taylor and certainly with Duncan Edwards could have won the World Cup in 1958. Duncan was big enough to have outshone the fabulous Pele. And Duncan would still have been young enough to have led his country in the World Cup in 1970. All this is now conjecture and speculation. What I do know is when managers, trainers and scouts, and all the vast army of football professionals who try to keep the wheels turning, get together for a chat about old times there is always one name that crops up. Duncan Edwards. The Real Professional. They will tell you there has never been anyone quite like him. Indeed when I hear Cassius Clay proclaim to the world, 'I am The Greatest,' I have to smile. You see, the greatest of them all was an English footballer named Duncan Edwards, and he died following an aircrash in a Munich hospital at the age of 21."

Matt Busby steered clear of the sort of 'Grand National' predictions made by Murphy, besides saying he was certain that "the youngest England player would have grown to be the eldest". "Goodness only knows what impact Duncan Edwards would have made on the game had he been spared," Busby said sorrowfully.

The pain of the disaster was clear. Duncan died two weeks after it. The distance provided a reason for him to be mourned separately. Busby himself described his death as "the biggest single tragedy that has happened to England and to Manchester United". Neither Busby nor Murphy would put one loss above another but it is easy to see why they felt especially bereft for Duncan. They saw themselves in him. They were wing-halves of international class. They believed the position was the most important on the pitch. In a team that was renowned for its pattern and togetherness, he stood apart with his distinctive contribution. They recognised he was that rare example of a player they felt they could not teach. They liked to believe he was the most shining example of their system. For almost six years they had heartily indulged in the prodigy, for five they had put him in the first team and spoke of a multi-functional system with the unspoken exception of it always being a team built around one. He was Busby and Murphy on the pitch. It stood to reason that the incomprehensible loss of that presence left them wondering how they might possibly ever go on. If he hadn't survived for as long as he did – well, they might not have gone on. Even with a scratch side remaining, it was Duncan's fight which inspired Jimmy to continue; it was Jimmy's continuation which inspired Busby to work again.

It surely does Duncan's memory most justice to recount what he did and marvel at both that and how he did it. There is no need to sensationalise it. The truth is remarkable enough. When he made his debut as a 16-year-old, it was as rare then as it is common now. He was a normal lad doing extraordinary things.

In two short years Duncan had emerged as one of the best players in the country. In the last two years of his life he was among the best in the world. That much is beyond any question.

Because United were so good with such a young team, there will always be conversations about the endless potential of that side. You could call it unfortunate, but you could also define it as a beautiful, romantic tragedy – Duncan and his team-mates, the Busby Babes, are crystallised in their youth for eternity. What they did. How they did it. What they stood for. It has been so inspirational to future generations and perhaps even more so because of the nature in which they were taken.

There is also an important element of something having to be created so it can be imitated or recreated. Manchester United would have greater successes and more dominant periods of success, and they did it following the fine traditions of the club, but it could not have been possible without those traditions being created in the first place. This writer was fortunate enough to interview Sir Alex Ferguson when writing a biography of Jimmy Murphy. Ferguson admitted he "absolutely" used Jimmy Murphy's visceral reaction to Munich to motivate his own players. "Telling them what Jimmy did," Ferguson said, "planting the seed of the work that man did, it's the most important thing you can tell a young player who is representing Manchester United. Telling them what their expectation is and helping them fulfil that."

If Murphy's drive was a holistic influence, then Duncan's on-pitch determination was the literal interpretation. It is fitting that the greatest triumph in the club's history, in 1999, was achieved by calling on the sort of spirit Duncan represented. One wonders if it would have even been possible without Duncan, as far-fetched as that may seem for an event that occurred decades after his death.

The identity of Manchester United was created in the years between 1946 and 1958. From 1955 to February 6th, 1958, the Busby Babes established a style of football that was unrivalled and a chemistry that was impossible to imitate. Duncan Edwards was the best player in a fantastic team, and on top of that he added a force of personality and a will to win that was so much a part of his own character that it seemed a separate quality altogether.

It is impossible to say what would have happened if there had been no Duncan Edwards in the Busby Babes. If Bolton or Wolves had been lucky enough to get his attention, or if they'd perhaps offered his parents something more lucrative than a washing machine. But within a conversation which so prominently features hypotheticals, we can take what *did* happen, and acknowledge that this period of history for Manchester United was beyond any question the most important with regards to its identity as a football club. That is as true today as it was in 1958, and it will forever be the case. If Matt Busby was responsible for the style, and Jimmy Murphy was responsible for the soul, then Duncan Edwards was the player who epitomised those two qualities more than any other.

BALL ASSOCIATION INTERNATIONAL MATCH

WALES
v.
ENGLAND

NINIAN PARK, CARDIFF

SATURDAY, 19th OCTOBER, 1957

OFFICIAL

THE "YOUNG ENGLAND" WHO VISITED ITALY

'Big Dunc'—finest of all The Babes

MANCHESTER UNITED FOOTBALL CLUB

D. EDWARDS

Cover Man — DUNCAN EDWARDS

'Greatest Youngster
I've Ever Seen'

Says Matt Busby

(Manchester United Manager)

SOCCER STAR, March 1, 1958

Duncan Edwards — the lad who had a big heart to match his husky

HERO OF A MILLION PEOPL

by
GRAHAM PAYNE

Floodlit Football Match at The Cliff, Brough...

FINAL — GILGRYST CUP

MANCHESTER UNITED v. ASHTON UNITED

WEDNESDAY, 1st APRIL, 1953 Kick Off 7-...

MANCHESTER UNITED
RED SHIRTS AND WHITE SHORTS

OLIVE

FULTON KENNEDY

WHITEHURST GREAVES BARR...

McFARLANE VIOLLET WEBSTER EDWARDS SC...

Referee: Mr. E. C. ALLEN
Mr. G. READLE (Stretford) Linesmen Mr. G. MERRIMAN.

WRIGHT MOSES ROSS RADCLIFFE S...

HOLDEN McNAB KNIGHT

BRICKELL

McBRIDE

ASHTON UNITED
YELLOW SHIRTS AND WHITE SHORTS

TO READ—HOLD PROGRAMME TO LIGHT

THE KENTISH C...
TRIANGULAR TOURNA...
ween the FRENCH, BELGIAN and B...

BRITISH AI...
v
FRENCH AI...

PLAYED ON THE GROU...
of
DULWICH HAMLET FOOTBAL...
CHAMPION HILL, DULWICH...

SATURDAY...

FOOTBALL
ASSOCIATION

DUNCAN EDWARDS of DUDLEY won his Junior International "cap" last season and has represented England in two full internationals this season. He will be playing for England against Scotland next Saturday. He has also played for the B'ham & District County side and the Worcester County side this season, and still has another year at school.

LEN COOPER has played for his area side for three seasons and represented the South of England against the North at Dudl... He has also been a regular member of the ...sides.

ENGLAND
—v—
SCOTLAND
(FOR THE VICTORY SHIELD)

THE FOOTBALL LEAGUE TEAM

MANCHESTER UNITED

McGuinness (7)
Charlton (10) Chapman (8)
Edwards (6) Harrop (5) Colm...
Rhodes (3) Beswick (2)
Clayton (1)

MANCHESTER UNITED
...A. Savl...C.
...TARJETA POSTAL